Disequilibrium

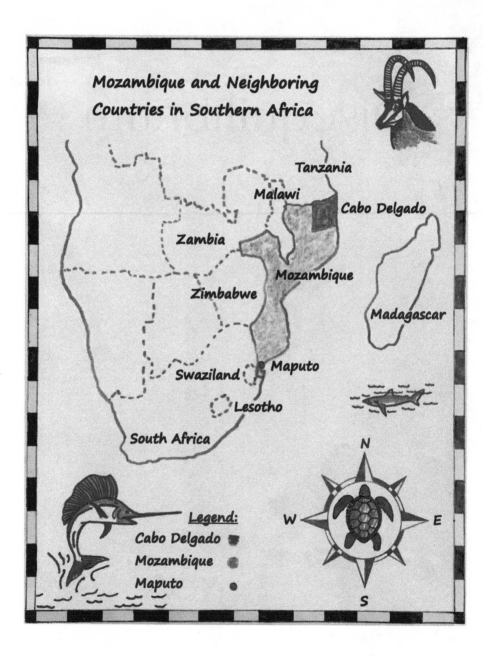

Mozambique and Neighboring Countries in Southern Africa

Tanzania

Malawi

Cabo Delgado

Zambia

Mozambique

Zimbabwe

Madagascar

Swaziland

Maputo

Lesotho

South Africa

N

W — E

S

Legend:
Cabo Delgado
Mozambique
Maputo

Disequilibrium

A Memoir of Africa, Wildlife,
and Bipolar Disorder

PETER H. BECHTEL

PELUTSI PRESS

PELUTSI PRESS
Philadelphia, Pennsylvania

ISBN 978-1-7334627-0-9

PRINTED IN THE UNITED STATES OF AMERICA

This book is dedicated to all those who have ever written a book, an article, a short story, a poem, hieroglyphics, a cuneiform tablet, or a pictogram on the wall of a cave.

Life would be less interesting without your efforts.

Disequilibrium [disē′kwilib′rē·əm]. Etymology: L. *dis*, apart, *aequilibrium*, the loss of balance or adjustment, particularly mental or psychological balance.[1]

Contents

Disequilibrium

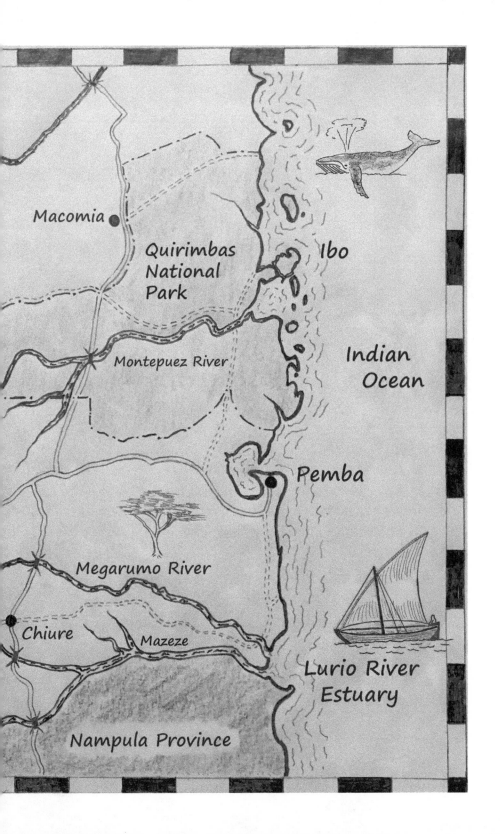

Macomia

Quirimbas
National
Park

Ibo

Montepuez River

Indian
Ocean

Pemba

Megarumo River

Chiure

Mazeze

Lurio River
Estuary

Nampula Province

Along the Cabo Delgado coast, it is not uncommon for hippos to live in estuaries or even the open ocean. They do require a source of freshwater for drinking; oceanic hippos generally leave the sea at night to graze and drink, returning at dawn. This family group lives in the brackish estuary of the Rovuma River.

CHAPTER I

Falling Apart

October, 2012. In which I take a work trip to Pemba and Macomia Districts, Cabo Delgado Province, Mozambique, and remember an earlier trip to Ibo District. I am living in Maputo, the capital of Mozambique, and working for the World Wildlife Fund (WWF).

MENTAL DISEASE DESTROYED the linear logic of my life. Cause and effect out the window. Emotions inappropriate to day and moment. Career derailed, family disrupted, self-respect gone. Muttering to myself and cussing out the driver's side window as passers-by look on in amazement or irritation. Ridiculous expenditures, ridiculous excuses. No concentration.

Multiple perceptual variations of the Heisenberg Uncertainty Principle.

On one of my clearer days, my daughter reminded me what this principle was, though not, of course, without some measure of satisfaction at getting one up on her old man. For her at least, I never lost my status as an authority figure, one worth besting.

"Geez, Dad, didn't you study this in High School? Didn't they have electrons back then?"

We did, Neli, but they buzzed around nuclei in comforting, elliptical orbits instead of blinking unpredictably into and out of existence within the guidelines of a multi-layered probability cloud. Electrons were things, too, actual bits of matter instead of some mystical modern-day hybrid of particle and wave.

"It's not mystical, Dad. The smaller things get, the more wavelike they become. Big things act more like particles, very small things act more like waves. Because electrons are very small and act more like waves, you can't really talk about them in ways that make sense to the casual listener."

She knows my degrees are in sciences. She is really enjoying this.

"The best we can do is to say that there is always a degree of uncertainty in what we know about electrons. If we pinpoint their position, then we won't know much about their momentum. At some point you just have to accept that knowing one parameter means knowing a lot less about the other. And they don't blink in and out of existence. Just sometimes they're more like a wave."

Which still sounds like leaping randomly around the nucleus, only without the leap, without any perceptible relationship between existence at point A and existence at point B.

Like me on a bad day.

The doctor at the Maputo Private Clinic takes one look at the X-ray and tells me that I will need a new hip.

"Cartilage gone and its bone on bone and that's why the leg gives out on you sometimes and hurts nearly all the time and why you can't lift it up to get into the front seat of the pickup sometimes."

I don't bother telling him that I can't throw the high roundhouse kicks anymore. I can work around that. That's tournament stuff anyways. TV stuff. The real stuff is elbows and knees and short, hard jabs and guarding your head and especially bringing the hips into it whenever you do anything important. The eyes and the head and the hands and the feet can fool you. Watch the hips and you know what's going to happen. Watch the hips and the future will become clear.

Except my hip never let me know what was going to happen. Or rather it tried to, but in those days I made a point of keeping myself jacked up on hormones and adrenaline and ambition and achievement. Running and swimming and diving and basketball with my son, and volleyball with my daughter and tracking elephants in the Park and building things at the farm. Point A to point B to point C D E F Z. Slowing down was going down and in those days once I went down I had no way to get back up, so I made sure I never slowed down. My momentum was clear; where I was, much less so. The reality of my deteriorating hip never flickered into the space-time continuum at a communicating point with the reality of what was going on in my mind.

Ruth, my wife, and I had flown up the coast to see our house on Ibo Island. It was a business trip for me, for Ibo Island is an historic town in the middle of the Quirimbas National Park in Mozambique, a national park I had invested many years and much of myself in making.

It was in our time of troubles and things were difficult between us. Still, she was herself, gracious and forgiving and tough in the way that bamboo is tough, slender and willowy and bending with the wind but unbreakable, and nearly impossible to root out. Of the ground, of the heart, or all of the above, and who would want to anyway?

A small delegation of friends and local citizenry awaited us at the Ibo airport, smiling and hugging us and even breaking into song as we descended from the chartered plane.

The Quirimbas National Park was established to protect nature as well as local people and their livelihoods; around 3,500 people live on Ibo Island, fishing and trading up and down the coast in hand-built sailing ships, much as their ancestors did a thousand years ago.

Things were going well in the marine part of the Park. Park rangers on Ibo were working together with communities to set up a series of no-take zones, areas of reef where everyone agreed not to fish or dive so that marine fauna could reproduce in peace and plenty. The effects of reduced fishing pressure in these areas were startling. Fish capture by local fisherman increased in surrounding areas and communities were delighted with these results.

Of course there were some problems. Patrol boat motors were inevitably broken, petrol was inevitably in short supply, and migratory fishermen down from Tanzania had been illegally harvesting cowry shells on some of the outer islands.

I was immediately captured, drawn into the details of marine park management on Ibo by rangers and community leaders alike. Like a fish into a net, I thought, and glanced at Ruth, but she smiled and gave me a little wave and so I knew it was okay to be caught.

While I worked with the local fishermen, Ruth went to see our house. It is an antique, constructed in an odd Arab-Afro-Portuguese style that reflects the cultural antecedents of the town and people of Ibo Island itself. While we loved the old houses of Ibo, we had never actually thought to buy one for ourselves. Then one day the leader of Ibo's Islamic Association called to say that they had arranged for us to buy an old house for the grand total of $3000.

It may have been the Muslim community's way of saying "Thank you." How could we refuse?

The house is built of coral rocks joined with lime; no cement was used in its construction. Lintels over the windows and doors are constructed of mangrove poles, which are impervious to rot. (Some of the oldest houses on Ibo have mangrove lintels that are more than 300 years old.) Ceilings are constructed of mangrove withies laid on mangrove beams and then plastered top and bottom with more lime.

In the old days, lime for plastering was soaked for up to a year to give it a smoother-than-silk texture. Builders these days have forgotten how to work with lime and so treat it like cement, using it immediately after mixing. What is best for cement is absolutely the worst for lime and recent repairs weather much more quickly than intact original walls.

We bought it sight unseen (OK, we knew where it was but had never been inside) and of course found an abundance of things that needed fixing. Despite the obvious advantages of using mangrove for construction, a previous owner had replaced all the original mangrove shutters and doors with pine imported from Portugal. Pine in the salt environment of Ibo is not a good idea, and so we contracted a local woodcarver to create some Zanzibar-style carved doors from local hardwoods, though not mangrove like original Zanzibari doors.

Since the declaration of the Quirimbas National Park in 2002, cutting mangrove is specifically prohibited, as it is an endangered species. Just one of the unexpected contradictions inherent in attempting to conserve culture and nature simultaneously.

Ruth found that our carver, Lucas, had outdone himself, mixing rhinos and cranes and swordfish with traditional Zanzibari geometric designs. Africa mixed with Arab with a hint of Portuguese, like the rest of Ibo, but something completely new. We went to sleep that night content, a little closer than we had been the day before.

The next day we went off to find the Cross of Vasco da Gama.

Mozambican history books say that he erected a cross on the northern side of Ibo Island in 1499 to celebrate his safe arrival. I had never found it, but several local fishermen informed me that they knew exactly where it was.

We set off early in the morning to avoid the worst of the day's heat, though it didn't matter in any case, for after an hour of walking I simply could go no further.

My hip just froze. I was mortified. I sat for an hour or so resting and stretching and tried again. Still no luck. Using the logic of those who refuse to acknowledge reality, I decided that if walking didn't work I should try running and managed to go about 200 meters before grinding to a halt. Ruth and the rangers went to fetch a motorcycle and I was ignominiously hauled back to town and fussed over.

And so it went for weeks. I tried everything except a visit to the doctor and an X-ray. An X-ray would be hard to ignore. An X-ray would be too much information. An X-ray would be too much certainty and so I leapt randomly around the nucleus, from rest to ice to heat to stretching to chiropractic without any indication of where I was trying to go except to get better and without any idea of where I was, except that I was someplace that hurt.

Then Ruth put her foot down and that was how I found myself at the Maputo Private Hospital, listening to a sad-eyed Indian doctor explaining in a sympathetic voice that I had no cartilage left in my right hip.

Too much wear and tear, he says, on top of an old injury. Too much running, too much jumping, too much climbing and falling and pressure and strain and stress. I hear the words but cannot understand them. Still no communication across the space-time continuum.

I was manic at the time. When you're manic, there's no such thing as too much.

The doctor is patient and repeats himself, and eventually some things start to get through. What seems to matter most is that he says I won't be able to run again. No more mountainsides in the cool of the evening after the day's worst heat, not really running but more leaping from rock to rock, heart pounding lungs on fire and mind blessedly still. Then the view on top which takes about two minutes to see because first there is the obligatory recovery with hands on knees and head down and breath blowing so hard that I can't even hear my tinnitus: another gift from a central nervous system gone awry, another challenge to be overcome every day on a minute-by-minute basis.

Red sunset in the northwest, better in the rainy season because you have a chance of thunderheads or rainbows to fracture the light into every part of the visible spectrum except blue, but you have that in the sky, and green, but you have that in the grass and the trees and the tiny orchids that wedge themselves between the boulders, safe from competition from other more aggressively career-oriented species.

Then racing the shadows down again, faster than I really can go, and praying not to fall. I carry an elastic brace to help me home if I tumble. My ankles are cobwebs of blue and red, relics from the times this lesser prayer was not answered.

I tell the doctor I run for the good of my soul. He says well you won't anymore.

Ten days after the doctor: a transition from employment to unemployment, only without the transition. The World Wildlife Fund says that now that I have Mozambican citizenship I no longer qualify to hold the post I hold.

It was designed for an expatriate, and I am no longer an expatriate. Now that you are one of us you no longer qualify to be one of us.

I really do not expect this. I had just been granted Mozambican citizenship after a fifteen-year battle. I had just negotiated a renewal of my two-year contract with the WWF, this time as a Mozambican national. We spoke about it on Friday. On Monday morning I fly to Pemba on a ten-day mission and my boss sends an official letter to our house in Maputo on Monday at noon, two hours after I leave.

Ruth calls me in the evening with the news. She opened the letter even though it was marked "Confidential."

I am glad she did. I think the idea was to inform me officially on the first of the month, to comply with applicable legislation, but not have me find out until the tenth, when I got home. Ten more days of passion and fire and parks and forests and conservation policy and practice.

Ruth frustrates that. She tells me to sit down and reads me the letter over the phone. Legalese in Portuguese. She is friends with the Minister for Labor, and wonders what Her Excellency would think if she knew that there were jobs in Mozambique that only expatriates are qualified for. Ruth is gentle and positive and says it is time for me to move on.

You worked for WWF for ten years, she says. You rode that horse as far as it would go.

I agree, but later that night I lose the plot. I kind of thought I would work at WWF forever. Be a good guy. Make more National Parks, save elephants and lions and the poor rural farmers who are in conflict with them both.

The WWF reasoning makes no sense. Something else is going on.

I call my boss and he says I generate too much controversy. I push too hard. I am too "entrepreneurial." I make nature reserves, but I also make enemies. Too much swashbuckling. Too much noise.

I told you three years ago to slow down, he says.

He doesn't say mania because I haven't told him about my bipolar. I can hardly admit it to myself.

He doesn't want to let me go, he says, but he received orders from above. My job or his. He says he wants to hire me as a consultant and also have a farewell dinner for me. He does neither. People think I left in disgrace. Maybe I did.

I go to the bush on Wednesday. It is sunny and raining. Only tropical Africa does this like this. Split light and sunbird colors.

Gentian sky. Chartreuse clouds. Ice up there. Sweat down here. As good as a sunset. Or better.

We get to the Pemba Sun forest concession on the border of the Park so I can see for myself the condition of the forest. It's beautiful of course. Elephant tracks everywhere, warthogs in the mud wallows. Tsetse all over the car.

The poachers haven't reached here yet. Bamboo soaking our shirts as we push through to see the trees, but the beauty hides the fact that all the good timber has been cut and sold at ridiculous prices to cowboy foreign buyers.

With care and love and patience it might recover.

Over the weekend there is nothing to do but write my forestry report for WWF, and brood.

I do a little of the former and much of the latter. Betrayal cuts deep. The worst part of it is that some of it is my own.

I think of Ruth and I think of the WWF and I decide that if I can't do the work I was put on this world to do and if I am not who I thought I was and not who she thought I was, then what is the point? I have no idea. All I know is I am tired of waking up and wishing I hadn't. Tired of fighting to keep going when all I want to do is be done. Tired of trying to get WWF to deal with the fact that thirty elephants per day are dying up north and we are doing nothing about it. Tired of wondering what will become of me with my leg that hardly works and a mind that hardly works and a wife who I love dearly, and who is trying to love me despite myself, and too many poor people, and too many selfish people and too many people who deserve better than this world gives them.

And too many trees sold for too little money.

And no care nor love nor patience for the elephants, even though I have just raised $400,000 in donor funding for WWF for anti-poaching. Which my boss never manages to spend.

·   ·   ·

Saturday night I let go. If there is a purpose for me still in this world I will be alive in the morning.

I walk on the beach and feel the hard-packed sand under the balls of my feet. I remember running this beach, sprint intervals in the dark and wind like phantoms falling away behind me. Outrunning the wind. Exhilaration. The joy of flight on a dark beach at night. I try a few steps but the phantoms stay right there, right on my shoulder. It's not my leg that's the problem.

Lidia says that mania is like that. You feel larger than life. Everything is possible. Nothing forbidden, nothing to worry about, no regrets. Flight.

Depression, of course, is the opposite. But that's what running is for, what booze is for, what cheap bars and cheap companions are for. What adrenaline is for.

To put you right back into mania.

It's taken me a long time to understand that the phantoms are not just the wind. And that there is no outrunning them.

Lidia gave me three kinds of medication to take. One to prevent depression. One to prevent mania. One so I can sleep.

I add one more. A bottle of White Horse whisky—George Adamson's tipple. Just the thing for the African conservationist.

I stand on the beach in Pemba and look north to the Quirimbas National Park and think that whatever happens I will have left my mark on this world. Whatever happens I did one thing right. Whatever happens my name will not die. The Park is there because I lived and I fought for it.

Then I go back to my room and take all the pills and drink all the whisky.

·   ·   ·

Tomorrow I am still here. Not until four in the afternoon, but I am still here. I stay in bed and think about that until after dark. Lidia later calls it a suicide attempt, but then she is a shrink who is trained to see things that way.

What I think is more complicated. A ritual, perhaps? A vision quest? Not quite. A toss of the dice with death, maybe, with no way to lose. Blessed oblivion or the knowledge that I still have something to do in this world. I lie in bed and think some more. I should have the great-grandmother of all hangovers, but I don't. Instead, I have a curious peace. A stillness of mind. A certainty that I will go on to find whatever it is I am supposed to do next.

After a while I get out of bed and go down to the beach. It is night and low tide and there are women trying to catch hermit crabs and minnows with mosquito netting out there on the mud flats. They do this because they are poor. And hungry. I remember better times. And worse. Alas for the bipolar, peace of mind and certainty never last.

Addenda to Chapter 1

I STARTED this manuscript in 1999. And yes, I know it's a mess. Bits of now, bits of then, all jumbled up together, flotsam and jetsam on the beach.

Bits of several different "thens," really. And I guess several different "nows," too.

I'll try to signal when "now" is at the beginning of every chapter, sometimes the month, always the year. I'm sorry but I can do nothing about the Heisenberg leaps forwards and backwards in time that occur within and between chapters. That's how my mind works, or fails to. That's what reality is for me.

I will also try to signal where things happen, though, like electrons, my family does not seem to actually live in any one place; rather, we have a collection of places where it is more or less likely that we will be found at any given time. Our own probability cloud.

Still, I owe you an attempt at clarity, so here goes. My wife Ruth and I moved to the north of Mozambique at the end of 1996, contracted by an international aid agency, the Swiss non-governmental organization (NGO) Helvetas (using funds provided by the Swiss Development Corporation) to help rebuild the country after nearly forty years of war. Prior to that, I had spent sixteen years living in Swaziland, first as a Peace Corps volunteer and then working for an American NGO, the Near East Foundation, supporting the Swaziland Ministry of Agriculture and Cooperatives.

I met Ruth at Ministry Headquarters in 1991 on her first day of work in our mutual supervisor's office: she was sporting a smile so wide she had to turn sideways to get it through the door. She and I were both in other relationships then, but something clicked in us, a Heisenberg leap, or a quantum twinning of electrons perhaps, which hinted at our future momentum, our paired trajectories over time.

We married on 25th June, 1993.

In 1996, Helvetas sent us to Chiure District in Cabo Delgado Province in the north of Mozambique to implement a rural development project to alleviate poverty through support to education, agriculture, health, and other important sectors. We went there with our two smallest children, Neli, our two-year-old daughter, and Lunga, our five-year-old son.

Our two older daughters, Tiny and Khulile, stayed behind in Swaziland in boarding school. We were worried about them but they told us many years later that they loved it: I guess we were restrictive parents, when we were around.

In any case we must have done something right and we are all extremely close now. My adopted daughter Licinia was by then away at university in the United States, my adopted son Dumisane at university in South Africa.

. . .

We were told that Chiure District was at the time the most neglected district in the most underdeveloped province of the poorest country in the world.

This was only a small exaggeration. Mozambique was actually 167th out of 174 countries ranked that year by the United Nations Human Development Index,[2] which measures human well-being according to a variety of indicators, including expected lifespan and degree of education. Measured on GDP alone, Mozambique was 169th.[3]

There is no question that Cabo Delgado Province and Chiure District were poorer than the rest of the country. According to the Plano Estratégico de Cabo Delgado, 2001–2005, the provincial government's strategic plan, life expectancy in the province at the time of writing the plan was 37.8 years, while the under-five mortality rate was 295 per thousand, or just about three out of ten children dying before age five.[4] By way of comparison, the national life expectancy was forty-nine years[5], with the national under-five mortality rate being 162.5 per thousand.[6]

The adjustment was hard, our work of poverty alleviation in the rural areas even harder. Only in mid-1999 was I ready to start writing about the things we saw there and the things we did there.

I wrote sporadically over the years, with big gaps for work, parenthood, and mental breakdown. And only now, eighteen years later, am I able to complete what I started those many years ago.

KEY DATES, EVENTS, AND PLACES THAT
ARE MENTIONED IN THE BOOK

1991 Mbabane, Swaziland. I meet Ruth—a life-changing experience.

May 1993 the mountains north of Mbabane, Swaziland. We buy our farm, our family home, the nucleus. We go there when we can. None of the events in the book actually take place at the farm, with the exception of Christmas, 1999.

June 1993 I marry Ruth at the office of the Justice of the Peace, Mbabane, Swaziland. We spent all our wedding savings to buy the farm. Our Justice of the Peace is arrested for corruption the day after our wedding, so we do not actually get our marriage certificate until three months later.

September 1996 We begin employment with Helvetas. Our work takes us to five Districts, but we have a house in Chiure Town and the use of the Helvetas guesthouse in Pemba, the capital city of Cabo Delgado, as our work in rural development often requires us to deal with the provincial government. Our two smallest children, Neli and Lunga, come with us. Our two older daughters, Tiny and Khulile remain in boarding school in Swaziland. Our adopted children, Licinia and Dumisane, are away at university.

February 2001 We end our employment with Helvetas. I stay in Pemba, working pro bono, to try to create the Quirimbas National Park. I borrow $10,000 from my parents, rent a house in Pemba, and begin to organize communities and lobby government to declare the Quirimbas National Park. Ruth returns to Swaziland to be with the kids.

December 2001   After nearly a year pro bono, I am field re-cruited by the WWF, which throws its full support behind the creation of the Park. Our family is three or four days from desti-tution at the time. Ruth earns her master's degree during the time period 2001–2005 without, mind you, having completed a bache-lor's degree beforehand. She returns to northern Mozambique in early 2002 to work with Oxfam. Lunga and Neli come with her. I spend most of my time in the six Districts that eventually became the Quirimbas National Park; Ibo, Macomia, Quissanga, Meluco, Ancuabe, and Pemba-Metuge.

June 6, 2002   The Quirimbas National Park is declared by the Mozambican Government. I become the first WWF 'Park Coor-dinator.' My job is to set up the Park from scratch. From this date until 2008 I am almost constantly in the bush. In about 2005 or 2006, local community members on Ibo Island find a lovely old antique house for us to buy and rehabilitate. This is the house re-ferred to in Chapter One.

2008–2013   We move to Maputo, and I take up a more senior position with WWF. I travel a lot. This is our 'time of troubles': Ruth had noticed my mental health problems before this, as did my children. These years were however the most difficult.

April 2012   We live in Maputo. The doctor tells me my hip cartilage is destroyed. I lose my job with WWF. The events of Chapter 1 occur the week I receive my notice of termination. I was in Pemba doing a forest evaluation at the time. The visit to Ibo, mentioned in this same chapter, is a flashback that actually occurred prior to this, as is the subsequent visit to the doctor. I recount these two events in a scrambled, reverse order in the book. Non-linear brain function at work, I suppose. After leaving WWF and, between bouts of depression and mania, I try to start an environmental consulting business.

March 2013   My leg gets so bad I can no longer walk, even with a cane. I fly to India to have a partial hip replacement. I learn that it is much easier to run an environmental consulting business when both legs share the job of carting one about. I gain deep respect for all those who manage without the advantage of four functional limbs.

January–November 2017   The first drafts of the addenda are written. I am living in Maputo with Ruth and running my consulting business, selling most of my time to the World Bank Group. Our kids are all off at university and a collection of younger nieces and nephews have moved in. Why do I write? Same reason I exhale; something in me has to come out. Why write the addenda? Time and distance and perhaps the wisdom that purportedly goes with age means that I find myself with more to say about the things I wrote back then. And because the writing brings me both peace and joy.

October 2017   My father dies. I was with him at the time in Pennsylvania, USA. A kind man, a rigorous intellect. A carpenter turned university professor.

May 2018   This book is completed, life goes on. We are living in Maputo with visits to the farm in Swaziland. We still have the house on Ibo, though sadly do not get there often. I am still doing environmental consulting and supporting conservation efforts in Mozambique. Ruth is Mozambique Country Director for Village Reach, an organization that helps distribute vaccines and medicines to the distant rural areas.

June 25th 2018   is our twenty-fifth wedding anniversary.

MAIN ETHNIC GROUPS OF
CABO DELGADO PROVINCE

Muani   Fishermen and traders from the coast and islands of Cabo Delgado.

Macua   The people of the interior of Cabo Delgado, Nampula, and Zambézia provinces, hunters and farmers.

Maconde   The warrior nation of the planalto, the Mueda Plateau.

A NOTE ON NAMES

I have changed the names of a few people in the book to shield them from embarrassment, shame, or censure. And in one chapter, because there were too doggone many people named Peter.

The Portuguese Fortress on Ibo Island. Swahili settlement here dates from sometime between the seventh and the thirteenth century. Vasco da Gama arrived in 1499 or thereabouts, and the Portuguese occupied the island soon after. This Fortress dates from the mid 1700's. The silversmiths of Ibo work their magic here using techniques and tools that date from the middle ages: charcoal forges, goatskin bellows, blowpipes instead of blowtorches, and lemon juice instead of flux.

CHAPTER 2

Not a Very Good American

September, 1999. In which the reader is rather abruptly dropped into my past at the point in time when I started writing. I am in transit, via Maputo, to Cabo Delgado after a holiday visit to Swaziland. Ruth and the kids have flown to Cabo Delgado a few days previously. I visit the American embassy in Maputo on the way through town. Living in Chiure District, Cabo Delgado, and working for the Swiss NGO Helvetas.

F OR REASONS KNOWN only to themselves, the people at the American embassy asked me to be the US Warden for the Province of Cabo Delgado, Mozambique.

This means that I become the official contact for Americans living in or travelling through the province, and would be called to action if, for instance, travelers should be attacked or lost in the hinterlands, or should there be an emergency that requires the American population to be evacuated in totality to some safer location. In such emergencies, this service is apparently provided free of charge by the US government.

I was informed of my nomination in July by fax and had no qualms about accepting, since to the best of my knowledge there were only two other American families living in the province at the time. One was a family of Bible Translators from Cape May County in New Jersey. The fledgling Bible Translators had recently arrived in Cabo Delgado on a fifteen-year contract, to translate an Evangelical version of the Bible from (presumably) English into the local languages of Macua, Kimuani, and Maconde.

They spoke none of these. I figured that people with the gumption to assume fifteen-year contracts to fly to Cabo Delgado and translate the Bible into three languages they didn't speak for the purpose of converting African Muslims and Catholics to their own version of Christianity were unlikely to need help from me or from the American embassy for that matter.

The other Americans were an expatriate couple who had lived most of their lives in interesting parts of the world, at least fifteen of those years in Brazil. More recently, they had returned to Washington DC and bought a house near the Beltway. Alice at last had the opportunity to slow down, do the homemaker thing, and spend the holidays with friends and relatives. She enjoyed immensely the re-integration of herself into American society.

Meanwhile, Bob picked a living from the *corpus* of the United States Agency for International Development (USAID), in the manner of a cattle egret, and felt himself less of a man and more of a prisoner with every passing day. His discontent crystallized in the form of an intense hatred of Bill Gates. An eight-month's contract as Advisor on Urban Development to the municipality of Pemba was Bob and Alice's compromise, a last adventure for Bob, but it was no good. Bob grew more difficult with every passing day, most of which he ended at the bar of the Complexo Touristico Nautilus on the Praia de Wimbi just outside of Pemba, the capital of Cabo Delgado Province. Bob's wit grew sharp and his tongue acid.

Still, he was full of stories, an excellent drinking companion, and I figured that I would know where to find him in case of emergencies and that his finding would not be an entirely disagreeable experience.

.   .   .

I faxed a formal acceptance back to the American embassy the following day. I must confess that my existence has come to the attention of authority so rarely that the nomination delighted me, in the same way that children are delighted by balloons. No matter that for the whole of the following year my duties consisted of a single telephone call, asking me if I had heard from two missing Peace Corps volunteers hitchhiking down the coast from Tanzania.

It later turned out that they had come to no harm, and that the scare over their disappearance was in fact a product of vivid imaginations of overwrought parents. The volunteers, quite sensibly in my view, had neglected to inform their families of their travel plans. If one is determined to hitchhike down from Tanzania, it is better to inform loved ones only after one has safely concluded the journey.

No matter that the content of the American embassy magazine that, as a member of the official American community, I am entitled to receive, ranges from the merely abysmal to the thoroughly embarrassing.

No matter that the magazine itself is entitled *Piri Piri Palavres* and features a logo consisting of a computer-generated image of two chili peppers dancing in what appear to be Mexican sombreros.

No matter that the magazine affords my wife, who is not American, hours of delicious *Schadenfreude*, an emotional state that I had not previously encountered in a person of African descent. No matter all of it. After many years in the wilderness, I was an Official American.

It was in this state of mind that I called the Consular Office of the American embassy in Maputo.

I had no business with them, but I was in Maputo for a few days, transiting from Swaziland to Pemba, and thought it might be rather nice to have the opportunity to attach faces to the illegible signatures at the bottom of embassy communications and to the disembodied voices on the telephone. They thought so, too, and promised coffee and a muffin, and to add my name to the visitors list so I wouldn't have trouble at the gate.

I arrived at 9:15 for a 9:30 appointment. I parked my car several hundred meters down Avenida Kenneth Kaunda and picked my way to the gate between cement traffic cones, a metal security gate, several low concrete walls, and police officers of various nationalities, shapes, and sizes. On the sidewalk in front of the security gate I presented my identification and was scanned with a hand-held metal detector. The studs on my blue jeans provoked a buzz from the machine and I had to empty my pockets. I found my name on the visitors' list and so was escorted through the gate into the embassy compound.

At the door of the embassy building itself I traded my identification for a plastic clip-on visitor card and passed through an airport-style metal detector and another security gate.

Inside I found a Marine Guard behind bullet-proof glass who directed me to the Consular Office. More bullet-proof glass and a sliding drawer like in a bank stopped me in the anteroom. On the other side of the glass several embassy employees hunched over stacks of official-looking documents. A woman looked up after a while and smiled a smile so full of welcome that I felt a little better about all the gates and bars and bullet-proof construction. She opened a combination-coded, steel-plated metal door, and at last I was in there, where the coffee was.

It was good coffee, but I didn't have a chance to do much more that sip it. A phone call a few minutes later informed me that the Ambassador was ready to receive me.

I hadn't realized that I rated an audience with the Ambassador and had worn only a Che Guevara T-shirt of a design readily available in Mozambican street markets. There followed a few minutes of confusion while we attempted to determine which one of those present had sufficient authority to escort me to the Ambassador's office. Judy, the woman with the smile, encouraged John, a middle-aged mid-level official behind a desk, to take me on up. John was concerned that by so doing he would be treading on the toes of Judy-from-upstairs. Judy-with-the-smile felt that this would not be the case. John demurred. A large man shuffling papers ignored us.

I encouraged John to show me where the Ambassador's office was, so that I could go there myself, unescorted. John felt that this would be presumptuous. Judy-with-the-smile felt that John had full authority to accompany me. So it went until Judy-from-upstairs came downstairs to get me.

In the end Judy-from-upstairs and John accompanied me upstairs, but only John entered the Ambassador's office with me, at the urging of the Ambassador himself. The Ambassador greeted me with a politician's hello and a Politburo handshake, the sort of handshake that brings to mind Soviet era posters and statuary. Firm, proud, with more than a hint of Darwinian dominance. Also brief.

Americans still have trouble with the African style of long handshakes and/or hugs, or even holding hands for a while.

The Ambassador and I rapidly discovered a mutual interest in nature and wildlife. He was an intelligent, direct man who had travelled widely in the north of Mozambique in some of my favorite places: the Niassa Reserve, the coast, and the Quirimbas Islands of Cabo Delgado.

Earlier that morning I had visited the Director of the Coastal Management Unit of the Ministry of Environmental Affairs, Dr. Alfredo Massinga, who had informed me that the island of Ibo, the cultural and spiritual capital of the Quirimbas, was being promoted by his Unit as a new World Heritage Site, with the assistance and support of UNESCO.

Ibo had been in a state of decline for the past half century, despite the presence of coral reefs, mangrove swamps, wildlife, whales, Arab and Muani architecture, and a well-documented visit by Vasco de Gama in 1499. Such a designation by a UN organization would not only mean conservation and cultural preservation for the historic island, but would also attract badly needed tourism and investment.

I shared Dr. Massinga's news with His Excellency.

"Ahem," His Excellency said. "We actually believe that UNESCO's involvement in the development of Ibo would be the worst thing that could possibly happen."

I glanced at John but received only a diplomatic smile.

"The USA withdrew from UNESCO a couple of years ago. It's a mismanaged, profligate, inefficient organization that brings nothing but grief to the very people it tries to assist. You look at *Ilha de Mozambique*. It's in worse shape now than when it was declared a World Heritage Site several years ago."

His Excellency waved at his desk. "See that black folder there? That's the UNESCO project for *Ilha de Mozambique*. All that paper and nothing has happened. What would really help Mozambique Island would be to let investors—foreigners—buy land there. As for Ibo, the best thing would be for it to be left completely alone."

Oops.

I hemmed and hawed.

It was true that much of Mozambique Island resembles nothing so much as a dilapidated, overcrowded refugee camp with overflowing toilet facilities, but I couldn't see how UNESCO had contributed to the development of that situation. The civil war was the factor that had forced mainland populations to flee to the safety of the island, a civil war in which the ideological struggle between the USA and the Eastern Bloc had played a not inconsiderable role. When elephants fight, the ants suffer.

Once on Mozambique Island, refugees had occupied every available square meter of land, be it marsh, or beach, or ancient

Afro-Portuguese historical monument. UNESCO plans for development of the island had not gone forward because renovation of historical structures would mean displacing thousands of Mozambicans from their precarious homes. Free-market sale of land would involve the same. And Ibo has been neglected for fifty years without any apparent conservation or cultural benefits.

I searched for safer ground.

"I couldn't agree with you more about the importance of investment for the Mozambican economy," I said. "There will be no recovery without it. Everyone can be an investor: foreigners, small businessmen, even poor farmers can invest, by planting fruit trees, or coconuts. The end of the war and land reform mean that secure land tenure is finally a reality for the rural Mozambican. The new Land Law of 1997 means that farmers can plant trees with confidence, and businessmen can build with confidence."

I had participated in the process of field-testing the new Land Law and had even written a draft clause or two of the Technical Annex (which clauses were, mercifully, deleted, as I am neither a lawyer nor legislator).

The Law itself is a remarkable thing that, for the first time in Mozambican history, guarantees in clear and simple language the right of the peasant farmer to the land he uses. It also acknowledges the role of traditional community leaders—chiefs—in land allocation and allows for the businessman to obtain a title deed for land to be used for business or commercial farming, though any businessman applying for a title deed is obliged to obtain community approval if he wishes to occupy community land.

"Ahem," said His Excellency. "We actually believe that the new Land Law didn't go nearly far enough. Land should have been completely privatized. Everyone should have a title deed, so land can be used as collateral for loans from the bank. How you gonna develop without bank loans? Whatcha have here is a situation in which …"

His accent broadened as he warmed up.

Oops again.

. . .

Too late I remembered what Dr. José Negrão had told me about American opposition to the new Land Law.

Dr. Negrão is a professor at the University of Eduardo Mondlane, runs the National Land Reform Campaign, *Campanha Terra*, and is the principal author of the new law. No one deletes his clauses.

"The Americans were very much against the new law, Peter," Dr. Negrão told me. "They wished us to take as a model the American colony, the Philippines. Everyone has a title there; the records, the maps, the *cadastro* is perfect. But there are many arguments against this system for Mozambique. I will give you just two. In the first place, 40 per cent of the useful land in the Philippines is owned by absentee landlords, speculators, and is unavailable for development. Is this what we want for ourselves? I think not."

I had to agree.

"Second. How long do you think it would take to survey and issue title deeds to every farmer in Mozambique?"

In Cabo Delgado, the Provincial Surveyor's Department, Dinageca, currently has 300 applications for title deeds pending. Some of these have been pending for years. Their equipment dates from colonial times; Dinageca had no GPS until last year, when we donated them a sportsman's model for the purpose of rough estimation of community land boundaries.

"A hundred years?" I said.

"At a minimum. And meanwhile the communities remain undefended. With this new law, we acknowledge community land rights immediately, and the burden lies on the developer to show he is not occupying anyone's land without prior consent. We have created an immediate defense. *Claro*, the law will later have to be improved, but which law will not? This is an interim law, as well adapted to today's conditions as we can possibly make it."

. . .

I recalled this conversation as the Ambassador's discourse ground to a halt.

John's diplomatic smile never faltered. I decided to try a question.

"The office of the United States Agency for International Development told me that they had an environmental program," I ventured. "Just what are they doing in conservation in Mozambique?"

"Nothing," said His Excellency. "All the environmental program money has been allocated for associativism, for programs encouraging the collective marketing of agricultural products. Maybe we'll do something in the future."

Judy-from-upstairs put her head in the door and pointed to her watch. The Ambassador saw me out.

His handshake as I left was slightly less Politburo than on the way in, as if I had been sweating, or shoveling manure. Judy-from-upstairs saw John and me downstairs.

My coffee was cold, but the muffin still looked good. John sat behind his desk.

"Gee, I'd forgotten that the USA had withdrawn support to UNESCO," I said, and bit my muffin.

John smiled back as I chewed. Judy-with-the-smile was nowhere in sight.

"And gosh, I'd forgotten that the Americans were opposed to the new Land Law."

I took another bite. John held his smile, but it was starting to show some strain.

"And wow, who would have thought that all the American environmental budget would be used for collective agricultural marketing?"

John blinked at that one and shuffled his papers.

• • •

I picked up the remnants of muffin. "Well, I can see that you have work to do, so I'd better move on. I can eat this on the way. It's been great to meet you."

"Stop in again sometime," John said.

Judy-with-the-smile appeared, and she and John saw me out. The large man who had been crouched over the pile of papers, and who I hadn't been introduced to, gave me a secret, conspiratorial smile as I went out: I still don't know why.

I had a little trouble juggling the bits of muffin, the plastic visitor card and my identification documents at the airport-style security gate, but I managed, and soon I was out on the sidewalk.

I drove back to the Helvetas office and rang Bernard at the Swiss Development Corporation.

"Coffee," I said. "Immediately. Do you have a minute?"

"Even five or ten," he said. "Come on up."

I went up. His coffee wasn't as good as the American embassy's, but at least I got to drink it.

"Look, Bernard," I said. "If you accept the premise that law must have some relation to the culture and tradition of the society that it seeks to govern, then the idea of private land for peasant farmers is absurd. There are absolutely no cultural antecedents for individual land titles. Land is not owned; it is used, and who gets to use which piece is governed by clan and community. Clans and communities hold land. Not individuals."

"This is clear," said Bernard.

"What will a poor farmer do with a title deed? He doesn't understand what the damn thing is, or what it means. He'll sell it off for a pittance and migrate to some other location. Everyone does that, and pretty soon the rich will have all the land titles and the poor will have nothing. Privatization of land will kick off the biggest land speculation boom that Mozambique has ever seen. The poor will lose their land and starve."

"This is definitely a danger of privatization," said Bernard.

"Their only defense is this new Land Law." I paused. "You know, I should have drawn some parallel between what happened to the Native Indians in America and what might happen here. I should have said something about Manhattan Island and a handful of beads."

"Did you tell the Ambassador of your association with the Swiss embassy; that you were working on a Swiss Development Corporation-funded project?" asked Bernard.

The Swiss Development Corporation had contributed substantial funding for the development of the new Land Law and for the education of the general public about land issues.

"Of course. I gave him my business card."

"I wish you hadn't done that," said Bernard. "Thomas gets along quite well with the American Ambassador."

Thomas, as Chargé-d'Affaires of the Swiss embassy, gets paid quite well for getting along with nearly everybody, I thought.

"I thought you were with me on all this stuff," I said.

The Swiss Development Corporation had another project on Mozambique Island, a sort of pre-project to encourage the residents of the island to return to their farms on the mainland. This would mean vacating the historic forts and ruins, which would allow the UNESCO restoration project to begin. The project wasn't going very well. Twenty years of war makes a body cautious.

"I am, I am," Bernard hastened to reassure me. Bernard is an excellent diplomat, which was why he has an excellent job as a Sector Co-ordinator near the top of the Swiss Development Corporation institutional hierarchy, with a top-floor corner office full of art and sculpture by recognized Mozambican artists and sculptors.

I, on the other hand, have a short-term contract as a "Project Official" with an office in Chiure District 2,000 kilometers up-country, full of rats and geckos and bat droppings, and dust when the wind blows.

"Thanks for the coffee, Bernard."

"My pleasure. Stop in again sometime, next time you're in town."

I rushed to catch my plane. Ruth and the kids had flown up to Pemba on Wednesday and I was anxious to see them again. Bernard lent me a driver who got me to the airport on time and carried my bags and finessed all my baggage onto the plane, and didn't even ask for a tip. I gave him a large one.

In the departure lounge, a round, bald-headed journalist walked up to me and greeted me in Zulu. I hid my surprise and replied in siSwati, which is a closely related, mutually intelligible language.

"I saw you in '97 in the *Pensão Martins*, my brother," he said. "You had two kids and a beautiful Swazi wife and a plump young woman who looked after the children. I remember you well, my brother."

He told me that he'd been organizing and teaching a training course for young journalists for the past few weeks and that he needed someone to carry a parcel for him to Nampula. One of his students joined us, a soft-spoken man I knew from Cabo Delgado who was starting a provincial newspaper, reporting on development projects and governmental activities, and generally trying to fulfill the traditional role of the press in a democratic society.

The young man, whose name I am ashamed to say I have forgotten, works entirely without remuneration, as no donor or embassy has seen fit to fund his efforts and people in Cabo Delgado have no money to buy newspapers. We chatted a minute, the young man took the package, and he and I got on the plane.

It was cloudy so there was nothing to see. I slept. When I awoke two hours later, the plane was descending through bright sunshine and Pemba Bay gleamed below us.

Ruth was waiting for me in the crowd outside the baggage claim room, smiling her magic smile, a tall and striking beauty even in a country of beauties.

She abandoned her Swazi reserve and kissed me there on the tarmac, while gap-toothed porters in neon-yellow vests and Indian traders in spotless jellabiyahs and dignified Macua matrons in bright *capulana* cloths jostled us on every side, and little boys fought for the right to carry the bags to the car.

As we drove down the hill into town I saw the ocean winking through the cashew and mango and baobab trees.

Abudjate, my boatman, waited down there with the sailboat, and Stu with the diving gear, and the dolphins and the fish and the reef, and Nicolāu and Abdallah and José Dias from the Provincial Forests and Wildlife Department were out in the other direction, working with the communities to control both poaching and wildlife damage in crop fields. It all felt right, except for the Americans.

I was pretty sure they weren't happy with their new warden. The embassy staff were good people, hardworking, well intentioned. I had hoped they would like me. I had hoped they would find in me a kindred spirit, someone they could work with, someone they could still call their own.

Nope. Not a flicker of that. Just an unexpected gulf that I had failed to leap.

Maybe I shouldn't feel so stupid. Time works on all things. In some distant prehistoric swamp a mammal, a prototypical otter, perhaps, or a muskrat, left the land to return to the sea, to the element whence it came, and the sea has worked it and changed it, has scoured its hair and drawn out its body and gifted it with sonar, and there is now no going back.

I left the USA nearly twenty years ago. And since then I have lived in Africa.

Addenda to Chapter 2

THAT "TWENTY years ago" is now thirty-six, and land is still a contentious issue in Mozambique and in Southern Africa in general. The colonial notion that land can be owned is foreign to traditional Africans, who see land as a shared resource. One can occupy and use land for a time, and houses and cattle kraals can be passed from generation to generation, but the land itself belongs to itself, its allocation the responsibility of the Chief or King.

The Swazi nation was appalled to discover in the early 1900s that there was no land left in their country on which they could settle and build houses and raise crops and cattle and children. All of Swaziland apparently belonged to colonial settlers.

The Swazi kings thought they had been granting sheep grazing rights, while the incoming British and South Africans assumed they were receiving land grants and registered them as such with the colonial administration.

In 1907, the British were forced to reduce the size of each concession by a third, which opened some space for Swazis to live,[7] but enshrined the concept of land ownership within the legal system of a country whose residents had no notion of such a thing. No communication across the space-time continuum. Many Swazis still resent the imposition.

In any case, and soon after this decision, the Queen Regent, Labotsibeni Mdluli, publicly condemned British land policy and established the Lifa Fund, using voluntary contributions from the Swazi population, to buy back the lost land. This fund continued to operate until the 1960s, by which time sixty percent of the country was back in the Nation's hands and being governed in the traditional manner.[8]

The Lifa buy-back process was officially stopped in the early 1980s, when the then-King Sobhuza II saw that there were only 400 commercial farms left in the country, and he judged that to be a necessary number in order to maintain a healthy agricultural sector. Good farms come on the market only rarely, so that is why Ruth and I leaped at the chance to buy one in May 1993, even though financially it meant cancelling our white wedding scheduled for June, and settling for a Justice of the Peace with only three friends in attendance.

In the early 2000s my Swazi Chief asked me for help in a land dispute with a neighboring farm family, who were claiming half of the Mvembili chiefdom as their farm on the basis of a title deed issued in the 1960s by the High Court in Pretoria, just before the time of Swazi Independence.

I should explain that I am an adopted Swazi, as well as being both a Mozambican and American citizen, which is how I came to have a Swazi Chief, the late Prince Solani Dlamini. Adoption is a common cultural phenomenon in the Southern African warrior nations such as the Zulu and the Swazi. Thus it is possible to be a "white Swazi" or "white Zulu" (the South African musician Johnny Clegg is an example of the latter) in a way that it is not possible to be a "white Macua."

Adoption in warrior nations exists as a way for the nation to replenish itself after losses in battle: an adopted Swazi is literally no longer seen as belonging to any other ethnic group except the Swazi. And it is not uncommon: a recent census showed that there are close to a thousand white Swazis.

The hardest part of the adoption process is gaining the confidence and friendship of a Chief and his community. This usually takes years. After that, one requests (or is requested, in my case) to ally formally with the Chief—a process known as "kukhonta"—and by extension the King and the rest of the Swazi nation.

One offers the chief a cow, to cement the bond, and the Chief informs the King, who grants a formal audience. This may also take years.

In any case, my chief asked for assistance in the community land dispute, and I was oath-bound to provide it. I investigated the case. Community elders informed me that the family's father, who I shall call Jacobus Stephanus van der Merwe, had asked Prince Solani's grandfather for the land to graze sheep and to build a house for his wife. His wife was Swazi so both she and her husband were no longer welcome in apartheid South Africa. Prince Solani's grandfather agreed, which acceptance meant that, in Swazi reality, van der Merwe joined the chiefdom and became one of its subjects.

Fast forward now to 1950, and van der Merwe's Last Will and Testament. In it he leaves "his farm Mooiplaats" to his children. No mention of the old Chief in the will. No mention of the ongoing van der Merwe family obligations as members of the Mvembili Chiefdom either. No mention of a title deed, nor a farm number, yet said children, now adults, appear with a title deed in 1990— one issued in South Africa in the 1960s, before Swazi Independence from Britain, but still during the time of apartheid.

I took copies of the relevant documents to Prince Solani.

"I thought the days of turning sheep camps into title deeds ended a hundred years ago," I said.

"So did I," he replied.

The legal battle continues to this day, though my Swazi neighbors have simply voted with their feet and invaded the farm, and no governmental authority dares to throw them out again. Members of the van der Merwe family regularly pass by to growl and grumble.

The new Land Law of Mozambique (Law no. 19/97) was intended to sort out such problems for the Mozambican population.[9]

The law is excellent in that it does not require family sector farmers to have documents from the government to establish the rights to the land on which they live and make their livelihoods; these rights are assumed to exist, the presence of fields, orchards, and houses being proof of the right to tenure.

Poor rural farmers have these rights even without a piece of paper (and even though much abuse has occurred because poor rural farmers do not always know how to defend their rights). This right to tenure also exists even though in theory all lands belong to the Mozambican State, which fact reflects both African landholding tradition and Mozambique's post-socialist political sensibilities.

Things are more difficult for incoming investors. Since family sector rights are generally not documented, investors who wish to acquire lands must either engage in a lengthy process of identification and negotiation with individual families, or risk conflicts and accusations of civil rights abuse. It is estimated that only 5 per cent of land holdings nationwide have ever been registered in the National Land Cadastre, and these generally are those of larger size.

Recent estimates of the time required to register all landholdings in the National Cadastre, including the many millions of individual family sector holdings, have ranged as high as 275 years. The resolution of land conflicts is a slow process, one that I have been very much involved in over the past few years, mediating, educating communities, educating investors, and even educating government officials on the workings of the Land Law.

Perhaps the biggest weakness of the law is that it requires governmental approval for all land transactions involving investors, who are defined for purposes of law as just about everyone who is not a family sector Mozambican farmer. Since all land is defined as belonging to the "State," government approval becomes ineluctable, the post-socialist "State" having assumed unto itself the role of the Chief in the land allocation process.

I myself have three cases pending, cases where communities have agreed to cede small parcels of land to me for various investments, yet government approvals have been held up for, in one case, more than eight years.

Only influential political figures get their land transactions approved quickly. The rest of us wait.

José Carlos, my friend and real estate specialist, tries his best to educate me.

"Peter, know this. The corrupt never say 'No,' they just keep saying 'Tomorrow ...'"

Since I am dense, he explains further.

"You know that all land belongs to the State. It cannot be sold. But you can buy it."

He gives me a look over the top of his glasses and even I know what he is trying to say. I do not follow his advice however, as it goes against some of my fundamental views on how governments should be run.

So I wait.

Present-day readers might question why I was bemused by the extensive security at the American embassy.

That was 1999, remember, and we all expected that things were going to get better. The Mozambican civil war was over, the economy growing. The euro was launched that year, a landmark step towards international cooperation.

The Truth and Reconciliation Commission had just completed its work in South Africa, and Médecins Sans Frontières would win the Nobel Peace Prize in October, 1999.

Yet none of these developments meant that all groups of the disgruntled, all over the world, would suddenly be satisfied. Sadly, such a degree of security is no longer remarkable.

Kussi, our sailboat. Abudjate Selemane, master mariner, is at the helm, with an unidentified colleague standing near the mast. We built Kussi to have fun on weekends, but I ended up using Kussi as a full-time workboat up in the islands, for setting up and managing the Quirimbas National Park. Some boats have greatness thrust upon them.

CHAPTER 3

Sea Creatures

October 1999. In which we go sailing with our friends Stuart, Connie, Charles, Vera, and Paula, in Pemba Bay one weekend.

W E SAW DOLPHINS in the bay today. And whales. We went out sailing just before noon in light airs that quickly turned into a strong breeze with a cross chop.

The wind has been terrible this year, all up and down the coast. While we were in Swaziland in August a storm came through that took roofs off houses and schools all over the country and dumped a few centimeters of snow on the heights. We even had snow at the farm, for the first time anyone can remember. I woke up worried about the peach blossoms, but one glance across the valley reassured me. The only frost I saw was the pink frost of petals on bare branches, clearly visible even at a distance of half a kilometer.

The wind had been just as bad in Pemba. My fellow mariner and occasional drinking companion Steve L. lost the *Vumba* a day or two ago. There were no fatalities except the boat. He and his crew were on the way back from a fishing trip in the islands. They hit heavy weather and ran out of fuel just north of Pemba.

In the darkness and the wind, they mistook a jerry-can of drinking water for the emergency jerry-can of fuel. The motors died as they rounded Ponto Diablo. Steve and his crew nursed them to the mouth of the Rio Tari where they tried to anchor for the night. The anchor cable parted. Nuru, one of the boatmen, dove down and set the spare anchor in a crack in the rocks.

The south wind, the *kussi*, rose even more. Rollers up from Antarctica pounded the *Vumba*'s hull until the anchor line pulled its cleat from the boat, leaving a hole the size of a football. Within minutes *Vumba* was on the rocks; there is no beach to speak of between Pemba and Ponto Diablo.

Steve and Nuru and the others abandoned ship. The following morning, *Vumba* was in fibreglass pieces no larger than a bathtub.

"*Muito mau*," Abudjate. "A very bad situation. You were wise to build a sailboat. No problem with fuel."

Abudjate was from a family of Macua fisherman, born and raised on the water, and when you hire a Macua fisherman to look after your boat, you have hired him to do something very close to the core of his own identity. The job brought him great prestige among his fellow fisherman. Several times on the beach I heard them referring to "*o barco de Abudjate*"—"Abudjate's boat," as if for them I didn't exist, or my existence was an irrelevancy.

Of course the boat was Abudjate's: he worked on it every day, cleaning, scraping, painting, even diving down to rub algae off the hull and rudder. I was just the fool who Abudjate took sailing on the weekends.

Despite his expertise and my appreciation of it, Abudjate and I had at best an uneasy relationship. We were governed by different rhythms. Mine are terrestrial: the five-day work week, the clock, the calendar. His were all of the sea: the tides, the monsoon, the migrations of pelagic fish. Several times, early in our relationship, he turned up at my door, at night, or early in the morning.

"*Senhor*, we must go to the islands, *Ilha Quipaco*, tomorrow. The north wind is blowing and the weather will be fair. My brother has just returned from there with a *marlin*, and several large *xereu*."

Or, "*Senhor*, it is time for the *campanha camarão*. They are catching much shrimp in the islands. We will fill the bilge with ice, and bring a tonne of shrimp down every week ..."

But I couldn't. There were meetings, and the accounts to settle before month's end, and endless reports and proposals and meetings with the Swiss. After a while, Abudjate stopped suggesting trips. My failure to respond pained us both, I think. Or perhaps the death of his wife in a cholera epidemic changed him.

Her family was from the wild *mato* north of Pemba, several days' walk from the sea. When she died, Abudjate journeyed inland to be with her clan from the time of her burial until the cleansing ceremony forty days later. He did not inform me of his departure and I was angry with him.

But this too was my fault, for it turned out that everyone knew that he had gone, except me, and it was clear to them that an absence of forty days was only to be expected. Ties to clan are as strong as those to the sea.

When he returned it was better. Maybe his time in the bush had taught him how it is for those of us who live by the land. He became more conscious of time, more aware of the need for communication with me. If he missed a day, he would tell me. If we agreed to meet, he would be there. Until today.

Today I drove to the beach with the lunch and the fishing tackle and found Abudjate gone.

Home, the fishermen said. He went home. We told him you would come, but he went anyway. Who knows why? I turned around and drove back to the house, growing angrier every minute. I wanted to sail with Ruth and the kids, and it went better if there were two experienced hands on the sheets.

I'll sack him this time. Too many missed trips. Too many times I find the boat on the beach when I want to sail. Too many funerals, and weddings, and sick kids, and ceremonies. Too many excuses.

I found him at the house and I was short with him. He said he had come to get me because he thought I might not come. We drove back to the beach. He stopped me before we arrived. "Look *Senhor.* There she is. There. And her baby."

"What? What is it?"

"*Balea, Senhor.* Whale. We go to see her today."

A long black shape rolled in the swell, far offshore.

Stuart and I rigged the boat in record time. My hands were shaking. The kids jumped around and got sand and water all over everything that should have stayed clean and dry. Ruth and Connie managed to protect the lunch. We met our friends Charles and Vera and Paula on the beach and invited them to come along. Then we ran up the jib and mainsail and ran downwind to see the whales.

Charles hadn't been on the boat before, as he had only started work at the Pemba Shipyard after it had been launched. He cast a professional eye over the deck and the mast and the fittings.

"Nice," he said, and she was.

She was a 21-foot pocket cruiser made almost entirely out of *mbila*, African mahogany, a medium-heavy, reddish wood that has a nearly unlimited lifespan in salt water, provided it is protected from rot and sun and shipworms. Even the mast was *mbila*. Stuart, my co-owner, lamented that we couldn't have a light spruce or aluminum mast, but I found the solidity reassuring, for there is no Coast Guard in Pemba. The weight up the mast also slowed the rolling of the boat, giving her an easier motion in the swells.

We built her last year in Pemba.

I say "we," but most of the work was done by *Senhor* Cabrito, the shipyard foreman, and his crew. The *Estaleiro Naval* had never built such a boat before; commercial fishing vessels were their trade, and so Cabrito built her as he would a fishing vessel, plans and dimensions and hardware specifications notwithstanding. He is as capricious and as stubborn as his name suggests, but he looks more like a well-fed shorthorn bull, and he has a temper like a buffalo. All this exasperated Stu, for he had carefully selected the boat plans and had imported them from Boston at a cost of $175 plus $64 postage, but I didn't mind too much.

I wouldn't have expected an English hydrological engineer and a Portuguese boat carpenter to have the same ideas on much of anything, especially the building of boats. In the end, Cabrito's version came out some 10 centimeters wider and 30 centimeters longer than specified. She also had an enormous keel hewn from a trunk of *chanfuta*, a dense hardwood that sinks in water and is impervious to shipworms, and her planking, much thicker than required, was braced for the squalls of the open sea, and for carrying tonnes of fish.

Nothing was under-built, and for that I forgave Cabrito the hideous green color of the hull, and for painting the toe-rail, which we had planned to varnish. The only time my confidence in him wavered was when Stu found him using sheetrock screws for the planking. We put one in salt water and it rusted within days.

"I didn't have any boat screws," said Cabrito, and so we imported some from the USA. Cabrito replaced all 600 sheetrock screws with number eight stainless steel, without complaint.

In the end, Cabrito may have been right about the toe-rail. Both Stuart and I are that curious blend of the quixotic and the practical that makes a person want to live in the underdeveloped areas of Africa and enables him to thrive there. The varnished handrails and ventilators of the boat look good, but re-varnishing every six months or so is something we have neither the time nor the inclination for. We maintain the boat as a fisherman would; everything seaworthy, nothing ready for the regatta.

We have the boat to sail it. We'll probably paint the handrails and the ventilators next time the varnish wears off.

Stuart and I took some days off work for fitting the mast. Cabrito and his merry men glued it together, but the intricacies of pulleys and shrouds and stays and sail-track were beyond them. Stu and I had never fitted a mast either, but it had to be done, so we did it. The spreaders were aluminum tubing that Stuart scrounged somewhere at the Pemba City Council. Cables were affixed by hand-carved *mbila* fittings and electrical tape; Abudjate and I were the carvers.

We fashioned the chain-plates ourselves out of stainless bar stock; at the time there was no chandler nor outfitter in all of Mozambique. We had to erect the mast three times before we got everything right, and even then the backstay pulled out after a few months.

Stu wanted to drop the mast again, but I had another idea. We put the boat on the beach and Abudjate and I ran Stu up the mast in a bosun's chair. The sight of an angular, 2-meter-tall English hydrological engineer dangling from the mast all elbows and knees with a spanner in his hand was something I wish I had captured on film. All in all, we learned why the local fishermen to a man use the lateen rig. It is cheap to make, easy to rig up and in a pinch, the whole thing can be dropped on the deck and repaired, even at sea.

Sailcloth was also an issue. We had to import ours, but the locals sew their sails out of emergency tents donated by the UN for disaster relief or to refugees, who do not need them. They build their own houses out of stick and mud adobe so the tents can be sold at a tidy profit to sailors. Stu and I found out the hard way that UNHCR tents do not withstand the stresses and strains of modern sail design.

Still, our boat does have some advantages. We make better time against the wind and there is something in the clean lines of a Bermuda rig that pleases our First-World souls. Friends tell me the boat looks like it belongs in a Bacardi commercial.

Naming the boat proved to be a bigger problem than rigging the mast. I wanted to call it *Sarafina*, which means nearly the same thing in all three of the languages we speak at home (the bright star, the angel, the blessed one), and is a beautiful name, capturing exactly the feel of bow cutting clear blue swells under a fluffy, cumulus sky.

Stuart preferred something more along the lines of Joshua Slocum's *Spray*, which he felt was the perfect name for a boat, unfortunately already taken. Connie, his wife, put forward some unpronounceable Ugandan name, so my wife countered with a difficult Swazi one. Nationalism was overtaking our unanimity.

We came to our senses and agreed that the name had to be Mozambican. But what? Eagles, terns, gulls, waves, wind, peace, serenity—all were proposed. Stuart finally went to the *Capitania* and registered her as *Kussi*, the south wind, but it didn't really work. The *kussi* is no great friend of mariners. Only people who do not know her call her *Kussi*, and we have yet to paint the name on her stern. We call her simply "the boat," and think of her as a man thinks of his wife, if he truly cares for her.

The boat understands and knows that she is not the same thing to all those who love her.

The boat danced down the wind to where the whales were. Neli and my son Lunga were nearly dancing themselves on the foredeck, while the adults spilled out of the cockpit and over the gunnels, binoculars in hand. Abudjate scanned the sea, while I kept my eyes on the sails.

"*Esta ai! Balea!* Over there!" someone shouted, and there she was, 200 meters out on the port bow. I set course to pass behind her. I had an idea that she would sound if approached too closely, so we passed fifty meters away, the calf clearly visible at her side.

Melville has written probably all that ever needs to be written about the size and strength and sheer presence of whales, so I feel no need to go into great detail here. Suffice it to say none of it was preparation for the sight of this black apparition surging through the water, rolling and blowing on the surface like a dolphin, but so much bigger and without the obvious dorsal fin.

I say surging only in retrospect, for she moved with deceptive grace and slowness. It was only when we tried to overtake her that we realized that we approached only at her whim, for she outpaced us without any apparent increase in effort.

Her calf was more believable, for he was still small enough that the vigor of his tail movements appeared to have some relationship to his speed through the water.

I turned to make another pass and the wind hit us like a hammer. I hadn't noticed how much it had risen since we left the beach. The boat heeled right over on her side and the adults clustered by the rail grabbed for handholds and got their feet wet. I brought her nose into the wind and she stopped the heeling movement but didn't right. I leaned and had time to think about the weight up the mast and the heavy *chanfuta* keel before the quick-thinking Abudjate slipped the mainsheet from its jamming cleat and the mainsail swung free.

We righted. Abudjate was laughing; we had lost the life-ring overboard.

"Leave it," I said, "We'll come back for it later. Let's go by the whale again."

We did, getting even closer this time, close enough to see the barnacles on mama's chin.

Then it was too close and mama sounded, but not too deep. We could see the aquamarine light reflecting off her back as she hung two or three meters under the surface. We gave her a rest and ran down wind to collect the lost gear. Charles enjoyed the unique experience of leaping overboard to rescue a life-ring.

· · ·

The whales surfaced and came back towards us. They were occupying a narrow, sandy channel between the inner and outer reefs, about fifteen meters deep, where we had dived often.

Mama let us come very close this time. She rose to the surface thirty meters upwind and lolled there. She exhaled and a cloud of white spray hung in the air for a moment before the wind snatched it away. Her calf came up on the far side of her body. Then she arched her back and the island that was not an island sank into the sea.

I thought of Sinbad, and Ibn Battuta, and remembered a voyage we made to Vamizi Island last May.

We met a fisherman there who sold us ambergris and offered us fresh coconut milk as we sat on whalebones in his yard. The islanders do not hunt whales; the ambergris and whalebone he had plucked from the sea-wrack after a storm the month before.

Another fisherman offered us a turtle shell, and we found precious red coral on the beach. Gum copal we found on the back shelf of a grimy bamboo stall in the market at Macomia, thus completing the four traditional treasures of the Indian Ocean.

We bought the gum copal, for incense, but not the turtle shell. Turtles are protected in Mozambique, but there is no enforcement on the islands and the fishermen are very poor. We surprised one group with a sack of 200 turtle eggs. They were going to eat them. The fish they caught were all for sale; evidently none could be spared for breakfast.

The wind carried us past the whales and we beat upwind, preparing for another pass. The bowsprit leapt and plunged in the chop and we took a sensual pleasure in the motions of boat and wind and waves.

"*Golfinhos,*" cried Vera. "*Ai!*"

"What? Where?" No one else could see them.

"*Ai!*" She pointed and switched to English, as if that could help us to see more clearly. "Dolphins!"

We looked where she pointed. A dolphin flung itself clear of the water, and then another, and another. We couldn't miss that.

"One. Two, no three! Four!" Vera called, and my daughter Neli chimed in:

"Five. Six—seven—eight!"

The dolphins came in a flood. They were all around us, blowing and leaping on every side. East of us, a group had trapped some redfish near the surface and were taking turns bursting up through the terrified school. Their attacks carried them three or four body lengths clear of the water. Then they would fall, some more gracefully than others, back to the sea.

One could see individual personalities at work: this one was a clown; that one an athlete; this one was showing off; that one simply wanted to eat.

The biggest clown of all tossed his fish into the air at the height of his leap. The bright red dot soared as high as the palm trees on the beach behind.

"Twelve! Thirteen, no fourteen! And two more over there! Nineteen! Seventeen! Twenty!" Neli and Vera were still counting, but it was starting to break down. There were too many dolphins and neither Neli nor Vera had enough numbers. Neli was limited by her age (she was five at the time), and Vera by her excitement and her command of English.

Charles chimed in, "Twenty-three! Fifty-one! Forty-eight! Twenty-leventy thousand!" We all laughed.

Charles has no problem with numbers. He speaks Zulu like a Zulu, Portuguese like a Portuguese, and English like a South African.

Then the dolphins found the whales. They were all over them, leaping and tumbling like a litter of over-excited Labrador pups. The water boiled white. It really did look as if there were twenty-leventy thousand dolphins out there.

Some of the cheekier ones leapt clear across mama's back, but she did not sound. It may have been a family reunion of sorts, or a meeting of old friends, and we were privileged to be a part of it.

I asked Charles if he knew anything about the social ecology of marine mammals, if whales and dolphins hang out together the way zebras and blue wildebeest do, but all of his experience has been in game parks. He didn't know. We didn't even know at the time what species of whale they were, though the long pectoral fins should have been a dead giveaway that they were humpbacks.

All too soon, the dolphins moved on. One minute the sea was alive with bright shapes, the next we were alone with the whales.

We passed close to say goodbye and this time mama let us come right in, close enough to smell her breath when she exhaled. She snorted, a bit like a hippo, and warm air washed over us. I expected the smell of fish, but it was nothing like that. It was all mammal. Not like dogs or lions, who have the breath of carnivores, but something vaguely familiar; something evocative yet completely unidentifiable; something that emphasized our kinship yet under- lined how little we could ever know of each other; something that said that it is ever thus with those we love.

Mama sounded for the last time. Her tail hung above the water as we waved goodbye and we parted, drawn apart to our separate destinies. We were sad, though the day had been perfection.

At the beach we dropped the sails and raised the center-board and the boat came to rest in sixty centimeters of water. Abudjate and I stowed the gear and put away the sails. I noticed in him a crispness of movement and a lightness of step that he had lacked in the morning. He felt my look and looked back, and his eyes told me that I was wrong about the whales.

His eyes told me that sometimes, if we do everything right, we can know the creatures of the sea, and they us; and sometimes, if we do everything right, we can know something of those we love.

And I had done everything right. I had been there when he needed me. I had let him show me something of himself. I had let him show me whales, and twenty-leventy thousand dolphins.

Addenda to Chapter 3

IT IS hard, now, to remember exactly what happened when. Part of it is time and distance, part of it is advancing age, but part of it is most certainly the fact that bipolar, for better or worse, does not lend itself to the conversion of short-term to long-term memory. Things that happen when I am up and things that happen when I am down are sometimes retained and sometimes not. And some things which are retained are scrambled. And other things, which never happened at all, I remember as clear as day.

All this was complicated by alcohol. Lidia tells me that "self-medication" is common among the bipolar. It is certainly true that I "self-medicated" to an extraordinary degree. What I mean here is simply "beyond ordinary"; I use the word "extraordinary" in a descriptive and not a superlative sense.

No one except Ruth really noticed just how much I was drinking. I was, and still am, more functional drunk than sober, though prescription pharmaceuticals now take the place of most of the booze. Something in the alcohol slowed my thoughts down, dampened my emotions, dulled my anxiety, and helped me fall asleep at night.

I tried to describe this to Lidia. I told her to think about the worst hangover she had ever had, headache, dung on the tongue, aching limbs, dry heaves, visions of Armageddon.

Then I told her that, day in and day out, every day for nearly twenty years, I chose that reality rather than sobriety. It hurt less. And I could do more. But the alcohol added to my memory issues.

.   .   .

I cannot guarantee to tell the truth here. I can only tell what I remember, though perhaps not in any linearly comprehensible fashion. Heisenberg uncertainty is with me still.

That being said, my family confirms that this chapter is essentially true. We did go sailing that day. We did see the wonders that the Quirimbas Archipelago has to offer. Ruth and the kids and Stuart remember the day, remember the whales and the dolphins and the life-ring going overboard.

I cannot ask Abudjate, for he is long dead of malaria. We miss him.

A typical village well in Cabo Delgado. Water is collected by a gourd on the end of a long stick. The woman collecting water is wearing the traditional white makeup known as mussiro, an attractive traditional face paint that is the height of fashion in Cabo Delgado. Two community leaders with rainbow sashes pose formally in the background; everyone dressed up for this photo. Alfredo Gonsalves, Quirimbas National Park Ranger, gestures at right. Poor me, I am cut in half at left.

CHAPTER 4

Kids

October, 1999. In which Ruth and I return to Chiure after our Swazi holiday and sailing adventure. We find problems with the Girl's Education component of our rural development project.

THE WEEK DID not begin well.

Ruth and I got hung up in Pemba on Monday and Tuesday. We ran around at full speed—meetings, phone calls, banging on keyboards, terse faxes—but for the life of me I cannot remember what we were so determinedly trying to do. It was not until Wednesday that we made it back to the project site in Chiure.

We found Chiure much as we left it. Our dog greeted us enthusiastically, though her five puppies fled in terror.

This may not have been such a bad idea, for the kids spent the entire afternoon pursuing them around the compound. Captives were subjected to hugs, kisses, bike and wheelbarrow rides, and generally everything else that young children find delightful and dogs don't. We tried half-heartedly to name the puppies but settled for giving them a tick-bath instead.

Christening failure is something of a family tradition, for we had had only limited success in naming their mother the year before. In theory she was "Old Yeller" (Lunga's choice), but as she was neither yellow nor old, no one managed to call her that. For a short while Neli called her "Yeli," as this was sort of "Old Yeller" rhymed with her own name.

Eventually the exigencies of day-to-day reality defeated all ambitions and she became "Doggie."

"What a fitting name!" exclaimed Connie, and there could be no argument with that. But Cabo Delgado does this with all things. There is no fat here. Only the leanest and hardest, the fittest, survive.

We walked to the office and found that the project had not collapsed in our absence.

'The project' was not, as the name might suggest, a coherent set of actions that lead to a defined goal. Rather, it consisted of a rather eclectic collection of activities having little in common save that they were all necessary in restoring the shattered rural economy. Oilseed production and oil pressing so people could have cooking oil. The revitalization of the cashew industry, destroyed by war and a powdery mildew epidemic: it was impossible for farmers to buy fungicides and knapsack sprayers while the war was on. Restocking of goats throughout the District, as all livestock had been lost in the war. Construction of schools. Promotion of Girls' Education. Community forest management. The construction of a town market in Chiure itself. And a few other things.

The name of the project was "Support to Local Initiatives and Empowerment" and, with a name like that, I suppose it was inevitable that the project would be a collection of oddments (Helvetas may also have been suffering christening failure at the time of the project's conception). Ten Mozambican full-time staff members worked directly for Ruth and me. We also engaged a variety of subcontractors for specific tasks, such as our developmental theater group.

All concerned pretty much agreed what "support to local initiatives" meant: the oddball set of activities was in fact a result of the various initiatives for which the local people and local government wished support. It was however a shame that Helvetas refused to allow us to address the main problem in Chiure, which was the lack of a community water supply. Helvetas at the time had a long-running community water supply project in Cabo Delgado and the powers that be assured our team that this other project would address this issue. In the meantime, people queued for hours to access a single spring, 5 kilometers outside of town. Ruth and I would wake up at midnight, when the queue was at its shortest, to drive to the spring to fetch water.

Empowerment proved more difficult to define; the word "empowerment" covers a multitude of sins. Economic empowerment may be achieved through improved agriculture or better negotiation and marketing. Educational empowerment may be achieved through building schools and supporting parents and society to allow girls to study. Political empowerment may be achieved through strongly-worded letters to the editor, sit-ins, the waving of placards, or the hurling of overripe tomatoes.

We puzzled over the issue and eventually decided that our agriculture, education, and other efforts needed to be coupled with some rights-based activities. Land rights were an issue that directly affected food security and agriculture, so we added land rights campaigning and awareness-raising to our project and hoped in some vague way that this would make it seem more coherent to the outside observer, or at least our superiors in the Swiss institutional hierarchy.

.   .   .

Although the project had not collapsed while we were away in Swaziland, there were a few crises. The worst of these was that one of our team, Juvencia, had abandoned her post in Mecolene village and returned to Pemba without informing anyone. She had accepted a posting to Mecolene as a teacher, to open a new program to promote primary education for girls.

Since our arrival in Chiure in November 1996, Ruth and I had been concerned about gender issues and the position of girls and women in Macua society, for they appeared to be treated simply as beasts of burden by their husbands and fathers and, furthermore, refused to speak to us in the presence of men.

We had not expected this, for in theory, the Macua are matrilineal, and in the past this meant real power for women. A man moved to the woman's family on marriage and land and fields and cashew trees were passed from mother to daughter. Children belonged to the mother, and thus a child's ties to his mother's brothers were more important that those to his or her father. In the south, in Zululand and Swaziland, children address strangers as *Babe*, or "father," but in the lands of the Macua, the proper honorific is *Tio*—"uncle."

So how could a society in which economic power was vested in women oppress those same women so completely? The answer is that there were other forces, equally strong, at work on women's lives.

Islam came to the Macua nation, *Macuana*, from Oman, near the end of the first millennium AD, or perhaps near the beginning of the second.

Sultanates were set up in the Quirimbas Islands and on the mainland, and from this marriage of Arab and African cultures and peoples sprang the *Swahili*, a unique people with roots in both. The Swahili language reflects this. Speakers of Arabic and Southern African Nguni languages will understand many individual

Swahili words and occasionally a complete thought. It is wonderful and frustrating at the same time.

The Macua nations, farther inland, had less interaction and less intermarriage, but nonetheless many adopted the Muslim religion.

The Swahili coastal sultanates dominated large portions of the north of Mozambique until they were expelled by the arms of the Portuguese in the colonial period. The sultanates left behind a system of Muslim, patrilineal chieftaincies, overlying the older, matrilineal clan structures. There were several Chieftancies within Chiure District.

Chiure Town itself lies within the chieftaincy of the *Regulo* Megama, a young man with a ready smile and a delightful sense of humor who lives in a grass-roofed hut indistinguishable from those of his subjects.

His grandfather had been a famous opponent of the Portuguese and had died in prison on Ibo Island in the 1960s.

Megama showed us a picture of his grandfather taken before the War of Independence. The old *Regulo*, resplendent in full Arab ceremonial dress, gazed at us as an eagle might. There was a ferocity in the hook of his nose and a determination in the set of his jaw that would have been overpowering were it not for his regal reserve, as if even these most kingly of characteristics were inappropriate for him to express. His parchment skin stretched tight over high cheekbones and there were stories in the lines around his eyes. Old Megama had not moved to his wife's family lands after marriage. He had migrated to Chiure from Namuno and had carved an empire out of what had formerly been uninhabited bush.

After the Muslims came Portuguese colonial rule and its successor, socialism. These, based as they were on centralized, top-down decision-making hierarchies, weakened clan structures still further.

The War of Independence and the civil war that accompanied the Portuguese and Socialist regimes delivered the final blow, destroying the local manufacturing and agricultural economies and pushing the survivors to the absolute limits of human endurance. During the war years, many people lived in the bush in improvised structures, for any permanent structure simply invited attack. Many wore tree bark, as clothes were unavailable.

When the civil war ended in 1994, Macua women found themselves almost completely disenfranchised. The fields and cashew trees that had sustained their families for generations were overgrown, decrepit and decimated by disease. Their ancestral villages were nothing but ashes. Uncles and brothers were dispersed over the countryside and many were refugees in neighboring countries. Male Village Presidents appointed by the dominant political parties fought traditional Chiefs for influence at village level.

Macua men returned from war fully aware of the persuasiveness of power, and equally aware that they had very little, except of course the advantages of size and strength over their women.

What could women do? The only thing they could. Submit.

We did a study in four villages in 1997, comparing the day-to-day workload of men and women. It made for incredible reading.

The average woman's workday started at 4 a.m., when she woke to prepare her husband's breakfast and fetch water for his bath. It ended after 10 p.m., when she had fed him and the kids, fetched water, washed the dishes, cleaned the houses and swept the yard, weeded the fields, done the laundry, collected firewood, and, in the more enlightened households, spent several minutes at the end of the day "conversing" with her husband—though why she would want to do this after all the other services she had been obliged to provide must remain a mystery to the outside observer.

The men arose later, worked in the fields in the morning, rested while the wife prepared lunch, and had afternoons free for drinking or work on income generating activities such as mat-weaving.

We called a meeting to share these results with the District Administration and local leaders. The first answer we got was that men in general worked much harder, when they worked, than did women, so the time inequality was fully justified. Then we looked at one little component of the day's labor, that of carrying food back from the field to the house. The men were forced to concede that on a daily basis they carried only a hoe or a bush knife back from the fields, while the women carried maize, greens, cassava, and firewood.

Great silences ensued.

Adamo, our Helvetas colleague and a Macua from the coastal area of Mecufi, explained some other facts of life to me after the meeting.

"They marry young in Chiure, *Senhor* Peter. On the coast it is an offense to violate a virgin before the age of eighteen years. You would be taken to the Islamic court and fined very heavily. Only a few people in my village ever did this."

He was quiet a while, then his voice hardened.

"Away from the coast it is different. They give their daughters away at the age of five years, or eight years. They believe that the breasts will not grow without the proper stimulation."

We had heard the same thing from other sources, including the young girls themselves. One of the international donors had had problems with a program to distribute agricultural implements because this had provoked a wave of childhood marriages. When men had more hoes they simply took more wives, so they would have the labor force to use them.

Then Adamo asked me about my traditions.

I did the best I could, out of my jumbled background, but my mind was working on his comments.

There it was in a nutshell, all the contradictions laid bare in a few short sentences, a few sparse threads teased from the tangled mass of Macua and Arab and Swahili and Portuguese cultures that had muddled together to create the things we saw around us every day.

A completely male-dominated matrilineal society. Leadership in tatters, created by successive waves of conquest. Clothing in tatters, or created from tree bark. Islam used to defend women's rights, while the supposedly matrilineal tradition sends young girls off to marry, because now there are extra hoes.

Take Mecolene, the village which Juvencia had abandoned.

It was a village midway between Chiure and the sea, 70 kilometers from the coast, situated on an ancient trade route from the fishing villages of Mecufi to the ancestral lands of the Meto Macua nation in the Montepuez area.

Caravans of slaves had carried cloth, iron, salt and fish to the interior, and grain, beans, and ivory to the coast.

The old trail wound along a ridge, avoiding the swamps and brush of the river margins. By 1974, when Independence came, followers of the Megama had installed themselves in the fertile lowlands along the Megarumo River to the north.

The post-Independence Frelimo government resettled this population to the ridge, to allow for the opening of roads and the construction of public infrastructure, and to allow for political control of the population during the civil war. While the resettlement plan did bring schools and a road and a village political structure, it also meant that women had to walk for hours fetching water and food, for there were no water sources nor fields on the ridge.

The village created was called Mecolene, the "place of the palm tree," for a single palm grew there, marking the caravan track. We passed through this village several times a week in the course of our work.

Earlier in the year, in June, one of our teams had visited the village to evaluate our goat-breeding and school construction and forest management projects.

The Village President received us with great hospitality, offering us the use of his kitchen for the preparation of our meals and his yard for relaxation away from the eyes of the village children. As there was, of course, no television and there were only one or two radios in the village, visitors, particularly visitors with cars and tents and a variety of different skin colors, were a ready source of much-needed entertainment.

We accepted his offer with gratitude. We all found it difficult to be stared at, especially while eating.

In the president's yard there was a young girl of fourteen years who kept her head covered with a cloth and kept her face painted white with *mussiro*, a root extract, and never spoke. I didn't notice her, but Ruth did. It took her several days of questioning to get the girl's story.

She had been a student in the primary school when her first menstruation came. Her family immediately withdrew her from school and sent her off for her initiation ceremonies, where she was taught all that was required for her to be a good wife. Upon her return, she was to be married to an older man of the village. She didn't want to.

She wanted to continue at school.

This was just not on. Her family insisted. So did she. The elders weighed in and told her that it was impossible for a girl not to be married after her initiation ceremonies. Unheard of. Unthinkable.

They told her that until she married the man, she would not be allowed to talk aloud. She would have to whisper. All girls of the village had to do this, from initiation until the time they were married, but this was usually only a month or two. The idea was to prevent them from crying out when the husband entered them for the first time, though I forget why it was so important not to cry out.

If this particular girl wanted to spend the rest of her life whispering, said the elders, that was her decision, but in any case, she could not go back to school. How could she go to school if she wasn't allowed to talk? How could she answer the teacher's questions?

The girl ran away to the house of the president of the village, who was some sort of relative of hers. I must confess here that the only African kinship system I have come close to mastering is the Swazi one, and that only because everyone in Swaziland is related to everyone else, so you can call anyone brother or sister with confidence. Except of course for older people: these can safely be called mother or father.

The Village President was not an elder; he was a political appointee, but he was a kind one. He couldn't do anything about the whispering or the head covering or the face painting, but he could offer the girl the hospitality of his home until the situation was resolved, one way or another. By the time we entered the picture, this anonymous, remarkable girl had spent nearly a year in silence.

We were all affected by her story, perhaps more than we were by the regular round of malnutrition and malaria and death and poverty. Her suffering seemed so unnecessary, so wasteful.

Malaria and malnutrition have a certain inevitability in Cabo Delgado, but for our team, as outsiders, there was nothing inevitable about the girl's fate, the elders' opinions on the matter notwithstanding. How can a culture survive that is so profligate with its human resources?

But it was not only this. We had also failed. We, as a team of professional development workers, male and female, Mozambican and expatriate, were charged with implementing a project that prioritized women and children, and we had worked since 1997 in this village without discovering this girl.

And for the past year she had been under our very noses, in the house of the Village President, a man with whom we worked on a regular basis. How much more repression would there be in more remote homes, in more traditional families? We left the village at the end of the trip with a determination to do something.

It was tricky.

There is a razor-thin edge between promotion of the status of women in traditional societies and the destruction of local cultures, and no two people can agree on exactly where this edge lies. Some people, including a high percentage of local men, treat any attempt to address these issues as a neo-colonialist attempt to overthrow survival systems that have worked for generations. Others, including many well-educated, well-meaning expatriates, believe that culture must submit to the pursuit of fairer societies. Both these extremes beg the issues.

On the one hand, the future will be different from the past, so change is inevitable, and it is wise to prepare all members of society for it, not just male members. On the other hand, the future of any society grows on the roots of its past, and modern attempts to uproot the past and plant new ideologies have often been messy, bloody, and unsuccessful affairs.

In a society in flux, the powerful find opportunities to make themselves more powerful. Mozambique itself is a case in point.

In the light of this analysis, our decision became much simpler. Education for girls and improvement of the status of women became a survival issue, not a moral one, and so we achieved a unanimous position, both within our team and with our local governmental partners. Still, there remained the question: how to move forward without alienating the male half of the population?

Not for the first time, we looked to the female members of the team for leadership.

Ruth was by now very emotionally involved in the development of the campaign and she had my full sympathy, though I regret to say very little of my time, busy as I was with my natural resource management activities.

Ruth had grown up the hard way, only making it through school due to the exceptional sacrifices of her mother and father, who endured debt and poverty and her father's tuberculosis to provide her with the best education that Swaziland could provide.

Ruth started the team off with a survey. She and a group of female colleagues returned to Mecolene, without us men, and had long talks with the girls' mothers.

Ruth came back and said, "It's poverty-driven. The mothers want a better life for their girls, so they try to marry them off to the richer men of the village. They know that they don't have money for school fees and even food for girls, but maybe the husbands will have food for wives. And the husband will be a benefit for the whole family, because he comes to live with them, in terms of tradition."

"But five or eight years!" I said.

"That's an exaggeration. They marry the girls off at first menstruation so they won't get pregnant before marriage. It's a great shame for the girl. It is true that sometimes girls are given younger, but not until the breasts start to push out. They return to their mothers and grandmothers for initiation rites at first menstruation. Then they go back to the marital hut."

Ruth and her team laid their plans. They prepared a theater presentation with our developmental theater group, a story written by a local girl about the life of local women and illustrating the advantages and importance of educating girls. Then they organized a seminar for teachers, based on the United Nations' "Sara" program (a gender resources kit for education professionals, parents, and students) to create a girl-friendly school environment.

They set up a scholarship fund for girls. Lastly, they decided that a few female teachers would be essential. There are no female professionals in the villages, no women who have jobs. Women are wives; men are everything else.

This division of labor is so clear that when we arrived in Chiure for the first time, we had no female applicants for the job of housekeeper though nearly a hundred men.

One old man we interviewed said that he had never done housekeeping nor looking after children, but because it was a job that paid he could do it. He was well known in town as an honest man, so we tried him.

He lasted one day.

He hadn't a clue how to clean a house, and his supervision of the kids consisted of lounging in the kitchen doorway with the screen door open as flies poured in and shouting at the kids to be good. Ruth almost had to go house to house to find a young woman of the Maconde tribe to help us, so we could both devote ourselves to our development work.

I did not help Ruth with this search. No one would have understood a man going from house to house looking for a young woman.

Juvencia, mentioned earlier, was the first female teacher we contracted. She was hired to pilot the "Education of the Girl Child" program in Mecolene, as Mecolene's (and Chiure District's) first female teacher.

We invested quite a lot of time and energy in preparing for her arrival. We took her to visit the village, we renovated a house for her, and we gave her a bicycle, a bed, and kitchen utensils, luxuries that male teachers had to save their pennies for. Then we dropped her off on her doorstep and flew blissfully away on holiday.

Juvencia was golden-brown in color, soft spoken, and well groomed, a beautiful young woman who could have been Ruth's younger sister. She and Ruth shared the same long frame, the same trim figure, the same graceful awkwardness possessed by all long-legged creatures: by herons, and by giraffes. Juvencia's brow was unfurrowed and her clear, intelligent eyes shone above unblemished cheeks and chiseled oriental cheekbones. She fooled us completely.

She lasted all of one week in Mecolene. She got up one morning, told the Village President that she was going home for the weekend, and vanished. No communication with us, no message to the Ministry of Education, no announcement of her death on the radio. This was the situation we came back to. We hunted her down in Pemba. She had a thousand different reasons, all contradictory, to explain why she hadn't gone back.

"I was going to go back, but I had problems with transport, and I was sick."

"Why didn't you tell us, so we would know what was happening?"

"Anyhow I couldn't stay in that house. It only had a bamboo door. My things were not secure."

"Juvencia, you told us to give you the money to repair the doors and you would do it yourself. Why didn't you fix the door?"

"I had to use that money because you didn't give me my supplementary allowance."

"Which allowance is that?"

"The extra money you were going to pay me for teaching there."

"Is that allowance in your contract with us?"

"No, it isn't. But in any case, the place is too far from Pemba."

"We took you to see the place so you would know what you were getting into."

"It was my husband who told me I had to leave."

We were getting nowhere.

We asked about the bicycle and the rest of the stuff, and got nowhere there, too. Ruth eventually threatened her with the police and an action for breach of contract. Juvencia promised to bring the stuff and the money, and left, but not before squeezing out a few pitiful tears that were calculated to melt our hearts.

Our hearts didn't melt. They were with that anonymous young girl. She had returned to school when Juvencia started teaching, and dropped out again when she left. She couldn't face down the entire village alone.

At least we had some success in other villages. The program of scholarships and training for teachers eventually reduced the dropout rate for girls in the schools in which we worked by 40 per cent. And in Ncuerete village, a dynamic headmaster had arranged for sixty girl dropouts to return to school.

.   .   .

We also had problems of a different sort with our own kids. Lunga decided that the inside walls of the storage shed merited a first ascent. Halfway up he fell and hooked his calf on a steel spike coming out of a piece of machinery, a motorized maize grinder. He dangled there like a slaughtered sheep, then managed to climb up and off the spike and call us. We found a very subdued boy and a hole as big as a squash ball and bits of meat falling out of his leg. The spike had rammed itself 10 centimeters up into his calf muscle.

We bandaged him and rushed him to Pemba. The Helvetas doctor had no thread so we had him sutured at the government hospital. We were shown into a filthy, cramped cubby that had once been a staff toilet. There was one chair and no table. No anesthetics either.

Ruth sat on the chair and I on the remains of the toilet bowl. We held Lunga across our laps while a male nurse sewed up his leg, assuring him all the while that the stitching wouldn't hurt, though it most obviously did.

Then we took him home to Chiure, fed him antibiotics, and fervently hoped that the needle had been sterilized. We spread a blanket and some pillows on the sitting room floor for him to play the next morning.

We needn't have bothered.

He couldn't walk, so he rode Neli's bicycle instead, and crawled in the sand pile and swung on the rope swing. Ruth had fits, but then of course she had to go to work, so Lunga could do whatever he wanted.

The next day he ran away and played football, despite all maternal remonstrations to the contrary. (The paternal remonstrations had ceased when the bicycle-riding started—I know when I'm licked.)

Over the following weekend, back in Pemba again, he went swimming and the bandage was lost in the water. We didn't bother putting on another one, I guess we'll cut out the stitches ourselves after a few days, or maybe he'll find some rodents or lizards or something to gnaw them out.

Sunday afternoon we sailed across Pemba Bay and landed on a small beach below Ponto Saide Ali. It was a fascinating beach: white sand and flat blue water surrounded by low cliffs, with an old dugout canoe and campfire marks and coral and mudskippers and a big shell midden. We clambered around and scraped our elbows and I found a fossil shell in the rock, about six centimeters across. I remembered the tiny fossil shells we found in Pennsylvania when I was young, and I called the kids. I was pretty proud of myself.

"But look over here, Daddy," said Neli. She showed me a fossil clam at least 50 centimeters across, in perfect condition.

"And here, Daddy," said Lunga. He had some other kind of shell, a bivalve, an oysterish-looking thing, even bigger.

At least I was the one to spot the leatherback turtle in the bay mouth, nearly 2 meters long.

Neli fell asleep on the way home, and I carried her into the house and to bed. Her golden head lay in the crook of my arm and her breath fanned my chest. The simple act of holding a sleeping child in my arms brought feelings of strength, and tenderness, and obligations gladly assumed. This, as all fathers know, is one of the best moments of being a parent.

I imagine that marrying a daughter off for food is one of the worst.

Addenda to Chapter 4

NELI IS in university now, with an intention to go to medical school. I cannot quite fathom how she manages A grades in Organic Chemistry; I tell her she must have been switched at birth.

Mozambique has instituted free primary education for all children, yet the girls of the rural north fare little better now. Poverty and custom continue to limit girls' opportunities.

There are signs, however, small things, paw-prints in the riverbank, tufts of fur on a twig, which give me hope. Small things, which show me that something new is here, a new creature in the forest that with care and stewardship might survive, might stay, might thrive.

I went to see the former Minister of Justice several years ago at the request of a mutual friend, to talk about the conservation of several offshore islands near the town of Angoche. I was getting back into the conservation game, finally healthy enough to be able to pick up where I left off, to think of life and community and the blessed bounty of nature instead of despair and dread and the red-hot sizzle of steel on skin in the darkness.

I thought I went there to discuss marine turtles and reefs and waterfowl, but he wanted to talk about his *Fundação José Ibraimo Abudo*, a new non-profit foundation dedicated to fair and just social development.

I must admit I was intimidated. He looked just as one would expect a former Minister of Justice to look. Age and authority and whatever it is that old elephants have.

"We are just getting started, Peter," he said. "We have courses for boatbuilding and sewing for the youth, to ease the unemployment situation and preserve traditional skills."

• • •

Wooden boatbuilding has been practiced for centuries in Angoche. Just south of town in the channel west of Catamoio Island, my team and I had discovered the remains of at least six large seagoing vessels from antiquity (but that is another story). Fabrics from Mozambique have been in demand in India and Arabia for an equal length of time.

"We also sponsor sixty girls. We help their families so they can stay in school."

This was not the sort of sensibility I had come expect from politicians of his generation. The first time Ruth had suggested a special scholarship program for girls in Cabo Delgado, the Governor's advisor has suggested we start one for boys as well. Boys have poor parents, too, he said. Why focus on girls?

I looked at His Excellency the former Minister.

"You sponsor sixty girls?" I said. I was pretty sure this was a donor-driven activity, an effort by a CARE or an Oxfam to ensure that there was at least some small gender focus embedded in a larger grant the Foundation had received. "Where does the funding come from?"

His eyes fell and he looked vulnerable and somehow younger. "I don't have any donors yet, Peter. I am funding this out of my own pocket for the time being. Maybe we'll have better luck fundraising in the future."

My heart went out to him and his sixty girls. I didn't see a politician, or a former Minister of Justice, or a judge, or even an old elephant. I looked at him and I saw a father. Strength and tenderness and obligations gladly assumed.

We men need too much from our wives to set them free and rejoice in their freedom. We learn the joy of doing this from our daughters, if we can. And, exceptionally, like His Excellency Dr. Abudo, we learn to spread this joy to other families, other fathers.

A new creature in the forest. I hope it thrives.

I pose with the Cabo Delgado Provincial Director of Wildlife, Jose Dias dos Santos Mohammed, after a successful anti-poaching operation. He has been a good friend for many years, and at the time of this writing is serving as the Warden for the Marromeu Game Reserve, a 10,000 km2 freshwater swamp which is home to thousands of Cape buffalo as well as elephants, lion, and smaller species. "dos Santos" means "of the Saints." No one seems to find it strange to link this name with the surname "Mohammed." Only in Mozambique.

CHAPTER 5

Poachers

October, 1999. In which I visit the remote mountainous areas of Ancuabe and Meluco Districts and discover an unexpected richness, and unexpected threats.

•   •   •

It was time to head out to the Districts, Ancuabe and Meluco, to supervise the new field staff subcontracted from the Environmental Association, the *Associação do Meio- Ambiente de Cabo Delgado*, better known as AMA.

This past year the Helvetas team, working with AMA, managed to set up five community nature reserves and the new staff are involved in setting up wildlife and forest management programs as well as community development projects in these areas. The idea of community-based resource management has been tested in other African countries, most notably Zimbabwe, but had never before been tried in the north of Mozambique. We used the New Land Law, the New Forests and Wildlife Law, and the collapse of the Southeast Asian economy to assert community rights over more than a million hectares of prime *miombo* woodland and dense Swahili coastal forest. I realize this requires some explanation.

•   •   •

Prior to 1997, rural communities had no rights whatsoever to the land, wildlife, and forests upon which they depended for their survival. All was the property of the state, which could, and frequently did, allocate these resources to other interested parties, parties who themselves not infrequently had close business or personal relationships with high-ranking government officials.

When I arrived in Cabo Delgado in late 1996, there were fifty-eight timber companies bickering for logging rights in the choicest areas.

By the end of 1997, this number had risen to seventy-five, and almost the entire land area of the province had been handed out in the form of renewable one-year *licensas simples*. The short-term nature of these logging licenses did nothing to engender long-term management strategies and sustainable-use policies.

Quite the reverse.

Giant old *umbila*, *chanfuta*, and *jambiri*[10] trees were hacked down as fast as the chainsaws could be driven. This was frequently faster than the timber lorries could be driven, and it is not uncommon to come across, in the middle of the bush, stacks of beautiful timber left to crack and rot in the dry white sun.

The majority of local timber companies sold their logs to Southeast Asian buyers, though some few sold through South African intermediaries, and others existed only on paper and sold no logs at all. These latter sold their *licensas* and quotas to other, slightly more legitimate, operators, and pocketed a tidy profit simply from having the connections or the authority to acquire a timber quota, without going through the bother of acquiring the actual timber itself.

Processing for export consisted of painting creosote on the cut log ends, to prevent splitting, and then numbering the logs with white paint. Logs were loaded whole onto the decks of cargo ships in Pemba Port, and sawing and processing were done in the destination country. The buyers offered any number of plausible reasons why this had to be done there—quality control, evolution of the timber dimensions required as public tastes in furniture evolved, specialized skills available only in Southeast Asia—but the real reason was that the local timber operators didn't want to run sawmills when there was easier money to be made, and the Southeast Asian buyers wanted all the added value of processing for themselves.

That local government took so long to do something about this situation is not stupidity, nor moral cowardice, but simply a sad, predictable result of centuries of exploitation. After the gold rush of the Portuguese in the 1600s, the ivory boom a century later, and the slaving boom, which ended only in the 1800s, export of whole logs may have been seen as a harmless lark, detrimental though it was to the economic development of the Mozambican nation.

But something was eventually done.

The first rumblings of change came in early 1997, when the Forests and Wildlife Department began formulating the new Forests and Wildlife Law, which called for a phase-out of both annual *licensas simples* and the export of unprocessed trunks.

Timber quotas for 1998 were reduced drastically, to allow for a proper forest inventory to be undertaken, and new regulations called for replanting of harvested species. The Governor of Cabo Delgado, who had presided over the logging mess (later dubbed the "Chinese Takeaway"),[11] was replaced with an educated man of honest reputation.

Battle lines were drawn between the loggers and the Forests Department when the Southeast Asian economy collapsed. Suddenly there were no buyers. Fifty timber companies went out of business or left the province in 1998. They left a vacuum, both in the corridors of power and in the paths of the forest.

Suddenly, there was room to maneuver at the political level. Suddenly there were forests without "owners." And there was the New Land Law of 1997 to help communities assert their rights. The same law the American Ambassador and I had knocked heads over (see Chapter Two).

. . .

Nicolãu from the Provincial Forests and Wildlife Department and I got our heads together. He showed me a circular from the National Department of Forests and Wildlife that called for the creation of Community Management Areas, in which all timber and wildlife rights would be invested in the communities themselves, though the circular unfortunately provided no legal basis for the creation of these areas.

We decided that possession was nine-tenths of the law and ploughed ahead. We used as our model the CAMPFIRE program in Zimbabwe,[12] which empowered communities to conserve their forest and wildlife resources and generate income through sustainable use. In the first stages of the program, wildlife usage was contracted out to hunting operators, with the money derived from the contract going to benefit communities, with health clinics, schools, and other public benefit projects.

As time went on, animal numbers increased and a conversion to game-viewing tourism was possible. I should explain that sport hunting is oriented towards the off-take of large males, which has little impact on population growth if hunting quotas are set correctly and observed rigorously. So, despite the hunting, and because of the patrolling, wildlife numbers grow until animals are numerous enough to provide a good game-viewing experience for the visitor.

All of this creates opportunities. The conversion from hunting to game-viewing means a large increase in jobs available, as tourism creates many more jobs than hunting. Communities eventually start running the tourism operations themselves.

We hoped to launch the same type of process in Cabo Delgado, though timber-cutting would substitute sport hunting in the early stages of the program, as Mozambique's *miombo* has valuable timber resources which Zimbabwe's savannahs and woodlands do not. This also solved my considerable moral dilemma on sport hunting, a dilemma I have never satisfactorily resolved. My head tells me that sport hunting as a path to increased wildlife and biodiversity works; my heart mourns the blood price involved, the loss of magnificent large males. I know it makes no sense. I eat beef and chicken and pork without a qualm. Or maybe it's because I am a large male myself, though no one, not even my wife, has ever called me magnificent.

We called a meeting of eleven interested government departments and non-governmental agencies. Nicolãu presented the idea to create Community Management Areas to them. The response was breathtaking. Spokesman after spokesman came out in favor of the idea. Together, we resolved to create a consortium with the inelegant name of the "Working Group for Community Resource Management in Cabo Delgado," with the goal of creating five Community Management Areas in 1999 (by now it ought to be clear that I am hopeless at naming things, with the single notable exception of my daughter Neli, but that is another story).

I congratulated Nicolãu with all my heart after the meeting, embarrassing him thoroughly in the process. We were in business. He, as the ranking member of the Provincial Forests and Wildlife Department could make the government work for us, while I, as a representative of a major donor agency, could motivate money to start work.

His job turned out to be easier than mine. The Community Management Areas were marked on the Surveyor-General's map within a month and the supporting documents sent to Maputo. Thus more than a million hectares of land was secured, albeit somewhat precariously, for we still had no clear opinion on the legal status of that land. On the operational level, though, no more timber or other concessions were granted in those areas.

On my side, I had to battle furiously to convince my colleagues that the scheme was not a hare-brained, grandiose delusion, brought on by too much sun and not nearly enough calm consideration. I was ready to resign to make my point, but it didn't come to that. In the end, the support of ten other provincial organizations swayed the day, and we won a budget from the Swiss.

One of the ten organizations was the *Associação Meio-Ambiente*, the Environmental Association of Cabo Delgado. They were a young bunch with a somewhat improvisational management style, but I was impressed by their dedication. They were running a project in one of the poorer areas of Pemba to discourage defecation on the beach, with some success.

The habit in the coastal zones had always been to use the ocean as a latrine and Stuart and the rest of the Water Department people had studies to show that this was probably the most hygienic practice for small communities. Not for cities of a 100,000 people, however, and not when one is struggling to launch a tourist industry.

Without any budget at all, the *Associacao Meio-Ambiente* was succeeding where other more illustrious and wealthy organizations (who shall remain nameless) had failed miserably. They did this by community education, highly amusing theater presentations, and by being so earnest and dedicated that their neighbors and friends and relatives could hardly refuse to respect their messages. And when the smell at low tide improved, the whole *bairro* noticed.

We needed fieldworkers, and so Nicolãu and I offered the *Associacao Meio-Ambiente* a contract.

"Look here guys, we need ten of your best volunteers plus two supervisors. We offer salaries, training, bicycles, a microscopic budget for administration, and all you have to do is waltz off into five of the most remote corners of the province to launch community resource management programs, convince people to stop burning the forest every year, stop hunting out of season, and help them with agriculture, woodcutting, and other projects of economic benefit. And don't forget to convince them that it is in fact good that elephants attack their fields every year, for one day, sometime in the future, it might be that a tourist might come by and want to see them ... OK we don't have any tourists in the province yet, but when airline flight fees go down and the bridge over the Rovuma River is built to Tanzania, maybe then ..."

What could they do?

They accepted immediately, and after two brief months of training, the brave volunteers were willy-nilly unleashed upon their respective Community Management Areas. I had flown blissfully off on holiday, as I mentioned in the previous chapter, and now I wanted to see how they were doing, count the bodies, and pick through the carnage.

I actually wasn't so negative. I remembered my own Peace Corps days in Swaziland and knew that in rural Africa, good intentions could make up for all sorts of other failings. Probably in many other parts of the world as well. Maybe good intentions could even make up for the fact that we had done all this maneuvering without any community consultations at all. We had broken every rule in the book. No one in the communities concerned even knew that we existed, or that they were now living in official "Community Management Areas."

We were playing God, and our only consolation was that we were exploiting a window of opportunity that could snap shut at any moment.

We started in Ngura village. The fieldworker there was a young man of twenty-two called Dionisio, or Dio for short. His father apparently had the same problem that I do with names, for there was nothing about Dio that suggested revelry or even merriment.

Dio was an organized, serious young man. He met us in the village and presented us with his report.

"I started with calling a meeting in every village and informing the people about the project," he said. "I told them the land was now theirs, and the timber and the wildlife as well, but that they had to respect the land and manage it and the animals in accordance with the law of Mozambique. I told them I was here to help them earn a better livelihood, but at the same time respect the environment."

A crowd had gathered around us, pressing in on every side, old men and young women and the inevitable swarm of young children, all staring and touching and completely unaware that all this might make a visitor uncomfortable, particularly a visitor who had come to deal with such delicate subjects as land and wildlife.

"And? ..."

We were almost afraid to ask.

"It went very well."

Dio gestured around him, and it was only then that we noticed the smiles. "I have friends here."

A short man in a red T-shirt pushed out of the crowd and pumped my hand.

"The Village President," said Dio.

More men pushed forward.

"And his assistant, and the man in charge of agriculture, and the teacher at the primary school, and my neighbor over that side, and this one is a hunter who will go with us today to see the area, and ..."

I shook each and every hand, and then went to the edges of the crowd, and shook the hands of all those who were too shy to come forward. Nicolãu and Celestino (the Chairman and Field Supervisor of the Environmental Association volunteers) did the same. Then we went to Dio's veranda for a drink of cool water and the rest of his report.

"I did exactly what you told me to do," said Dio. "I started with the New Land Law, and everyone was my friend after that. Then

I talked about economic problems, what projects we could start so people would make more money—carpentry and agriculture and goats and whatnot. I have a list of names of people who are interested in all of these projects. Then I talked about land management, how important it was not to burn the forest in winter, and to hunt only in season. The Village President agreed ..." Dio waved at him, and he nodded his head, "... so we set up a system of community forest rangers, older men, hunters, men who used to be poachers. The local Department of Agriculture gave them all credentials."

"They gave them credentials?" I couldn't believe my ears.

"Yes, and we had only three fires this year. We caught two of the people who set the fires, but not the other one."

"You caught the people who set the fires?"

"I think, *Senhor* Peter, I think this idea of community management is going to work," said Dio.

"And I think, Dio, and *Senhor Presidente*, that you two have done a terrific job," I said.

Nicolãu smiled and said nothing. But then he hardly ever did. His presentation at the formative meeting of the Working Group for Community Resource Management in Cabo Delgado was the first time I had heard him string together more than a sentence or two.

The President spoke up, in Macua, and Dio translated.

"He says that if the land and the forests are really ours, how come a timber company is logging over that side, by the mountain there?"

Dio pointed.

Nicolãu and I looked at each other.

"And there is another problem. Five elephants have been killed on the other side of the river, in the village of N'tephu. Some people passed by early this morning with meat, and I heard them talking," said Dio.

• • •

Poachers. Elephants and timber.

We collected all the details, then climbed the mountain behind the village to get a fix on where the poachers might be. Nicolãu promised the President that he would look into both matters, and we drove off the next morning to the next community management area, in the District of Meluco, around the village of Minhanha.

Dio came with us, for his counterpart there, Djini, is a good friend of his. We arrived at night, as Minhanha is far off the beaten track. We gave a lift to some women returning from selling tobacco in the district capital who showed us to Djini's hut.

Djini leapt into Dio's arms when we arrived, literally squealing with delight.

"Dio! And *Senhor* Peter! And *Senhor Celestino*! And *Engineiro* Nicolãu! *Que honra!*"

He rushed off to organize a chicken and some rice for our supper. My back hurt after a day in the car, so Dio and I walked around the village to stretch out the bits of us that had been folded all day. There was just enough light to avoid falling into erosion gullies and rubbish pits. All was silent.

We reached the edge of the forest and stopped. It was one of those pregnant African nights that other writers have described much more evocatively than I ever could. All I want to add is that all the clichés about the mystery, the mystique, the magic of night in Africa are absolutely true. We stood for several minutes.

Then a drum started from the direction of the village square, and we turned back. We found a crowd, and Celestino, under an enormous mango tree. The dance was a girl's dance of the Macua tradition, though both Macua and Maconde nations were represented in Minhanha.

We watched for several minutes. The girls leapt to their feet in pairs and danced a quick, shuffling step across the centre of the circle and back. When the first pair sat down, another pair leapt into the centre. Though the dance involved a lot of shaking of the hips, it was not at all erotic, because the dancers were all little kids.

After a short while it was not even interesting, as there was no variation in the dance nor the rhythm of the drummers. Not interesting for me, I should add, because everyone else watched, rapt, from the edge of the circle.

A group of lovely young mothers beside us, all still in their teens, shuffled and clapped in time with the dancers. Then the prettiest, a rounded, almost muscular girl with very dark skin, had to go sit and nurse her baby. It was only then I noticed that her breasts hung nearly to her waist.

The Swiss Development Corporation had instructed us to prioritize the development of programs for "youth," but what was "youth" when girls married at age fourteen, were grandmothers by age thirty, and were dead by thirty-five?

The dance must have bored Celestino too, corrupted as he was by life in town, for he began to quiz Dionisio about Macua tradition.

"Do you know why the dance is always held under a tree, Dio?"

"So the firelight reflects back down from the foliage and everyone can see?"

"Wrong. It is for the drums. They boom better in a partially enclosed space. Back up a few steps and see for yourself."

We did, and Celestino was right, but I didn't think that meant that Dio was wrong. The light certainly did reflect down off the waxy surfaces of the mango leaves.

Dio fought back with special knowledge of his own.

"Did you know, *Senhor* Peter, that this dance is only done by girls, and that their leader is always a woman? The drummers can be men," he nodded at them, "but the dancers are always girls."

He pointed at a fat woman seated behind the drummers.

"That one is the leader of this group."

The woman had presence, and unquestionably a degree of relative wealth. No one but a wealthy person could be fat in Minhanha.

"I knew that this was a girl's dance. I have seen a similar dance in Chiure," I said.

Celestino started to cut in, but Dio had not yet played his ace.

"Did you know, *Senhor* Peter, that in my village, that same village where you were yesterday, a man is in charge of the girls' dance? This man is a leader of all the women, and he is accepted everywhere, even in the female rights of initiation? He has large buttocks like a woman, and he lost his power of erection ten years ago. On nights like this he puts on a skirt and dances with the women."

"Is he a homosexual?" asked Celestino.

"He must be. They say that he has the spirit of a woman."

"Have you ever seen anything like this before, in your country?" asked Celestino.

"In USA I have seen it. One of my uncles lives with another man as man and wife. I guess it could be said that he has the spirit of a woman."

"Does your relative show himself in public as this man of Dio's village does?"

"I think so. Yes. In some places in USA this is more accepted than others."

"There was a woman in Pemba who was married to a Portuguese some years ago. She took female lovers and was eventually sent to jail for it."

"To jail?"

"Yes. Homosexuality is illegal in Mozambique."

"But no one bothers this man of Dio's village?"

Dio answered. "They accept him."

"In Swaziland there are also men who dress as women, and women who dress as men," I said. "It is said that these are people who have been taken over by the spirits of their ancestors. It sometimes happens that male spirits enter a female and vice-versa. The person is sent to *kutfwasa*, to study to become a spirit medium. If not, the person will go mad. I have even heard of a female medium who lived completely as a man, even took wives."

Celestino and Dio seemed to have no trouble with this concept. We watched the dance for a time.

"Mugabe does not like homosexuals," said Celestino. "What you think?"

I had had a similar conversation in September with Ruth and her brothers. An older, unmarried man who lived near the family home had died, and had apparently been buried with a corncob inserted in his anus.

"This is always done," said Ruth, "so that the problem will end there, so that more members of the family will not have this problem of not marrying, and not having kids."

Cousin Zakhele was laughing.

"But why did the old Swazis, our ancestors, decide to do that particular thing to solve this kind of problem. Why that?"

Ruth's brother Bha was laughing, too.

"They know they like it," he said, and then we all laughed, but the conversation left me thinking. Clear that Swazis regard homosexuality with concern because it produces no children, but also clear that Swazis, as well as the people of Ngura village, have traditional mechanisms that allow societal roles and acceptance for all.

Was this a contradiction? Maybe, or maybe it was simply a pragmatic attitude of people forced by circumstances to be pragmatic. I decided that my attitude was also pragmatic.

I answered Celestino.

"I don't think about it too much," I said, "If a man has the spirit of a woman, what can be done? Africa, and Mugabe, have more important things to think about."

There had been another round of devaluations to the Zimbabwean currency a few months previously.

"True. É *verdade*."

"It is good when society finds ways for everyone to fit in."

"Not quite everyone. Not elephant poachers."

"Yes. Not elephant poachers."

．　．　．

We went to eat, then slept in Djini's hut. We rose at four the following morning to visit Xaxaxa, another poor village in Djini's area.

We hoped to see animals along the track but had to content ourselves with bites of the tsetse fly. I myself received five.

Tsetse is a strong indicator of the presence of game. On the way Djini gave his report, which was as positive as Dio's but, Djini being Djini, included much information about his personal life as well.

This part in particular took a long time. The gist of it was that he did not want trouble in the village, so he had decided not to go about looking for a girlfriend. He also did not smoke nor drink, and for this reason his new friends in the village worried about him. But we should not. He would do his best, and offered us an absolute guarantee that he would not be chased out of the village for sexual misbehavior.

I tried not to wonder why he felt it necessary to reassure us on this point.

After the meeting in Xaxaxa we went down to the Messalo River, which was completely dry, and walked around in the sand. There were no tracks, but Djini told us that there were elephants about, and that a poacher had been killed recently.

The poacher had tried to kill an elephant with an AK47. His companions had had to bury him in the bush: AK47s are underpowered for elephants, and rage is at least as common a result as death for an elephant attacked with an AK. It was still early, so we drove back to Minhanha and then to the capital of the district in which lay the village of N'tephu. The District Administrator ushered us into his office with a smile and called the District Director of Agriculture.

"Have you heard that five elephants were killed near N'tephu?" asked Nicolāu.

"It was only one," said the Administrator. "The elephants were in the fields there, and so we authorized the hunters to go and scare them off."

"But one was killed," said Nicolãu.

"Yes, but as I told you, the elephants were in the fields there, causing trouble."

"If you sent the hunters there to scare off the elephants then how come one was killed?" I asked.

The District Director of Agriculture cut in.

"Look here, Senhor Peter, it was in *'defesa das pessoas e bens'*—defense of people and property. The law says that killing of elephants is legal in defense of people and property. The elephants were causing trouble in the fields."

"In the fields?" asked Nicolãu.

"Yes."

"Not the village?"

"No."

It was the end of the dry season. There were no crops in any fields, anywhere. The worst the elephants could have done was leave footprints.

I started to say that I thought only José Dias, the Provincial Director of Wildlife, could authorize killing in *"defesa das pessoas e bens,"* but Nicolãu signaled me to shut up. I did.

We terminated the interview.

"They're involved," said Nicolãu.

We drove to N'tephu.

There, Celestino led the way, as Nicolãu and I speak little Macua. We greeted the village authorities and organized guides to show us to the river.

The normal crowd of little boys ran behind the car as we picked our way down the footpath in Nicolãu's Land Cruiser. The path got narrower and narrower and we finally had to stop. Nicolãu stayed with the car and Celestino and I walked towards the river.

Celestino let the guides go to the front, while he lagged behind to talk with the little boys. After a while he came to me.

"Our guides won't tell me where the poacher's camp is, but this boy did." He pointed to a boy of ten or twelve.

"It's just ahead, on the near bank of the river."

We looked at each other. We had no guns, no credentials, no authority of any kind to arrest poachers. I had a bush knife, but Celestino didn't even have walking shoes. He was nattily turned out in pleated chinos, a dress shirt, polished brogues, and a green satin and tweed waistcoat.

I have no idea why he felt that this was appropriate dress for fieldwork.

"So what's the plan ..." I began, but he had already turned away.

We cut off the main trail, over some boulders, and came out of the forest onto dry cotton fields. There were elephant tracks everywhere.

The little boy spoke to Celestino, and they pointed to a patch of brush.

"There," said Celestino.

"So how are we going to do this ..." I began, but Celestino had turned away again.

As we walked the last few hundred meters, I thought to myself that if one is determined to arrest armed elephant poachers while wearing a green satin vest and carrying only a bush knife, it may be best to have no plan whatsoever. A plan would only detract from the spontaneity of the moment, which seemed to be the only advantage we possessed.

We walked into the camp.

Four men lolled under a brush arbor, while several women roasted something that smelled good on a fire behind. Three high-caliber rifles lay on a mat, close at hand. On one side, the poachers had constructed drying racks for the meat. We noted parts of zebra, kudu, and wild pig, as well as other, larger chunks that had to be elephant.

. . .

Celestino greeted the men warmly. We shook hands all around and sat down. Celestino introduced us: Djini and Dio were with us, as well as an agricultural officer that the Administrator had sent along, probably to spy on us.

An old man in a white T-shirt and with a pendulous belly introduced the other men.

Only one of these men was a hunter. The other two were men from the village.

"You had a successful hunt," said Celestino.

The old man replied, "Yes, we did."

He picked his teeth with a twig.

"Tell me, what animals did you kill?"

"Pig. Zebra ..." he picked again, "Kudu."

"We heard you killed elephant," said Celestino.

"Yes." said the man. Rarely have I seen such a self-satisfied grin.

"We were in Ngura village," said Celestino. "We heard you killed five elephants."

"Yes," said the man. "We killed five."

Celestino looked at me. Time to improvise.

"That's funny," I said. "The Administrator told me that you killed only one. I talked to him just now."

"Very strange," said Celestino. "Tell me, do you have a license to kill elephant?"

"Yes," said the man.

"As I told you, I work with the *Associacao Meio-Ambiente*, the Environmental Association, and this man," he nodded at me, "works with the Working Group for Community Resource Management of Cabo Delgado. We would like to see your license."

"It's actually not with me. It is with the *Chefe* of our group, who is in the village now."

"Ah, you are not the *Chefe*?"

"No."

"I think," I said, "it would be good for us to see your *Chefe*. We can confirm your authorization to kill elephants and confirm your hunting license."

"Yes," said Celestino. "A very good idea. I am sure you will not mind showing us your hunting license in the village. Shall we go?"

The old man had to agree.

"Bring the guns, too," said Celestino, "so we can match the serial numbers with the gun licenses."

They tried to hide one gun under a sleeping mat, but we saw it, and told them to collect it, too. We took a piece of zebra hide, a pig's leg, and a piece of kudu hide along as evidence. We had plenty of time to think on the long walk back to the car.

I thought mostly about the fact that the poachers still had all the guns. No one spoke.

We arrived at the car.

Nicolãu woke up. He had been driving since four that morning and had stayed behind due to exhaustion. We climbed in the front of the car and told the poachers to climb in back. Nicolãu turned the car around.

"Wait a minute," I said, and jumped down. "It's not safe to have loaded guns in the car. We could hit a bump and a gun could go off."

I handed the youngest man a plastic bag. "Please take the bullets out of the rifles and put them in there."

The young man looked at the old man, and then at me. I tensed. Then the young man worked the breech and out came the bullets. The old man emptied the other two guns. We let them keep the bag of bullets. Celestino, Dio, and Djini edged closer to the poachers, ready to grab them. Nicolãu started to drive off. I stopped him.

"Wait a minute," I said, and jumped down again. "Let's put the rifles behind the front seat. They'll be safe there. They won't be damaged by the bumps."

I smiled and held out my hand. They handed over the guns.

The old man didn't look so satisfied any more. We drove to the village. It was pitch dark by the time we arrived.

Nicolău led the way in the village. We found the *Chefe* and told him to bring the tusks. We told him that we had to go confirm with the Administrator the number of elephants that had been killed. We told him that the Administrator authorized only one, yet he had killed five. He swore he had authorization for five.

"So let's go confirm this," said Nicolău, and there was no further argument.

Nicolău, the *Chefe*, and the others started off into the darkness to fetch the tusks.

"Wait a minute," I said. "Won't the two men in the car run away?"

"No," said Nicolău, and walked away, offering no further explanation. I let him go. I was used to him by now.

I passed an uncomfortable twenty minutes waiting for their return, but they did, and with the tusks. My two poachers had not run away. The *Chefe* jumped into the truck and we drove back to the district capital.

"OK, Nicolău, why didn't they run away? Or attack us? They must know by now that they're in trouble."

"It's the guns. They borrowed these guns from the police in Pemba. No one is allowed to own guns anymore. Only the police."

"So ...?"

Talking with Nicolău is always like pulling teeth.

"So if they don't take them back there will be no place to hide, except Tanzania. If they attack us ... that is even worse. The police will hunt them like dogs. They will never leave them alone."

"I see."

"And they still think the Administrator will vouch for them—*defesa das pessoas e bens*."

"Will he?"

"Watch."

The Administrator had gone to bed, but we found the District Director of Agriculture at the clinic. His child was ill.

"We visited your hunters," said Nicolāu, "but we found some problems."

"I told you, we authorized ..." started the Director.

"Not that," said Nicolāu. "We found them with meat of kudu, pig, and zebra."

"Look at my license," said the hunter. "I am authorized for kudu and pig."

"Until 30th September," said Nicolāu. "Today is 21st October, and you killed those animals on the 18th. And you are not authorized for zebra. It is a protected species in Mozambique."

Silence.

"We are taking these men to Pemba," said Nicolāu. "Just so you know."

We drove away.

"You didn't mention the elephants," I said.

"No. It would have just caused an argument," said Nicolāu. He smiled. "But I will mention them in Pemba."

We arrived after midnight. We went to José's house. As Provincial Director of Wildlife, he had to be informed immediately.

"*A final!* It's you!" he said to the *Chefe*. He turned to us. "I know this man. I was the one who issued him this license." Then back to the *Chefe*, "I told you not to kill elephant. Isn't it?"

The *Chefe* hung his head.

"You did."

We took the men to the police station and served them with a variety of processes, including hunting protected species, hunting out of season, and hunting elephant.

The new Law of Forests and Wildlife and come into effect on 12th October, so the fines and penalties to be applied had been strengthened considerably.

The poachers were looking at fines of $10,000 per elephant, sums they could only dream about. Failing that, they were looking at long prison terms, something I felt to be entirely appropriate, as did the rest of the team.

The adrenaline was wearing off. Nicolãu dropped us at our respective houses. We shook hands and shared the look that mountaineers share, and soldiers, and all men who come to depend on each other's strength and judgment.

I took a shower and drifted around the house, looking in on my sleeping family, playing the radio, touching things: a sandalwood bowl, a piece of branching coral, Lunga's T-shirt, a seashell, Neli's shoe. I made my way to the bedroom and listened to Ruth sleep. She didn't snore, but tomorrow I would tell her she did, and she would laugh and not believe me for an instant.

So much to do, so many to care about.

Then I fell completely and absolutely asleep.

Addenda to Chapter 5

THIS MAY have been the time when the idea of conserving the Quirimbas Archipelago and adjacent continental areas first entered my mind. Certainly, it would have been difficult to imagine how such a thing could have been accomplished earlier. It was only in 1999 that the local timber industry collapsed and parts of the province became available for conservation due to the cancellation of timber licenses.

There are two questions that people always ask me about the Quirimbas National Park. The first is why it is the shape it is, awkward and lumpy in places, long and thin in others, with some important habitats left out and some unimportant areas included.

The answer is that the Quirimbas National Park represents the largest area of the Quirimbas Archipelago and surrounds that was ever available for conservation purposes.

The important habitats that were left out were and still are subject to timber licensing; the "unimportant" areas that were included have turned out to be important, as climate change advances and species migrate along gradients of temperature and rainfall. Even plants migrate generationally.

The second question is why the Park was created with so many people living inside it. One of the things that makes a park in Southern Africa different from a park almost anywhere else in the world is that humans are part of the indigenous fauna of Africa. Human interaction has been shaping habitats and species for thousands and perhaps millions of years (depending on how you define "human").

This was illustrated during our first bird count in 2007. The team of ornithologists spent an entire day in the deep Swahili coastal forest, a rare type of dense forest habitat found only along the East African coast. The day's work yielded twelve species.

The following day the team moved 20 kilometers to a nearby village. In three hours, in a howling gale, the team counted 155 species in the fields, around the houses, and along the tree-line. It is not overstatement to say that in the Quirimbas, humans make habitat for animals.

There is another aspect, however, that also weighed heavily in the decision to consciously include villages and settlements inside the Park, and that was that human livelihoods and lifestyles were so closely based upon the natural resource base that separating them would have been not only cruel but also disastrous.

We consciously chose to preserve habitats, species, human livelihoods, and cultural traditions as a unit; the management plan I wrote for the Park specifically refers to the importance of conserving human lives and human culture. The idea was not to create a fortress for nature into which no one could enter, but rather, to build reverence and stewardship for nature into the day-to-day life of everyone associated with the Quirimbas National Park. And what a blessing for all concerned to find seeds of that reverence and stewardship all throughout the culture of the local Macua, Maconde, and Muani peoples who live there.

I will take just one example: my friend Momade Anli, a village leader turned ranger of the Quirimbas National Park, has always preferred prayer on the beach to prayer in the mosque. He says he finds it easier to talk to God there.

I think I agree with him. Lidia tells me that going outdoors and moving around is one of the fundamental management tools for depression, a remedy I require with distressing frequency as I leap without apparent motive or transition from up to down, from hyperactivity to immobility, from godhood to catatonia. She is right as always but it is more than that. Frail creature that I am, my dreams and hopes and prayers and visions cannot penetrate doors and windows and roofs and walls.

I am not at all sure that the gay, lesbian, and transgender members of my family will agree with, or even be comfortable with, the notion that a homosexual is a "man with the spirit of a woman" (or vice versa).

I do not doubt however that they will appreciate that the cultures described in this chapter have each created a way for societal understanding of a variety of gender identities. Gross oversimplifications perhaps, but effective ones, establishing accepted roles and identities for those who otherwise would have none. Would that more of these traditional notions had found their way into modern life and modern legislative frameworks.

I would love to tell you that this is a deadly green mamba, and that I took the picture while dangling one-handed from a tree limb over a cliff, my camera lens inches from the snake's flickering tongue. In reality, I have no idea what kind of snake it is; Mozambique has eight or nine snakes that look quite similar and I am not herpetologist enough to tell them apart. But I did take the picture while dangling one-handed from a tree limb over a cliff, my camera lens inches from the snake's flickering tongue.

CHAPTER 6

Campaigns

November, 1999. In which our Helvetas team extends the
"Support to Local Initiatives and Empowerment Project" to
the isolated and remote area of Mazeze, in eastern Chiure
District.

CAMPAIGNS STARTED THIS week.

In the rural areas, eggs appeared for sale along the
roadsides, piled on rickety bamboo tables or hanging
from tree limbs, cradled in scraps of plastic.

As we drove to Chiure, ragged children and old women lurched
unsteadily towards the car, waving and shrieking *"Ovos! Ovos!"* as
if their lives depended on it. It took me a few tire-squealing skids
to realize that these poor unfortunates were not intent on throwing themselves bodily into my path, but merely wished to sell me
something which I sincerely desired to buy. As it turned out, my
sincerity was no match for Ruth's, and we ended the journey the
proud owners of something like five dozen fresh, cream-white
eggs, some of which were almost immediately transformed into
omelet sandwiches.

. . .

We had arrived too late and too tired to contemplate the preparation of anything more ambitious for supper, partly because the egg-buying process and the screeching stops, the negotiations (with associated arm waving and gesticulation if the seller could speak no Portuguese), the careful examination and selection of each individual egg, and the frantic search for something to put the damn things in (as the sellers invariably refused to part with their plastic bags) added something like fifty minutes to the journey.

We cared not, for in Cabo Delgado, eggs, like rain and tomatoes and onions and green maize and cholera and even fish, have their season.

They weren't hen's eggs.

No one who is not desperate, or a great fool—like our former employee Bernabe, who we sacked last year—willingly sacrifices a potential chicken for the momentary pleasure a few cents or a few bites of protein will bring.

But then Bernabe was trying to buy his way back into our favor after a remarkable series of escapades that included simultaneously setting fire to a pile of blankets on our sitting room table while locking himself out of the house, breaking down the front door, stealing gin from the pantry and encouraging our other staff to drink it, and offering a prostitute to a friend visiting from Zimbabwe.

His gesture of atonement consisted of an early-morning offering of five eggs, all of which turned out to contain nearly-hatched chicks in various states of embryonic development, and which we later found to have been stolen from under a neighbor's hen. You may well ask why we hired such a clown, and if you do I will be unable to offer any response except that it seemed like a good idea at the time. (In the spirit of complete honesty in which I desire to write this, I am forced to add that Bernabe was not the worst of our former employees, but that is another story.)

. . .

The eggs were those of helmeted guinea fowl.

As Bernabe and his ilk represent the reverse of the Platonic ideal of a household staff member, so do guinea fowl represent the opposite of the ideal of avian maternal care. Not for them the homely nest, the feathers so tenderly plucked from mama's proud breast, the squirming insect so lovingly proffered.

None of this.

The female guinea fowl drops her egg almost anywhere, and the farmer who desires to rear guinea fowls domestically must gather the eggs where they may be found and slide them under an unsuspecting hen, if he happens to have any that are sitting eggs that month.

Only once have I seen a mother guinea fowl with chicks at heel, and this phenomenon provoked much amazement and discussion among the Mozambicans who were with me at the time. Most people have neither the time nor the inclination to bother with the propagation of so hapless a creature, and so gather the eggs and sell them by the roadside. It is a sad economic commentary that so many are pressed upon passing motorists at this time of year, though I cling to the hope that the ragged children manage to consume a helpful number of eggs during the collection process, away from watchful adult eyes.

None of the five dozen we bought from the rural folk were rotten, unlike the crates of imported South African eggs that one buys from time to time from pushy young men in the market in Pemba, which invariably contain a bad egg or two.

The national presidential and parliamentary campaigns also hit full stride this week.

The campaigning actually began on the 19th, but I had been in the bush and so had not had time to give the campaign the appreciation and attention that a national democratic process in a newly fledged democracy really deserves.

The political campaigning affected our lives in a number of ways.

The first effect was a seismic uncertainty about the feasibility of a number of long-standing work plans, the first tremors of which we felt a week or two before the beginning of the actual campaign.

"I'm not sure the Governor will come to Mazeze on 13th November," Nicolãu would say to me. "That is close to campaign time."

"Will we be able to take so many members of government away from the campaign for two weeks for the seminar on the new Land Law?" José Dias would ask.

"Please change the dates for the Zimbabwe study tour," pleaded Carlos Mugoma, the Provincial Director of Agriculture and Fisheries. "I will be away, and most of the District Administrators will be busy with the campaign."

We scribbled corrections in the margins of our desktop calendars and sent a flurry of faxes to Zimbabwe and Maputo. Problems with the campaign, we explained, but I'm sure our friends and colleagues in Zimbabwe wondered why we couldn't have foreseen such problems a little earlier.

We wondered the same, and wondered even more why our Mozambican colleagues had let us schedule such events during this period.

But perhaps this had much to do with the youth of the Mozambican democracy. This was only the second electoral campaign in Mozambican history, and the first that the Mozambicans had organized for themselves. The earlier election had been held in 1994 with the support and supervision of the United Nations (the 1999 campaign would only be observed by Jimmy Carter and a handful of assistants).

Thus, it is quite probable that only three or four people in the entire country had an idea of what to expect and how to prepare, and it is certain that none of these were in communication with us in early 1999, when our year's work plan was scraped together.

• • •

That being said, some aspects of the campaign were marvelously well done.

In the first place, the campaign itself was limited by law to forty-five days duration, a wonderful improvement on the American system (where campaigning appears to be continuous), though unfortunately not quite as well done as the British system (typically around four weeks).

It must be said, however, that the limitations on travel and communications are such that forty-five days are insufficient for a Mozambican politician to generate the same amount of noise and confusion as his British counterpart generates in twenty-eight (or that his American counterpart can generate in an hour and a half). The campaign also terminates three days before the actual voting starts, another sensible innovation which eliminates the possibility that an unfortunate citizen may encounter on election morning a Mozambican apparatchik of one party or another scrounging for a few additional votes.

At that time, the electoral law religiously defended the principle of equal radio time for all (I do not know if the same was true for television time, as I was never able to adjust our set to receive TV Pemba, the only station within range).

Thus, from nine to ten every night, each of the eighteen or twenty parties contesting the election were allotted three minutes in which to sway the hearts of their listeners. This policy was unquestionably fair, though whether it was a good idea nor not depends upon one's perspective. We as listeners found it tremendously entertaining, though for the parties involved it seemed an onerous burden, as indeed it was. Rare is the politician who can formulate three minutes of something intelligent to say, day in and day out, over a forty-five day period.

The wealthier parties (*Renamo* and *Frelimo*) were able to finance the production of catchy campaign jingles which could be used to fill up to one-third of the daily time allotment.

The poorer parties had to resort to the hesitant reading of (presumably) nearly illegible position papers, the wooden repetition of Mao-style slogans, and the inevitable accusations of corruption against the existing *Frelimo* administration. A typical evening's listening included the following.

1. The *União Democratica (UD)* promised to eliminate corruption in the health and education sectors, a significant promise in a country in which patients are often required to bribe to receive treatment, and students must bribe to pass. Unfortunately, instead of explaining how this might be accomplished, the UD went on to promise better salaries for all, but failed to explain how the Mozambican economy might be stimulated to support such a move.

2. The *Partido Social, Liberal, e Democratica (Partido SOL)* started well by preaching against violence in the electoral campaign—"Elections should not lead to the cemetery"—but after this were unable to maintain their momentum, for they went on to divulge the earth-shaking news that the objectives of *Partido SOL* were the development of Mozambique and the development of the *Partido SOL* itself.

3. The *Partido de Progresso Liberal de Mozambique (PPLM)* spent the first minute and a half explaining in minute detail what the party symbol looks like (illiterate voters mark their ballots by symbol, not by name). The symbol of the PPLM includes an ear of maize, a sheaf of wheat, and a representation of the Cabora Bassa dam wall, among other things. This is unfortunate, for nearly every other party's symbol contains an ear of maize as well as a mix of other agricultural and industrial motifs. The poor PPLM representative

was hard-pressed to distinguish his symbol from all the rest, and it showed in his presentation, which was peppered with umms, aahs, *alias, portantos, quer dizers,* and other symptoms of oratorical unease. From there he complained about inequalities of campaign financing, though he did note that at last the PPLM had attracted sufficient funding "from all over the world" to allow it to distribute T-shirts and caps, and post signs on walls and other suitable surfaces as the two major parties were doing.

4. The *Partido Ampliação Social de Mozambique (Pasomo)* started with complaints about the negative influence of money on Mozambican political processes. This concern turned out to be nothing more than an indirect way to complain about *Pasomo's* financial situation, for by the end of the three-minute period, the complaints were no longer indirect, and the suggestion was put forward that the government ought to finance the campaigns of all parties equally, even those, such as *Pasomo,* who seem to have nothing to offer to a national political debate.

5. The *União Mozambicana de Oposição (UMO),* after explaining its symbol, PPLM-style, complained about the punishments—*"castigamentos"*—that the Customs Department imposed on traders and importers, who were simply trying to "work for the economic development of Mozambique." As traders and importers in Mozambique are far richer than the vast majority of the population, this did not strike me as a populist message. Near the end, "improvements in salaries for all workers" were mentioned, again with no explanation of how this was to be accomplished.

By this time I was getting sleepy, and my notes are therefore less clear. I believe that it was the *Partido Liberal de Mozambique (Palmo)* that put forward a number of worthy national objectives, including the following:

- decentralization of political structures;
- passage of a new law to allow more self-government for municipalities;
- prioritization of Mozambican citizens in economic development programs;
- employment creation programs; and
- to have all provincial governors be natives of the province in question.

Palmo declined to elaborate how these goals might be achieved, on the grounds that every time they make sensible proposals, other parties steal them and use them in their own campaigns.

A catchy campaign jingle awoke me later on, followed immediately by a roar of applause and a bullfrog voice shouting, "Vote for me! Vote for Progress! Vote for Change!"

The candidate never did say his name (or maybe I was too sleepy to hear it) but did have time to mention that his name would be the second one on the electoral list (again, for the benefit of illiterate voters) before the music swelled and his time was finished. Not once during his speech did I hear mention the name of his party, nor did he offer a single reason why the discerning voter should choose him.

I fell asleep for good after this, before all parties had had their three minutes, thus losing this opportunity to make a fair comparison between all of them at that specific point in the campaign, something I regret to this day.

Although we enjoyed the radio, we as expatriate employees of a non-governmental development organization were contractually forbidden from participating in campaign activities, or even attending political rallies.

This did not stop our children from coming home nearly every day sporting *Frelimo* caps and buttons that they were given by friends, neighbors, and *Frelimo* party campaign workers, for Cabo Delgado is predominantly *Frelimo* territory. Nor did it keep us from pestering our friend Joaquim Nema, a senior official of the Animal Husbandry Department (and *Frelimo* party organizer), to give us a couple of the really extremely snazzy yellow *Frelimo* campaign T-shirts.

Eventually Nema gave us a couple of much less snazzy white ones, reasoning no doubt that the really snazzy yellow ones should be given to people allowed to wear them in public. And/or vote. We couldn't argue with this logic.

Neli and Lunga were quite taken during this time with "*Vota Chissano*" buttons, featuring a smiling President Chissano on a field of red and yellow. The photograph was an old one, as we found out when the Chissano campaign came to Chiure. Chissano himself passed by our house and waved to the kids who were sitting on the gate out front.

"Who is that?" asked Lunga.

"It's President Chissano," said Ruth, but Lunga disagreed, forcefully.

"No," he said, with a finality that only children can possess. "Chissano isn't bald."

I must say in all fairness that I found the interest and enthusiasm with which my Mozambican friends and colleagues approached the election to be nothing less than exhilarating.

They are in many ways better democrats than I am, the existing problems with Mozambican democracy (corruption, cronyism, etc.) notwithstanding, and I came to feel that my First-World cynicism did not entirely become me.

I envied them the pleasure they took in voting, a degree of

pleasure I have never felt, having never been deprived of the vote. I envied them their *Mozambicanidade*, their characteristic pride in themselves as Mozambicans, and I envied them what they have achieved under some of the most difficult circumstances imaginable.

In the middle of the week I went out to the estuary in Mazeze to work on yet another campaign. This campaign was to motivate proper resource management in the community nature reserve there.

The estuary is almost mythological. Though it really exists, it is hard to imagine such a place until one has actually been there.

The community reserve of Mazeze lies between the two rivers that make up the estuary, though we are working to expand it both north and south to encompass the entire ecological zone. The smaller (and seasonal) Rio Megarumo runs into the Indian Ocean a mere 3 kilometers north of the much larger (and perennial) Rio Lurio; the Lurio rises on the Malawian border and runs through the heartland of the Macua nation, separating the provinces of Nampula and Cabo Delgado.

It is hard to believe that the Macua, whom no one has ever heard of, are the largest ethnic group in all of Mozambique—five million out of seventeen million Mozambicans are Macua—but they are.

Hard to believe that Chiure District, which has a population of 190,000 people, nearly the most densely populated District in the entire country, has at its eastern end a largely unexplored forest in which are found buffaloes and lions and extensive stands of ebony timber, but they are there to be seen.

Hard to believe that an area two hours' drive (in the dry season) away from the provincial capital of Pemba can contain the village of Nacahe, previously unknown to the outside world, but my friend and colleague José Dias "discovered" it while on a wildlife inventory in June (in the same fashion as Columbus "discovered" America; one hopes that the population of the village will not be annihilated by its contact with us).

Hard to believe that the estuary contains a hippopotamus population that lives in the open sea, but there they are. (Adamo and I sleep on the beach whenever we go to the estuary in order to see them returning to the waves at dawn.)

Hard to believe that the estuary supports a large population of sharks that breed in an abyssal canyon that reaches nearly to the mouth of the Rio Lurio; harder still to believe that the sharks occasionally kill a hippo; hardest of all to believe that the locals go to sea with tiny dugout canoes and home-made hooks to do battle with these monsters; impossible to believe that they regularly win.

The shark fins are sold to Tanzanians who re-sell them to oriental buyers. The meat is sold locally or consumed on the spot.

Mazeze is the poorest and most isolated Administrative Post in Chiure District, and our early investigations showed that it had the worst set of developmental indicators: kwashiorkor, growth stunting, and various other nutritional diseases are almost universal.

We decided in early 1997 to prioritize Mazeze, to start work in Mazeze before we started anywhere else.

It didn't work out that way. We spent an entire year being thrown out of meetings.

"You people are liars. You come here talking about help with food and goats and tools for the woodcutters, and schools, but you won't do anything. We know all about people like you. We have experience with people like you."

"Wait a minute," we said. "We just got here. We haven't lied to anybody yet, and we aren't going to lie in the future, either."

An old man snorted.

"Another lie," he said. "Last year I registered my name with you to get a loan for carpenter's tools. I paid ten *contas*. Then nothing. When do I get my tools?"

"I was in Swaziland last year," I said. "You didn't register your name with me."

Another stood up. "I don't know about that, but the man beside you once fined me for not having a carpenter's license. Where am I supposed to get the money for a carpenter's license when I don't have all the tools I need? My tools were destroyed in the war."

I looked at Adamo.

He shrugged.

"It's true," he said. "It's my job. I'm a forest ranger. I let that man cut a lot of wood before I fined him."

A younger man stood up, the *Chefe* of one of the *bairros* of Mazeze Town.

"You government people are all alike. The Governor himself came here last year and promised us a new roof for the school. Where is this roof? When will you put on the roof?"

I tried again.

"I told you I'm not from the government, I am from Helvetas, a Swiss Non-Governmental Organization that ..."

Seven or eight people were all shouting at once.

"What about the road? No one can pass on the road in summer. When do you fix ..."

"We need hoes and bush knives. How do we plant food without hoes?"

"The government put up a lot of water pumps, but none in Mazeze. No one ever does anything in Mazeze. No one cares about us..."

When things quieted down I tried again.

"Look, we are here to support local initiatives. That means that we are here to help you, like a neighbor. You don't tell your neighbor to build your house for you. You ask him to help you build. So you can't tell us to put a roof on the school, and then just sit and wait. If you want to fix the school, then we must work together. We can buy the cement and roof tiles, but you must get the sand and the stones and the poles ..."

The old men, the *velhos*, walked out of the meeting to go smoke under a tree. They'd heard enough. The young ones still had some more frustration to work through. We let them shout at us a few more minutes and then we left. It went like this for twelve months.

In the meantime, we started in the neighboring Administrative Post of Chiure Velho. We set up agriculture and goat projects, and made loans to woodcutters and carpenters. We started building a school. Now and again we'd meet an old man or a *Chefe* from Mazeze on the path. When one of them demanded to know why we were helping people in Chiure Velho, but not in Mazeze, we knew it was time to try again.

"We aren't working in Mazeze because you and your elders keep throwing us out," I said.

"Oh, that," said the *Chefe*. He laughed. "That was when we thought you were liars."

We laughed too. There was no point holding grudges. We'd learned enough about the history of the area to understand why the people in Mazeze were the way they were.

It had been a rebel area during the war, closed to the outside world. Renamo had used the estuary as a harbor, taking advantage of the depth inshore to land war materiel practically on the beach. To keep this fact a secret, anyone caught entering or leaving had been killed. When the war stopped, there had been a few half-hearted attempts to develop the area, including a failed project to help the woodcutters and carpenters. Even our employer, Helvetas, had ignored Mazeze: of the 1,300 village water pumps that Helvetas has installed in the province since Independence, not one is in Mazeze.

We'd started in 1998 with a goat project (to replace stock lost in the war), tools for woodcutters and seeds for farmers, and a water supply in Milapane village. We also spent a lot of time listening: listening to people's problems; listening to their complaints; listening to their dreams; but mostly just listening so they would feel listened to.

We began to make friends. By mid-year, confidence was high enough to make us feel ready for more difficult interventions.

We organized a group of woodcutters in the five most distant villages, near the mouth of the Lurio River, and submitted a request for a license to cut ebony.

Ebony *(Dalbergia melanoxylon)* is one of the world's rarest and most precious woods; only Mozambique still has it commercial quantities. The harvest is strictly controlled by the Mozambican government, the annual quota being something like 600 tonnes (fewer than 3,000 trees).

Because profit margins are high, there is tremendous competition for licenses. We held our breath. In the meantime, several commercial operators heard about the ebony in Mazeze and prospected in the area. We wondered if our newly-created "Community Management Area" could stand against the power of the timber lobby.

In September Carlos Mugoma (Provincial Director of Agriculture and Fisheries) called me to his office.

"Congratulations," he said. "You've got twenty tonnes. We can't give you more until you make a proper forest inventory and management plan for the area."

He shook my hand.

"How in the world did you do it?" I managed to ask, but he only smiled.

"You have to cut it all before 31st December," he said. "Get going."

I did.

. . .

Adamo and I went straight out to the Lurio Estuary to arrange for the ebony harvest and to start work on the management plan. We didn't want to manage only the ebony. We wanted to work out a comprehensive plan that included all types of timber, wildlife, fisheries, biodiversity preservation, and agriculture.

For this last we would have to devise a sustainable cropping system, for slash and burn agriculture works only in areas of low population density. All this planning is difficult enough in First World countries, never mind countries in which new villages are still being discovered.

The ebony harvest was both easier and more difficult than I had expected. The easy part was cutting down the trees. This is done by hand, for the wood is too oily to use chain saws.

The villagers had a more difficult time of the sawing than I did. I blessed my parents and my uncle Ernie for raising me with tools in my hands, and for feeding me on a regular basis. Out of respect to the villagers, who brought no lunch, Adamo and I also ate nothing during the workday, but nevertheless were shocked at the differences in our respective energy levels.

The hard part of the job was finding a tree to cut. There were thousands of trees, but only a very few with long, straight trunks. It took us half the first day to realize that the best trees were found on the edges of the ebony stands, near to dense forest. Competition makes the trees in these places grow straight and tall.

Pure ebony stands in general contain trees that look like something out of Tolkien; one expects Tom Bombadil to come whistling through the brush, axe on his shoulder. But it is only Juma, bucket in hand, offering water and mangoes.

We sit in the shade of a gnarled old forest patriarch to eat them. A bateleur eagle wheels overhead, and two green parrots dive for the safety of the lower branches.

Juma points out yesterday's buffalo tracks, and I realize, not for the first time, mind you, that I am a long way from New Jersey.

. . .

By Thursday, Adamo and I are feeling unnecessary. The community leaders have the work well in hand; one of the woodcutters is in fact the *Rainha*—queen—of Soma village.

We set off to find the mouth of the Lurio River. We drive as far as we can, then abandon the car in the shade of a baobab. The tide is out, so we trudge down the riverbed, sand dragging at our feet and sun in our eyes. The tide rises and we head for the near bank.

This is tougher going, for it is mud, and one must pick one's way forward using roots and clumps of grass for purchase.

Now the mangroves begin, and the hard going begins in earnest. Roots and branches form a three-dimensional lattice that can only be crawled through. Small oysters are everywhere, slicing hands and knees and foreheads.

We decide to return to the river. Adamo climbs a mangrove and ties our clothing above the high-water mark. The water is knee-deep, then waist deep, and then we are swimming. Four hundred meters farther along we round a clump of trees, cross a small, clear pool, and touch down on a long finger of sand that separates ocean and estuary.

We hear surf pounding on the other side, and female voices. We climb the sand spit and find ourselves in a fishing camp.

For the first time, we meet the shark fishermen of Mazeze.

We spend the day with them, marveling at their skills and the beauty of the estuary, swimming, laughing, and talking. We hold a meeting to talk about management of the fishery. We use a number of the techniques of Rapid Rural Appraisal—mapping, semi-structured interviews, transit walks—to help us form a picture of village needs and initiatives.

An old man paddles in with a 2-meter hammerhead shark. He offers us a piece, which gladdens Adamo, for back in camp we are down to noodles and coffee powder.

I am dubious, for I have never liked the smell of shark—a glutinous, oily, cartilaginous smell—but Adamo says it will be delicious. Someone offers us a ride back to the truck in a sailing dhow. No one mentions that we are wearing only our underwear.

Back in Soma, clothed again, Adamo busies himself with the pots. I make notes on the day. My stomach growls. The food, when it comes, looks great. Adamo has fried the shark meat and mixed it with spaghetti and some tomatoes he has bought somewhere. It looks like Kentucky-style chicken spaghetti, but it tastes like shark—ammonia and grease. So does our coffee the next morning. So does everything else we cook in that pot for the next few weeks.

I decide I can survive another day with no food.

That was 1998.

In early 1999, we completed a full resource inventory of the Lurio Estuary area. The woodcutters and the shark fisherman participated for the full three weeks of the survey. We brought ecologists up from Maputo to supervise. The report we produced on the biodiversity there was interesting enough to attract the Governor's attention. We arranged for him to visit the estuary on 13th November. We wanted to present the results of the inventory to him and to all the community leaders on that day.

I went to the estuary on a Wednesday night to begin preparations. Adamo came along, and Celestino and Paulo, the leaders of the *Associacao Meio-Ambiente*. Celestino left his green satin and tweed waistcoat at home.

We awoke early and spent the day with community leaders choosing the best site for the Governor's visit.

Some of the leaders wanted the site to be in the palm forest, others in the *miombo* bush, others out on the beach. I liked a small hill that rose just behind the mangrove swamp. We climbed it, but the bush was too dense to see anything. Paulo took a photo of me perched in the tree-tops; or rather he took a photo of my torso. Paulo always chops the heads off his photos.

Several species of raptors were about. I saw bateleur, gymno-gene, osprey, and yellow-billed kite. We saw tracks of hippo, civet, jackal, kudu, and sable in the mud by the river.

On Thursday, we drop formal invitations at all of the villages in the estuary. The community leaders have decided that each village must bring samples of what it produces. The shark fishermen hope to bring a whole shark, but it will depend on the day.

On Friday we visit our development projects in the area: goats, rice, sesame and sunflower production, ebony cutting. All are making progress. No one calls us liars. On the way back to Pemba, I spy a bat hawk circling above a dilapidated primary school in the village of Murrebue, waiting for the bats to come out.

I stop the car, and we follow the hunt until it is too dark to see. The bat hawk is actually a falcon, jet black, with a falcon's speed and agility.

The bats are the smaller, insect-eating type, and they hug the tops of the cashew trees, darting inside the canopy when the hawk dives. The hawk hunts for fifteen minutes without a kill, though there are several near misses. We don't know whether to cheer the hawk or the bats. The hawk is a relatively rare species (though one hunts above our house in Chiure), but the bats eat both flies and mosquitoes.

I arrive home several hours later.

Ruth is tired and frustrated. The Swiss Development Corpora-tion has decided to spring a surprise inspection on us next week, the same week that the Governor will visit. As if we weren't going to be busy enough with His Excellency.

A small mountain of faxes and emails have arrived from Ma-puto in my absence, detailing the documents and reports that must be prepared, and urging us to go through the accounts with a fine-toothed comb in preparation for the visit.

I am specifically instructed to prepare a document describing *Aspects of the Project that Contribute to Sustainability.*

I am supposed to have this in Maputo by yesterday. Our life often seems like a sprint from weekend to weekend, but this time there is to be no weekend.

I write *Aspects of the Project that Contribute to Sustainability* on Saturday and email it on Sunday. No one ever mentions this document again. It vanishes into the bureaucracy without a trace.

Addenda to Chapter 6

I AM a Mozambican now, having won my citizenship in early 2012. My Mozambican ID is one of my most precious possessions, and I am prone to make far too much of my *Mozambicanidade* when being introduced to new colleagues and acquaintances.

The topic excites me, so in true bipolar fashion, I show too much emotion, talk too much, and even go so far as to show them my identity document. Most remain unimpressed. Ruth reminds me, when she can, not to continue doing this.

I am not nearly so excited about how Mozambican politics has evolved.

As I write this, a forensic audit is underway into two billion dollars' worth of hidden national debt. The government of the former President saw fit to incur this debt and hide it from the International Monetary Fund as well as the parliament and people of Mozambique.

Most of this money is unaccounted for, and Mozambique is probably the world's most indebted nation, per capita, in the world right now. Frelimo politicians are having an awkward time trying to explain how and why this happened and have even used their parliamentary majority to retroactively approve these loans. Constitutional lawyers note that post-facto parliamentary approval is irrelevant; the loans are unconstitutional on at least three grounds and thus are "un-approvable" ... meanwhile relief for the rural poor seems as distant as ever, though we do have a shiny new airport and a multi-billion-dollar bridge going up in the capital.

You may be wondering by this point when I am going to address the harsher realities of being bipolar. Black depression, inability to cope, self-mutilation, suicidal thoughts, impulses, plans.[13]

At this point in my latest review of the manuscript I was wondering it myself; these things are an integral part of my life after all and not to mention these struggles is not only dishonest, but belittles all those who face similar struggles, whose lives are similarly encumbered.

So where is the depression? The only explanation I can find is that in 1999, when I started this, I was in complete denial, maintaining myself on an extreme diet of risk, booze, adrenaline, and hyperactivity.

I never let myself slow down, never acknowledged the negative, never acknowledged that something was wrong, though all who knew me knew there was.

Want proof? I just found some.

I was looking back through old emails a couple of minutes ago, trying to remember just what happened when. When I collapsed, when Ruth found out about my infidelities, when I broke her heart, when breaking her heart broke mine. Trying to put a date on disaster. I did not find what I was looking for. This is what I found instead, a copy of an old email to my mother.

To: Bechteljo@aol.com
Subject: Re: Bad news
Date: Mon, 27 Sep 1999 12:17:00 +0200

Hello all. We have had a bit of a disaster this past week—the past couple of weeks really. Dumisane Tsabedze [my adopted son] died on Friday the 24th September after spending two weeks in a coma following a car accident. He was struck while crossing the road. Apparently neither he nor the car saw each other—he was in a hurry and so was the car. Broke both his legs and his skull—he never regained consciousness. He was twenty-seven, and had been married only six months and four days.

We went to see him the day before he died and we tried hard to hope. He was on a respirator and his head was swollen and there was absolutely no response to anything—eyes open but not tracking, no movement, nothing.

We stayed an hour talking to him and to his wife. She is a nurse and knew the score, but was trying even harder than we were. His blood pressure was low and fluids would not stay in him. Another nurse said that the parts of his brain that control metabolism were affected, but that he was stable.

He needed a brain scan, and we arranged to come on the following day to make the required payments and whatnot for him to be moved to Jo'burg. We came back the next day at 2 p.m. and found him gone—he must have slipped away as we were parking the car.

His wife collapsed and we all just stood around—no will, no powers of decision, no nothing. Everybody numb. They let us go in and say goodbye. We only knew it was him by his body. The funeral will be next weekend.

We have spent the past few days trying to figure out what to think about all this. Ironic and cruel that the one of us who was the most confident in God and fate should have been the one to be plucked like this. Rage has seemed as inappropriate as platitudes about a better world and life everlasting. It was only this morning that I found a line from Karen Blixen that seems to have some relevance:

> ... *Africa, amongst the continents, will teach it to you: that God and the Devil are one, the majesty co-eternal, not two uncreated but one uncreated, and the Natives neither confounded the persons nor divided the substance.*

Poor Dumi tried hard to help us believe otherwise, and while he was here, sometimes we could. We were better for knowing him.

September 1999, if you will recall, is when I started this book.

September 1999, the same month my son died. September 1999, when I wrote about the Americans and the embassy and the land struggles of the African poor, and did not mention that my son had died. My son, newly graduated, newly married, his whole life ahead of him, was struck by a car belonging to the Red Cross Society that was being driven at excessive velocity past a bus stop where people were getting on and off and crossing the road.

My son, who I adopted when it became clear his birth family could not take care of him, could not even feed him. I started my career in Africa as a Peace Corps agriculture teacher and he was my most brilliant and most malnourished student. And then I talked to his grandparents (his parents had passed away), and he became my son. Funny, caring, a heart as big as the universe, he studied to become a pastor and had launched a new church and a feeding program for poor local children within four months of his graduation.

Dumi, I am ashamed. How could I have started this book without you? Why did it take me eighteen years to remember that I only started writing when you died? And when I did, I wrote about the Americans, and the Swiss, and the new Land Law. And diving, and fish, and bat hawks, and sharks, but not you.

. . .

I remember your wedding.

A riot of joy and Elvis-inspired bad taste. You were wearing a hand-sewn double-breasted suit of purple satin with yellow trim and a yellow mandarin collar, and I had just that morning decided that I need to be much cooler and had thus bought a pair of iridescent insectile wrap-around sunglasses, and I see you there and realize that the only way to make you look more hideous and more joyful is for you to wear the sunglasses. So I hand them to you and your whole face lights up and you put them on and your grooms- men shriek like bridesmaids and your look is pronounced to be perfection.

The groomsmen are wearing satin jackets in a variety of pri- mary colors, all but one who only has a white shirt on, because his wife sewed his jacket so badly that nobody will let him wear it. It is used for polishing your shoes and the bonnet of the hired BMW that you will ride away in.

Your bride is late, as can be expected when the bride lives three hours away and is a Swazi. All is forgiven when she arrives, how- ever, because someone has taken her in hand so that she comes out looking like a bride instead of an entrant in an Englebert Humper- dink lookalike contest. She is beautiful, and when she enters the church we all jump up and roar like football spectators instead of guests at a wedding, and when you walk down the aisle to collect her from her father you take off the sunglasses and someone has to hand you a tissue because you are crying and about half of the guests are crying too and the band abandons all pretense of per- forming a wedding march and lets rip with some back-beat boogie gospel medley with electric bass and Hammond organ and the rhythm-master and the preacher leaps to his feet and starts doing an awkward elbow flappy jiggle-jump, the sort that only African preachers can get away with, and I tell myself that my hay fever is acting up again and I remember the old days when you were so skinny that if you turned sideways we couldn't see you, and here you are a man almost as tall as I am, dancing down the aisle of a church in a fluorescent purple zoot-suit with your bride on your arm and it is simultaneously the most tasteless and the most wonderful thing I have ever seen.

It takes you about half an hour to get down the aisle because everyone is whooping and hollering and jumping up and down like something out of Huck Finn, only no one is poking fun and it is not satire and we are moved.

Later when we all bow our heads and pray I know that I am either getting old too fast or maybe something else is happening that is too much for me to wrap my head around.

It takes about four hours for us to get you married off and everyone is exhausted. There is an hour's break between the wedding and the reception and Ruth and her cousins and I sneak out to get some wine and breath mints because all of this is happening, believe it or not, in a church in which no drinking is allowed. When we get back I have a couple of minutes alone with you and I tell you that I am as proud of you as I can possibly be. And then the reception and the toasts (Ruth doesn't let me make one) and off you drive in the BMW and we stand there in the night and feel the dew come down and things feel just right in the world.

I remember your funeral, clear, crisp, yesterday.

Six months later. The sun was yellow that day, not white, and there was dust in the air and haze over the mountains. We buried you high on a hillside, in your ancestral graveyard, looking north over the valley where you were born. I was the first one to speak over your grave. I was the first to throw a handful of dirt on your coffin, forced by that act to acknowledge that you were gone from us and that we would henceforth have to soldier on without you. I was trying so hard not to cry that I spread the dirt with my left hand. It should have been my right, the hand of respect in Swaziland, but I used my left and I wish I hadn't. I meant no disrespect. Just love, but I showed it badly. I do that.

After we had covered your grave the other mourners crowded around, offering condolences, well meaning, caring, intolerable. I excused myself. Abruptly, I remember. I went to sit by your grave. Ruth came and sat with me. The other mourners trickled back to their cars and we sat for a long time. Then it was down the hill, to find everyone gone and our truck sitting empty, alone by the side of the road.

So where is the negative in this narrative? The depression? I don't need Lidia to answer that one. I blocked it from my reality. Blocked my own son from my reality. No perceptible relationship between existence at point A and existence at point B.

A Heisenberg Gap, a gulf of my own making.

It's a pathetic excuse, but I had to. In 1999, I had no other tools to use to go on.

My son, Dumisane Tsabedze, and his groomsmen on his wedding day.
He is third from left. He died in September, 1998, six months after
being married.

CHAPTER 7

The Powers that Be

November, 1999. In which we host the Provincial Governor's official visit to the Lurio Estuary.

O N Monday morning I went to see Carlos Mugoma, the Cabo Delgado Provincial Director of Agriculture. I wanted to confirm his participation in the seminar with the Governor at the estuary the forthcoming Saturday, on the 13th.

"I don't know," he said. "The Governor and all the Provincial Directors will be in Montepuez until late Friday night. I doubt if we'll be back until Saturday."

"Have you talked to the Governor about this?"

He gave me the look one gives to one's teenage children when they ask to borrow the family car.

"Helvetas is hosting the seminar. You're supposed to coordinate with the Governor, not me."

"Rolf had a verbal agreement with the Governor. They met on the road to Mueda and talked about the visit. The date of the 13th came from the Governor himself ..."

"Then everything is fine, *não é*?" he said, but he was laughing.

Mugoma and I are friends, but this didn't stop him from enjoying the fact that here at least was one problem that was not his.

I went to find Rolf. Rolf sports the portentous title of "Helvetas Provincial Coordinator for Cabo Delgado," and may or may not be my boss. In the hierarchy of Swiss international development, it is difficult to be sure of such things. Rolf summons us to meetings and occasionally issues instructions, but nothing worse than interpersonal friction results when we miss the meetings and ignore the instructions.

He also serves as the communication channel to Marcus in Maputo (National General Coordinator of Helvetas, Mozambique), who is the man who signed our contracts, though not our paychecks. These come from Zurich. Also in Zurich is Albert (Helvetas Country Desk Officer for Mozambique), who is incidentally the man who issued the instruction to write *Aspects of the Project that Contribute to Sustainability.*

Albert neither signs my checks nor is Marcus's boss, yet he comes to visit us once a year and his visits are moments for hurried preparations, suppressed nervousness, and suppers with local dignitaries (and, Albert being Albert, jokes and stories and very good times in local bars when the meetings are all done).

What is most clear about the hierarchy is that Helvetas gets the money to run our project from the Swiss Development Corporation, the overseas development arm of the Swiss government. This adds another small army of people who feel obligated to issue us with sometimes unwanted, usually unsolicited, and always contradictory instructions and advice.

And to spring surprise inspections upon us.

Aside from Bernard in Maputo (the SDC *Bureau de Coordenação*), and Michel of the *Delegação Norte* in Nampula (though his role was defined last year as not supervisory in nature, but merely that of "coordination"), there are a great number of khaki-trousered, white-shirted delegates from offices with names like "Southern and Eastern Africa Regional Office" who pass through from time to time and offer comments that range in quality from insightful to stupid.

Only the Swiss are comfortable with this arrangement, for they govern their own country in more or less the same fashion.

The Swiss and Ruth, I should add. Swazis are expert at finding spaces within hierarchies to do exactly as they please; the Swazi monarchy has over time given the average Swazi hill-man many opportunities to refine this skill.

Early in our time with Helvetas, Ruth found a clause in an official document describing Rolf's role in our project as that of "discussion partner," and she has managed to treat him as that, and little more, throughout most of their relationship. Rolf obliges her by being a good discussion partner, balancing her field perspective and creativity with a more global outlook and solid administrative backup.

I fare worse with Rolf. We alternate between productive brainstorming and out-and-out war.

"Mugoma says everyone will be in Montepuez," I told Rolf. "He said you were supposed to coordinate with the Governor, not him. Have you been in touch with the Governor?"

"I told you I talked with him on the road to Mueda last month. His Excellency himself is the one who chose this date. I haven't talked to him since."

This was not what I wanted to hear.

"We seem to have a problem, Rolf. Mugoma thinks no one from government will come. I thought the idea was to get all levels of leadership together, from village level up to Provincial level, to work out an agreement on the future of that area, legalize it as a national marine park, keep it as a community reserve, or whatever."

"Now I'm thinking that maybe the best thing would be if the

government people didn't come," said Rolf. "Once they come everything is more complicated, everything becomes political, and it is election time ..."

I stopped listening.

I thought of the invitations I'd sent, the food I'd bought, the cooks I'd hired, the radio and TV coverage I'd organized, the road we'd opened so vehicles could reach the estuary, the promises I'd made everyone that yes, the Governor will be there, so come, you shouldn't miss it.

All because Rolf and the Governor had had a conversation on the road to Mueda.

"I don't know what we'll do all day if they don't come," I said. "We've already spent a lot of time talking to the communities. Now we need a broader consensus."

"I'll call the Governor," said Rolf.

"Good idea," I said, and walked out.

I spent the rest of the day and all of Tuesday preparing for the surprise inspection. I figured that if the day in the estuary was going to be a mess, at least we could do well on the inspection.

Faxes continued to arrive with instructions. The most bizarre of these was a request for Ruth and me to organize contracts and job descriptions for all staff members (something I thought Helvetas had done when the staff were hired), and send copies to Maputo and Zurich.

By Wednesday morning there was still no word from the Governor. My nerves were shot and I was exhausted from paperwork and from avoiding everyone who wanted to talk to me about the preparations for the thirteenth.

Until I knew what was happening I wasn't going to say anything to anybody. I went home with a fever at noon. I stayed home until dark, when Rolf came by.

"It's on," he said. "The Governor is coming. A protocol officer goes with you to the estuary tomorrow to review the plans for the day."

We set out at dawn. My flu had vanished.

In its place were the protocol officer and three policemen, but they turned out to be no trouble at all. We took them to the beach where the governor would visit and they discussed the possibility that he might want to swim.

We took them to the Lurio River and they marveled at the view and waded in the shallows. We took them to the shaded forest where the meeting would be held and they pronounced it beautiful. No one mentioned the difficult access, the lack of toilet facilities, the bamboo benches on which we would sit. I began to think that everything might work out.

Rolf came out on Friday to make his own review. The volunteers of the *Associacao Meio-Ambiente* had constructed a thatched meeting-room near the river, and there were five pavilions scattered in the forest behind.

We planned to present the overall results of the seminar to everyone in the meeting room, and then divide in small groups to discuss the results of the resource inventory and brainstorm about plans for the future.

Each aspect of the survey had a pavilion: one for timber and forest resources; one for wildlife; one for fisheries; one for agriculture and soil issues.

Each pavilion was manned by a translator from the *Associacao Meio-Ambiente*, a specialist from our project, and several community members, also specialists in their fields. The fisherman brought nets, dried fish and prawns, hooks, lines, spears, shark fins, and stories of the monsters that got away.

The hunters brought bows and arrows, excrements, and animal

skins, and rigged a variety of traditional snares, one of which the Governor agreed to step in the following day, to the satisfaction of everyone.

The timber cutters brought samples of each kind of timber found in Mazeze, a log of ebony and a saw. Everyone but the governor had a turn sawing ebony; the governor had a touch of the flu himself and made his excuses.

The farmers brought samples of their crops, their medicinal plants, and their homebrew (I don't know if the governor sampled the homebrew, but he ought to have done; it would have been just the thing for his flu).

The farmers made a map of the entire area in a clearing, using different colored sand and bits of twig and shell and stone to represent the resource base of the entire estuary.

There was also a pavilion for tourism, to introduce the idea of tourism to the local folk. The members of the *Associacao Meio-Ambiente* had set up a campsite with a tent and fishing poles and binoculars and prepared a display of craft items—wooden bowls, candlesticks, baskets—from elsewhere in the province, things that the people of Mazeze could make and sell in the future. Everything looked great.

We sat and had a drink of water in the bamboo meeting room.

"Now," said Rolf. "The presentations. I assume you're presenting the marine survey?"

I nodded. "With Paulo Mualimo, yes." (Paulo was the Coordinator of the *Associação Meio-Ambiente*.)

I waved at a thick pile of reports.

"Casimiro presents the socio-economic survey, Nicolãu the forest survey, and José the wildlife survey," I said.

"Let's have a trial run," Rolf said. "I want to see the presentations now. Remember everyone has only fifteen minutes, plus ten for questions."

I looked at Casimiro who looked at Nicolãu who looked at José who looked off into the middle distance. Nobody had had time to prepare yet.

We'd all burn the midnight oil.

"Or maybe we should just head back to town," said Rolf.

"Good idea," I said.

I created my presentation that evening. Ruth arrived home after nine, Swiss inspector in tow, and collapsed across the bed.

I could only envy her as I pressed on into the night. We woke up in time to greet the governor at six-thirty the following morning in front of his official residence. The entire provincial government had come; the *coluna* was twenty-five cars long, flanked by police and driving at breakneck speed. I suppose it is a point of honor that Governors must be driven faster than other mortals.

We dropped off the back of the column, not catching up until the village of Murrebue where everyone stopped.

This had not been a part of the plan.

There was too much dust in the air to see anything, so Ruth got out of the car and walked up to the front. As Project Director, she was charged with escorting the Governor on the day.

She arrived by his side just in time to be filmed by *Televisão de Mozambique* shaking hands with a group of village leaders, all wearing Frelimo T-shirts and chanting party slogans. His Excellency gave a short campaign speech while Ruth tried to disappear into the crowd.

The first planned stop was the village of Milapane—"the place of the baobab trees." We turned off the main road and onto a track (non-existent the week before) that ran from the village out to the mouth of the Megarumo River.

There we parked and walked down the river to the beach, where we met Paulo Mualimo and a group of community leaders. Paulo was supposed to show the Governor around and explain that the area represented a confluence of a wide variety of habitat types, but he spent most of the time introducing himself to the Governor and listing his own qualifications in great detail.

> "... I am a *Técnico Medio* in Secondary Education, I also have a Diploma in Environmental Education and Development Management; I am a qualified *Técnico* in Conflict Resolution, with an additional Trainer of Trainers Certification, I have attended courses in Environmental Evaluation, Erosion Control, Reforestation, Accounting ..."

Then it was the turn of the *Chefe de Capitania*—the local representative of the provincial Marine Administration. The *Chefe* was supposed to tell the Governor about the history of the area, how people came to live there, and how they use the marine resources to stay alive. The *Chefe*, a tall, thin man, stood at attention as I introduced him to the Governor.

"Pleased to meet you," said the Governor. "Tell me, what do you do on this beach?"

The *Chefe* winced, or shrugged, or maybe it was neither. At any rate, he made a small gesture with his arms and shoulders.

"We fish," he said. "We kill chickens."

We waited, but no more words came out. We waited some more.

"You fish," said the Governor. "You kill chickens."

The *Chefe* stood to attention before the Governor, eyes cast down and to one side. He had nothing more to say.

I thought of the years of socialism and war and realized that nothing in this man's life had prepared him for a conversation with a governor. Nothing had prepared him for the possibility that anything good could come from being noticed. He had said all that he could. Time to rescue him. I went and stood by his side. I took out my binoculars and handed them to the Governor.

"There are at least six marine habitats represented in this bay," I said, "And the local population exploits all of them, under the supervision of this man here. There, at the northernmost point of the bay, lie the ruins of the Limbuiza lighthouse. In front of the lighthouse are coral banks, ranging from the shoreline to a depth of forty meters. These extend far out into the sea and constitute a hazard to navigation. It was for this reason that the lighthouse was built in colonial times. The local population fishes there with lines, spear guns, and traps. Women and children collect mollusks in the intertidal zone. The area comes under intense pressure from the four villages of the area, and several species of mollusks have already disappeared. Fishermen complain that the catch is lower every year."

The Governor looked.

The *Chefe* nodded. Paulo, who should have said all this, was nowhere to be seen.

"Just north and south of the lighthouse, on both sides of the coral bank, lie beds of seagrass. It was in these beds that signs of grazing by dugongs were noted in June, 1999, by a team from the Ministry for the Coordination of Environmental Affairs. No dugongs have been seen here for five years, though they were common in the past. Our guess is that the animals live in the open ocean now, only coming in to the shallow water to feed at night."

I looked at the *Chefe*. He nodded.

"The local name for dugong is *empuva*. The local population will eat dugong, and it is considered a remedy for a variety of diseases."

Strictly speaking, a Muslim should not eat dugong, but Islam here has been Africanized, in the same way that Christianity was Romanized under Peter and his successors.

"Coming south now, there lie the beaches and the sandbanks, from the lighthouse to the river mouth, where we stand. This zone has several unique characteristics. The dunes contain a variety of unique flora, and support populations of civet, jackal, and various gazelles. The dunes also serve as feeding grounds for hippo, which here live in the open ocean."

There were murmurs of surprise from the guests, and murmurs of agreement from the locals.

"The beach is used as a breeding ground for sea turtles, four species of which are found here, including the rare hawksbill turtle. There is conflict over sea turtles, for they are considered a delicacy by the local population, though all are protected internationally by the CITES treaty."

"Behind us lie mangrove swamps, home to monkey, baboon, fish eagle, herons, crabs, and fish. The swamps also serve as breeding grounds for a number of non-resident fish species. The estuary of the Rio Lurio just south of here contains prawns in commercial quantities, though there is no way to transport them to town after harvest, due to bad roads. Some are captured in fishing nets and dried for local sale. Boys spear them one by one with bamboo harpoons."

"Now look," I pointed. "Just where the dunes meet the mangrove. See the palm tree? That is a holy place. The *Rainha* Fatimah, Queen of the estuary, is buried there. In ancient times she ruled here. Those who want to fish in the bay place offerings of food or cloth by her grave, and she will help them. This must be done, for the bay is a dangerous place."

It dawned on me that the *Chefe* had been referring to these offerings when he spoke of killing chickens on the beach.

Paulo reappeared.

"Yes, Your Excellency. The bay is a dangerous place. There is a channel in the center of the bay, a place of great depth and vicious currents. Those who have trouble there are lost, and no one will go out to help them."

The *Chefe* nodded, and the crowd murmured agreement. Paulo pointed to the center of the bay.

"There is the dangerous canal. It runs to the beach at the Lurio Mouth. The depth there just by the beach is 250 meters. That canal is where the sharks live. The men of Nimanro village catch them from their canoes. Zambezi, *tigre*, and hammerhead sharks."

All man-eaters. All bigger than a dugout canoe.

The Governor looked impressed and said some suitably gubernatorial words.

Then Paulo led us back to the cars and we drove through the forest to the meeting site. I dug my elbow into the ribs of the *Chefe*.

"We fish," I said. "We kill chickens."

He gave me a weak smile. It may have been from relief.

The presentations were very well received, though the usually taciturn Nicolãu overshot his time limit by eleven minutes, which gave Rolf an attack of hypertension.

There were many questions about wildlife control, particularly monkeys and baboons. There seemed to be no easy way to keep these out of the fields. One old man suggested inviting members of the Maconde tribe, who eat monkeys, to come and live in the estuary.

This idea produced an uneasy laugh, for the Macondes are great warriors and traditional enemies of the Macua. I had anticipated problems with the concept of fisheries management, but everyone agreed that something had to be done to preserve fish stocks in the area.

What to do was a little harder to decide, but we resolved to meet again with community leaders to work on the problem. Everyone was impressed with the quantity of precious wood the forest inventory had found. The Governor read a speech, which Paulo had written the week before.

After a break we went to the pavilions. Though I had participated in the marine survey, I did not man the fishing pavilion. Nicolãu had decided that I should run the tourism pavilion, presumably because I was a foreigner, and thus something of a tourist already.

I was a little irritated at this, but since then I have come to realize that Nicolãu knows absolutely nothing about the tourist business while I, at least, know what will be interesting for a visitor.

The first group came to my pavilion.

I sat them down and showed them the tent and the binoculars and the carved wooden bowls, and told them that yes there were people in this world who had time and money to visit other places just for fun. João from the *Associação Meio-Ambiente* translated. Three fetching young *Rainhas* were quite taken with my display. White teeth flashed as brilliantly as brass nose rings as they giggled and stared and fondled the alien equipment. I didn't mind at all that I had to come close and reach my arms round them to demonstrate the use of binoculars. When they knelt to enter the tent, it was a real effort not to kneel and crawl in after them. Lack of sleep must have been clouding my judgment.

There were no *Rainhas* in the next group, just fishermen. I decided to cancel the binoculars and show them how to use my fishing pole. Instantly all discussions of tourism were abandoned.

The men crowded round, testing my hooks on broken fingernails and rolling the line between callused fingers, staring at the flimsy "bamboo" and manipulating the strange "winch" attached to it.

Within seconds the line was wrapped around a bush and several of the men. A fierce discussion broke out, and not for the first time I wished that I had mastered the Macua language.

We eventually got everyone untangled.

"So, what you all think about this idea of tourism as a way of making money?" I asked.

João translated. The men looked at each other, back and forth. No response.

I tried again.

"Would you be willing to take people and show them where the fish are? They would pay you for every day you went with them.

People with money could come down from Pemba, and you would be their guides."

More silence, until the oldest and most respected shark fisherman in the group stood up.

"It won't work, *Senhor*," he told me. "In the first place, your hook is too small. You need a bigger hook to handle the fish here. The line is strong enough, but you need a bigger hook."

Nods and grunts and "mmms" of agreement from the others.

"And your 'bamboo' is too small. It is not right for the fish that we have here. These people that will come here from Pemba will not catch any fish with that bamboo."

He shook his head sadly and sat down.

A younger man stood up. He did not really have sufficient status to argue with a *branco*, a white man, but the older man's success had emboldened him.

"It would be much better, *Senhor*, if we catch the fish ourselves and sell them to these people from Pemba. All we need are more lines, like the one you have here, and hooks, but bigger hooks. We do not need this 'bamboo,' and we do not need this winch."

I tried hard to get us back on track, but how do you explain tourism to people who do not have enough money for food?

"No, no. You have the wrong idea. These people from Pemba do not want to buy fish. They themselves want to go fishing. But not all of them will want to go fishing. Some will just want to swim, or go sailing in your boats."

This sounded stupid, even to me. Fortunately another group of men arrived and the need for further discussion was lost in a round of greetings and handshakes.

"Take that pole and hide it," I said to João, and he did.

After lunch we walked to the banks of the Lurio. We found clawless otter, civet, sable, and cheetah tracks on a sandbank, and left our own there with them.

Mudskippers danced away from our feet, then crept back for a closer look, bulbous eyes above the water, tails curled for a quick getaway, goggling at us like schoolchildren.

We danced with them, feeling the mud balm between our toes. We cupped the clear water in our hands and splashed it on our wrists. Two sacred ibis hunted crabs on an islet in the stream. The sun glowed red through a dust cloud, painting the waters with the colors of Gauguin.

Great grey inselbergs glowered from across the river. A gnarled baobab reached for us, blessed us, and let us go.

We turned and picked our way back to the meeting place through a cathedral of mangroves. Adamo and I had to join hands to reach around the largest of them. These had grown here undisturbed for centuries, undaunted in spite of erosion and tides and salt water and men with axes.

At the end of the day the Governor spoke again, this time from the heart. He praised our work and the interest and energy of the local leaders. He marveled at the beauty and the richness of the estuary. He promised the full cooperation of the government in the development of sustainable resource use schemes and conservation activities in the province.

He threw some banknotes on the table and declared that he wanted to be remembered as the first tourist of the estuary. He challenged us to build a tourist camp.

Then he was gone, and the day was over.

I sat on a bamboo bench while the young volunteers of the *Associação Meio-Ambiente* cleaned up the papers and the plates and returned the meeting place to the forest, to which it had always belonged. The community leaders and the *Rainhas* stood by and looked awkward, not knowing what to do. Rolf fussed with a briefcase. I held my head in my hands.

Thank you, my young volunteers, for caring, for reminding me that even here, everyone has something to give; for making me feel like I'm not alone in the things I dream of; for making me believe that there may be something we can do together. I will do my best for you.

Thank you, *Chefes* and *Rainhas*, for talking, for listening; for lowering your defenses, for taking a chance; for ignoring a thousand of years of exploitation in the hope that there may be something we can do together. I will do my best for you.

Thank you, Your Excellency, for coming here, for listening, for talking; for walking on the beach, for walking on the riverbank; for believing that there may be something we can do together. I hold you to your promises. I will do my best for you.

Thank you, *Rainha* Fatimah, *Dona* of the estuary, for the day, for the white beach and the red sky in the water and the green shade of the raffia palms; for the hippos and the sharks and the currents and for what they demand of men; for the hope that there may be something we can do together. I will do my best for you.

And thank you, Rolf, for coming through for me. At last we have done something together. I have always done my best for you, whether you believe that or not. And I will do my best for you tomorrow, and the inspection will go well. The inspector will find nothing to criticize in our accounts and operational systems, and much to be happy with in our programs. And he will return to Switzerland and write a report that will be read by Marcus and Albert and the khaki-trousered men of the "Southern and Eastern Africa Regional Office," and they will nod and be well pleased, though none of them has ever walked down the Megarumo to the shores of the bay, nor passed by the grave of the *Rainha* Fatimah, nor danced with mudskippers on the banks of the Lurio.

Six months later we tried to further explore the estuary with a boat and a pilot and Mario, a marine ecologist from the Ministry of Environmental Affairs. We wanted to dive the drop-off and see the sharks. The dive boat motored down from Pemba while Adamo and I drove the Land Cruiser down with camping supplies.

We arrived to find the marine ecologist stranded on the beach and the boat struggling to stay afloat in the surf. The wind was howling and the waves were three meters high. We decided to swim out to the boat and head south to survey a sheltered point. We had planned to dive at the river mouth but this was out of the question. Adamo, Mario the ecologist, three local spear-fishermen and I made up the marine survey team.

Swimming out to the boat proved to be quite a process. I had little trouble with the wind and the waves, raised as I was on the north Atlantic with its storms and its nor'easters.

I got a little jolt from the pilot who waved me away from a dark shape in the water that I had assumed was a coral head.

"Hippo!" he shouted. "It can take your leg off!"

It didn't, though, and I climbed aboard, a little more rapidly and a little less gracefully than I had planned.

Adamo arrived at our boatside some time later. Although he is from a fishing family in up the coast in Murrebue, he has less experience swimming with big waves. Fishermen of the coastal region swim to spear fish, not for fun, and so do not go out on stormy days. The three local spear-fishermen stood on the shore and looked out at us as if we were mad. I waved to them to come on.

Adamo shouted something, perhaps the Macua equivalent of "Come on in, ladies, the water's fine!"

The fishermen couldn't hear Adamo, but it didn't matter. His laughter and his body language were unmistakable. Pride is a language that needs no words.

The fishermen struggled out to the boat. The last one arrived so tired that we had to lift him aboard. By that time the surf was breaking regularly over the gunnels.

I looked back towards shore. Mario, the ecologist, was stuck. At 1.2 meters tall and weighing all of forty-five kilos, he did not have the bulk to bull through the waves, nor had he learned to dive deep under them and let the undertow pull him out to sea. He was born inland, seventy kilometers from the coast, and only acquired a taste for marine biology in University. He struggled in the surf for a little while, pushing forward and being pushed back, until his gear sack was torn from his hands.

He made a forlorn little gesture with his hand … "You all go on without me…" and turned back to collect his gear sack, which was by now lodged halfway up a sand dune.

As he turned, a particularly nasty wave took him amidships and cast him up on the shore, seaweed, a rag doll, jetsam abandoned by our boat.

The pilot gunned the motors and guided us out to the relative safety of the offshore chop, his face as white as an African face can be. Adamo did his thing of standing in the bow and shouting directions that no one could hear. We arrived at the point and surveyed some indifferent reefs. Sediment and fresh water from the Lurio mouth were clearly having negative impacts, though we did see some large mountain corals (*Porites lutea*) that were holding their own.

The next day, the powerboat from the Ministry of Environmental Affairs broke down. We tried hiring a sailing dhow from local fishermen, but never managed to get very far. Dhows, though solid and reliable, do poorly upwind. We gave up.

Several months later we tried again, in a much bigger boat, which we had hired in Pemba. Yet another delegation from Switzerland accompanied us.

This time the estuary met us with a violent thunderstorm. The waves were so big and the movement of the boat so antic that the on-board GPS lost all precision. At one point it informed us that we were two kilometers inland and rapidly approaching the village of Nimanro. The rain and the fog were so heavy that the pilot lost his way and nearly grounded us on the beach. Nor was the compass any help; it had evidently taken up break-dancing.

Paulo Lucillo, the newest and consistently the most hapless member of our Helvetas team, was thrown from his seat by a wave and bruised himself on the far bulkhead. The next wave deposited him neatly back where he had started from, minus two shirt buttons and his tin of cold drink. He had never been on a boat before.

One distinguished visitor from Switzerland spent seven hours vomiting over the stern, while the other stayed in the cabin and grew steadily more silent and withdrawn as the hours passed. Perhaps in a desire to expunge all memory of the trip, he gave the presents the villagers had offered him to the pilot, thereby breaking one of the most basic rules of southern African etiquette; it is a terrible insult to pass on a gift one has given you to someone else. I rescued the gifts and now they adorn a wall in my house—two magnificent sets of Zambezi shark teeth and jaws.

One is big enough to put one's head into.

It was my right-hand man Casimiro, a non-diver himself, who offered what in retrospect seemed to be the obvious explanation for all our troubles in the estuary.

"Did you make a sacrifice at the *Rainha* Fatimah's grave, Peter?" he asked.

"No," I said, and he started to laugh.

"Then what do you expect? The people of Nimanro told you that no one could sail the bay without first making an offering. Aren't you the one who is always telling us about the importance of using local knowledge and tradition in the design of rural development programs? It won't matter how big the boat is if you haven't made a sacrifice."

We never did manage to dive with the sharks in the submarine canyon at the mouth of the Lurio River. The area remains unexplored, defended by the hippos and the sharks and the storms and the iron will of the *Rainha* Fatimah, reaching out from beyond the grave.

I still owe her a live chicken and a length of fine white muslin cloth.

Addenda to Chapter 7

UNLIKE THE Quirimbas, the Lurio Estuary was never officially declared as a protected area. Despite its beauty and its biodiversity, the terrestrial area simply had too many people to become a national park.

New immigrants arrived every day, chopping down the palms and the towering *messinge* trees and setting fires and scratching away the ground cover and pinning their hopes and betting their lives on a few grubby seeds cast onto the burnt red ground.

It was all hard to see, not only the felling of the forest but the bloated bellies of the little kids and the missing eyes from vitamin A deficiency and the rickets and the stunted bodies and the torment on the faces of the parents.

"Why do they come here?" I asked Adamo. "There's nothing here. Why don't people stay in Nampula or Mecufi? Why come here?"

"Nampula is full of people. Most of these people here were living on borrowed land. They come here because there is still land to be taken here, if you want to work. And people come down from Mecufi because in Mecufi the soil is just sand. Add cement and you can build houses with it."

Dropping down the trail to Nakarika village, we ran into an old school classmate of Adamo's, a young man with his even younger wife living in an improvised shelter alone in the middle of the bush. No health service nearby, no school, no water, no neighbors.

"I thought you were in Pemba," Adamo said.

"I was," said his friend, "but I was starving. I couldn't find a job and I couldn't grow anything there. My family was getting tired of feeding me. I've been here for two years."

He spoke excellent Portuguese.

"So you're going to stay here now?"

"Yes. Life here is more secure."

At least we managed to launch some agricultural support programs with the aid of the Environmental Association volunteers.

Ruth, Lunga, and Neli swimming in Pemba after a rainstorm, 1997.

Religious leaders on Ibo Island blessing the keel of a new Park patrol boat (shown at lower right). In the days before the coming of Islam to the islands, the blessing would take the form of a human sacrifice, a strong young man (presumably from an enemy clan) whose soul would guide the boat and keep it safe from harm. Nowadays, islanders ask Allah to undertake this task.

Our theatre group, Ndjagarimia, performing in a village. Mamudo Abudo, at left, was one of our two stars. He currently works as a community development official with the Environmental Association (AMA).

Omar with sun-dried fish, which provide eighty percent of the animal protein consumed by Mozambique's population. Dried fish is a local delicacy, but I think the taste must be acquired in childhood. Neither Ruth nor I can get past the smell, though Ruth (and the kids for that matter) happily eat freshly hatched queen termites, grasshoppers, and mopane worms. All roasted of course. Grasshoppers in particular smell like lobsters while on the grill.

Bernard from the Swiss Development Corporation visits our tree nursery in Chiure, where we produced fruit and cashew trees to distribute to local farmers who had lost theirs during the four decades of war. Adamo points at something while I try hard to look suave and nonchalant in my hat and sunglasses.

Baby humpback whale coming up for a blow just four meters from the boat. Mother quickly maneuvered baby away...

A school of giant kingfish juveniles off Quilalea Island. I dove frequently here after the Park was established and watched this school grow from fingerlings to young adults of five or six kilograms apiece. Giant kingfish grow to eighty kilograms.

Most of the fishing in the Quirimbas is done with traps like these, woven from bamboo slats and weighted with stones. Fish swim inside for shelter and become trapped; juveniles escape through the holes in the weave. It is a selective and non-destructive way to fish, a good example of traditional practice that kept people in harmony with their environment for centuries. Modern seine nets are dragged across the sea bottom, damaging corals and seagrasses. This trap is about 1.5 meters long.

A baby green turtle we rescued from a fishing boat. It is not so easy to hold a sea turtle. Turtle flippers are surprisingly strong and the turtles use them to beat the bejeesus out of your hands as you try to slip them back into the water. We finally just set this one on the beach and waited for a wave.

This is what afternoon feels like in the dry season...

A fish eagle on a rocky outcrop. There are hundreds of such outcrops in the Quirimbas archipelago. Fish eagles and other birds roost in them at night, moving every couple of months from one to another. We never knew why, until one of my rangers climbed a recently- abandoned rock to find out. He lasted about 3 minutes before leaping off the rock into the water, covered with bird mites.

I like to say, only half in jest, that the Quirimbas National Park is the only place in the world where you can still see giant coconut crabs without getting radiation poisoning. The giant coconut crab is rare in most of its range due to human predation, surviving in the Quirimbas only due to a local religious tradition. To the Muani people, it is taboo to touch or eat or otherwise abuse them. They are also abundant in the South Pacific on the Bikini Atoll, the site of American nuclear bomb testing. Coconut crabs are basically giant land lobsters, with their tails rolled up under the tummy. One of the Park rangers taught this particular female to come to his tent for a snack of coconut pulp every evening.

Ranger training, with the assistance of the Navy. Frigate Captain Eugenio Bento Bandeira, a dedicated conservationist, stands in the background, third from left, in dress whites. I am second from left. Also present are ranking members of the local administration and police.

Xavier Bacar Simba, friend and ranger extraordinaire, holding a crested guinea fowl that he has released from a snare. It was returned to the wild.

I pose with Aida, Omar, and five of my ranger team,
all former poachers, all experts in the bush.

Neli and Lunga doing a little rock climbing, personalities on display.

From left, Dio, Nicolau, Celestino (with waistcoat) and Njini, tracking animals in the Montepuez River basin. Nearly all rivers in the north of Mozambique dry up completely in the wintertime. Wild animals dig to find water; in the late dry season, the concentration of animals near the few remaining water points makes them vulnerable to poaching. Note Nicolau and Celestino holding hands. It is not uncommon for male friends to hold hands like this in Southern Africa, but it takes some getting used if you are a newcomer. The eagle-eyed reader will note the elephant tracks just visible, running from the left lower corner to where Njini is standing.

Tragedy in the Quirimbas. This particular group of poachers targeted a mother and baby. Senseless, wanton cruelty. The ivory of the baby is worth very little. And what kind of monster kills a mother and child? For money? This sort of poaching is not done by poor folks just trying to make a living. These are criminal gangs, with military-grade weapons.
PHOTO CREDIT: *Quirimbas National Park Chief Ranger Armindo Araman*

Joy in the Quirimbas.
Two young females with newborn babies, in the Montepuez River basin.
PHOTO CREDIT: *Quirimbas National Park Chief Ranger Armindo Araman*

Exceptional things happen now and again. My rangers and I heard some fishermen talking about "dogs coming out of the water." We jogged down the beach to find this Cape fur seal basking just above the high tide line, some 3000 kms beyond the known range for the species. We spent the day with it, resting and basking in the sun. By the afternoon, it accepted a drink of water from us and even let us scratch its ears.

A fishing canoe carved from a single tree trunk, and capable of carrying ten fishermen and their nets. Apparently canoes were larger in earlier times, but trees of sufficiently large size are becoming scarce.

A photo on the last day of our traditional wedding, the umtsimba, in 2012. The ceremony lasts for three days, which is why I look a bit disheveled. Ruth of course is serene and radiant as ever. My beaded necklace shows that I am a high-status "Umbutfo," or warrior, having undergone traditional initiation (and hazing) to join the warrior ranks. Ruth's brothers did not choose to be initiated, so I tease them mercilessly. PHOTO CREDIT: *Lunga Bechtel*

Daughters Licinia, Tiny, Neli, and Khulile, at my father's memorial service.
He loved bow ties.

Son Lunga in the mangroves, 2015. This is what Mozambique feels like...

Casimiro finds shelter on a camp chair under the tailgate of the land cruiser during a thundershower in the Mazeze Estuary area. The tailgate chain is missing and the stick beside him holds it up. No, the stick did not break, nor did I kick it away. He just sat there and worked on his notes while I got wet.

CHAPTER 8

Fatigue

November, 1999. In which, in the aftermath of both the Governor's visit to the Lurio Estuary and the Swiss surprise inspection, we return from Pemba to our house in Chiure and organize last year's Christmas party.

THE WEEK STARTED with a headache.

Mondays are hard enough without headaches. They're hard enough when you've had a weekend.

Mondays are hard enough when you don't have to drive to Chiure to organize a Christmas party which you should've done ten months ago, and buy goats.

Mondays are hard enough when you stagger into the bathroom and turn on the shower and water comes out. But it didn't, not that there was any reason that it should have, and so I staggered outside to the cistern and brought in a bucketful and poured it over myself. Then I leaned on the sink and tried to persuade the mirror above it to show me a newer model, something in slightly better condition, fewer rips in the upholstery, fewer dents, less rust, slightly firmer suspension.

Maybe something in fire engine red, or deep forest green. Or a racing stripe. Just not bloodshot and yellow and pasty white with smudges of grey.

There was South African chicory powder masquerading as coffee in the kitchen, and I used it and heated cistern water to make a brown beverage that I drank several cups of, and that allowed me to achieve a state that masqueraded as consciousness.

I walked back to the bedroom.

"Ruth, darling. Coffee."

It wasn't coffee, it was chicory and it tasted like burnt carrots, but love maintains itself upon gossamer webs of fiction, carefully spun and carefully believed, carefully proffered and carefully received, a cup of hot chicory passed from hand to hand in the throes of a Monday morning.

"Wake up, darling. Have some coffee. We have to go to Chiure."

"Shit," she said, or maybe "it" or "bit" or "hit" or "sit." Her head was in the pillow, so I couldn't be sure, but "shit" seemed the most likely given the context.

"Here. Drink this."

She rolled over. I lifted her and held the cup to her lips. We looked like something from the late movie, something starring a clean-cut young man with a firm jawline and a World War II uniform bent tenderly over the bedside of a young actress with a 1950s' coiffure. We looked like the touching scene in the final reel where he realizes she's going to live, if only because she never dies in movies made in the 1950s.

She's going to live, thank God. She's going to live. She'll walk again. She'll talk again …

Wait a minute. Her face is going down into the pillow again. Cut.

Give her ten more minutes. No sense wasting the coffee. Off to the bathroom again to shave and find an aspirin.

.   .   .

The world outside the house looked no better than the one inside. The sun was up in force. Hot white light sharpened the edges of things, made them seem closer, threatening; made a concrete fence post reach out and rake its claws against the wheel well of the Hilux as I backed down the drive.

I fumbled on my sunglasses and we drove to Chiure.

The office in Chiure was a mess. I hadn't set foot in it in weeks, busy as I was out at the estuary. The papers on my desk were turning into mulch. I picked through the salvageable bits and swept the rest into the dustbin.

Sr. José, the guard, brought hot water and more South African chicory powder. Oog. I opened my briefcase and prodded the contents with a pencil. They seemed safe enough. I shut the briefcase and sat at my desk, contemplating my empire.

Ruth slumped in her chair. I decided to keep my sunglasses on, perhaps for the next several weeks. Time passed. Then Aurora walked in.

"*Bom Dia Senhora Diretora! Bom Dia Senhor Peter! Bem Vindo! Como vai? Chegaram quando? Como foi a viagem?*"

Oog.

Too many questions. Too much volume. But we needed a dose of cheerful.

"Aurora. How are things?"

"*Normal.* All well."

Her smile was irresistible.

"Ronnie is fine? And the baby?"

"All fine."

"And our friends and colleagues? Nobody has malaria?"

In any randomly-selected group of ten people, at least one will be down with malaria. It's still the main killer in Cabo Delgado, getting worse every year as the parasite grows more and more resistant to chloroquine.

"No one."

Her eyes danced. "Mamudo has a new wife."

"No! Who is it?"

She told me the name, but it was no one I knew.

"I thought he had two already. And wasn't he fiddling around with Elsa earlier this year?"

Elsa was a member of our developmental theater group, the female lead. An enormous stage presence, but only four feet tall.

"*Senhor* Peter!" Aurora was shocked. "That was last year. Elsa has a new husband now, too!"

"What?" I was completely out of date, a throwback, something from the Paleolithic period.

"Six months ago. She's living with one of the government agricultural officers."

"Good for Elsa. She deserves a break. But Mamudo doesn't need another wife."

"It's not a real wife. It's unofficial. They're really just lovers. Mamudo spends nights at her house."

"When he's not with his other wives."

"Yes. Once a man has two wives it is difficult for them to control his movements. It is easy for him to take a third."

Mamudo was one of three young men on our team, the field officer in charge of school construction. He now has three wives, Adamo has two, and Paulo Lucillo, the oldest, and the only Christian of the three, has none.

This means that there is a reason for each of them to be teased, mercilessly, and we do.

Aurora turned to Ruth.

"I go today to buy the goats, *Senhora Diretora*. I arranged to go to Meluco."

Aurora is not well educated and she has endless trouble managing money, but she gives up her weekends and holidays to make sure the project runs as it should when we are busy with inspectors and the like. She hosts a Bible school in her sitting room in the evenings, and spends a large portion of her free time visiting people in the hospital and dosing them with food and affection and all the latest gossip.

Ruth and I have feelings for her that are something close to love, except of course when we want to kill her for buggering up the finances.

"Thank God," said Ruth. "Something going as planned. You have money?"

"Yes."

"Batista is driving?"

"Yes. He's filling the Land Cruiser now."

"Be back by Thursday night. It's the Christmas party."

Aurora held her arms up and jiggled her ample hips.

She whooped and managed to look sixteen years old.

"I'll be here," she said, and left, laughing out the door.

Aurora's name is not really Aurora. It's Maria Aurora, but we drop the Maria, for half the women in the Portuguese-speaking world are named Maria. She is from Pemba, a *mulatta* daughter of a Portuguese settler and a local woman of Macua descent.

Her mother apparently was famous as the most beautiful girl in Pemba in her youth, and is still known as *Menina*—young girl. She is still beautiful.

Aurora also claims to have been a beauty queen in her youth, though this didn't say much to me, as every second or third woman we know from Pemba claims the same.

Much more convincing was the photograph she showed us of herself in high school.

Aurora is now about thirty-five years old and twenty kilos overweight, but enough remains to her to have attracted Ronnie, her twenty-one-year-old husband, whose child she is now carrying, and by whom she also had a baby last year. No one has the heart to tease either of them about the age difference, even though we are dying to; the Swazis call such unions "i-chicken murder," which term evokes a series of wonderfully apt images without actually meaning anything at all.

Ruth must have been tracking my thoughts.

"Did you know she used to be a dancer in Nampula?"

"No. Tell me."

"You know her father left her mother when Aurora was small. I don't know the whole story, but after he left they had a lousy life, you know, living like rural people but in town, no money, eating cassava and leaves and grass and sticks and cooking outside on the fire and carrying water from the well, and no fields so you have to buy all the food except you don't have any money."

"Yeah."

"Somehow Aurora got through school—maybe her father sent them a little money for that—and after that she went to Nampula to make her fortune. She says she had a job, but I think she was one of these girls who hang around outside the disco and wait for men. Then after a while she was hired to be a dancer inside the disco."

"With or without clothes?"

"I'm not even sure she was hired. Maybe she just danced there and made money from the men. She said she had a lot of boy-friends. There was this one in particular, a tall, slim handsome Italian who fell hard for her. Well-groomed, beautiful hair, well dressed, a good expatriate salary. He was always there, always asking for her, always wanting to dance with her, but she wouldn't go home with him."

"Why not?"

"I don't know. Her friends were always telling her to go with the guy, maybe he would marry her, maybe he would take her to Europe, but she resisted.

"Her friends thought she was crazy. Finally she gave in and went home with him one night. He was very romantic. He swept her off her feet, kissing with tongues, caressing her, telling her she was beautiful. He really had her going."

"Then what?"

"Then when they got into bed together and he took off his clothes she realized that he was, shall we say, unimpressive."

Ruth started laughing. "Aurora was so funny telling me this. We were with Amelia. She made a face, a really twisted face, and spat the way Macuas do. She said she was in shock, but that wasn't the worst of it."

I was laughing, too.

"What could be worse than that?"

Ruth could hardly talk.

"She said he wanted her to use her mouth and she couldn't. All she wanted to do was get out of that bed and run away."

It took us a while to calm down enough to finish the story.

"And then ..." I said.

"The next night the guy came back and asked for her again. She refused and he got really upset, really angry. He couldn't understand why she wouldn't go with him again. Her friends thought she was crazy, so she told them the story. They still thought she was crazy. So what if he's like that, he has money, maybe he'll take you away from here ... think of your future ... you can always arrange something bigger on the side ... they said things like that. But she said she just couldn't cope."

"So what did you and Amelia say to that?" I asked.

"We said we couldn't cope either."

Ruth gave me a twisted little smile.

"I can't believe she told you all this," I said.

"Aurora is an innocent. She talks about anything and her face is so innocent and fresh and she looks at you with those big eyes and you just can't believe that all those things you are hearing are coming out of her mouth. She just treats everything as if it's *normal*, a normal thing to talk about. Remember when Ibraimo had syphilis?"

"Yeah."

"She said it was *normal*. She had no problem talking about it. She said everyone gets VD. She said she's had VD. She says if someone tells you they never had VD then it's a lie. *Mentira!*"

Ruth was laughing again.

"I hope you didn't try to tell her that you've never had a sexual disease."

"Of course not. She wouldn't believe me."

Sr. José came in with more coffee water and was greeted with the sight of his two *Chefes* bent double, clutching the sides of their desks and laughing like fools.

"Everything fine, *Senhora Directora?*"

"Everything fine, Senhor José," Ruth managed.

Monday afternoon by definition is not Monday morning, and so love, and hope, require a little less collusion, a little less self-deception.

Monday afternoon can sometimes take care of itself. As this one did. I audited the financial statements that should have gone to headquarters a week previously while Ruth organized last year's Christmas party.

The rest of the world sometimes perceives Africa as a slow-moving place, a place where things can be done tomorrow or not at all, a place that runs several hours behind schedule, a place that functions on African time. It is true that things run late, that things are not done, that some men (never women) have time to sleep under mango trees all afternoon, but that's not the whole story.

The reality of African time for us has been that everything runs late because it is hard to keep organized in an environment without modern transport and communication systems. Things happen that change the plans: the truck gets stuck; money doesn't arrive; a child needs to be taken to hospital; or forms may need to be filled in triplicate and signed in the presence of a commissioner of oaths.

Ruth and I long ago adopted the "twenty-four-hour rule;" one can be twenty-four hours late before the other one is allowed to start worrying.

Still, a Christmas party ten months after Christmas is for us something of a record.

We had originally scheduled it for November, 1998, but at that time there was an epidemic of cholera in Mozambique that had its epicenter in Chiure. None of us had time to dream of a party.

The epidemic subsided after the new year, but by then we were away in Swaziland, checking the farm.

We only came back from Swaziland in February, which meant that the month was spent getting the project going again after our absence. In March I went back to Swaziland for my adopted son Dumi's wedding, and then Mamudo and Adamo went on leave in April and May respectively. June was spent out in the villages, sleeping in tents. July was the same.

By August, we had forgotten that we owed the staff a party, but they hadn't. They reminded us of it in October. We'd wanted it on a Friday night, but that proved to be impossible. Everyone's calendar was packed—fieldwork, courses, seminars, deliveries, wildlife inventories, meetings.

It wasn't just us. With the rainy season about to begin, we had to get the agricultural programs going and the schools and the wildlife and forestry work finished before the roads turned into soup. No one on our team was taking weekends any more.

"OK," Ruth had said. "The party is Thursday night. No work on Friday. Everybody can sleep in."

"Good idea," I said.

"Except you and me," she said. "We have to be back in Pemba. Michel from *Cooperação Suíça* will be coming to town to talk about the external evaluation coming up next year."

· · ·

Aurora and Batista got back from Meluco on Wednesday night with the goats and drove out to distribute them to their new owners on Thursday morning, promising to be back by nightfall. Our old friend Jowett from the Oxfam project in Cuamba arrived as promised on Thursday noon. Jowett is an old Zimbabwean farmer who has managed to make a place for himself in the over-intellectualized world of international development because of, or perhaps in spite of, his considerable practical experience growing crops and tending livestock.

He walks straight, talks straight, and laughs loud enough to shake the roofing tiles when things go wrong. When I turn fifty, I hope to be just like him, except maybe not so stocky and definitely not so bald, and of course I don't have a chance of turning black.

Jowett is running a goat-restocking program in Niassa Province using methodology which he stole from us in Chiure. We didn't mind that at all—we felt rather complimented in fact.

What we did mind was the scale of his thinking. He had decided to distribute goats to 200 families simultaneously and had come to Cabo Delgado to buy 600 goats. This tapped out the market and meant that Aurora had to drive to all the way to Meluco to find goats for our own goat-restocking program in Chiure.

Despite our best efforts and all the delays, several important people could not be present. Yahaia Magido, the local veterinary officer (and one of the key players in the goat project), had been transferred to another district. He sent his new wife to the party to represent them both, and she was large enough and lively enough to do so quite adequately. The Administrator of Chiure District didn't make it, as he is also Provincial Director for Disaster Relief. As one can image, this second responsibility demands much of his time.

Everyone else came, though: the Agriculture Department staff; the doctors and Administrator from the clinic; the Director of Education; the members of the local tribunal; the land law team; and the developmental theater group, except they almost didn't come. Ruth and I walked through a light rain from our house to the office and found no theater group.

"They're waiting at Mamudo's house for a lift," said Luisa. "They won't come because of the rain."

"I thought parties and weddings and such were blessed by rain," I said. "I thought rain was a blessing in Africa."

"It is," she said, "but not when you have to walk through it."

We went to collect the group in the Land Cruiser. They piled in the back, laughing and joking and hooting and hollering, all dolled up in their best gear.

Elsa was there in 10-centimeter-high black platform boots, which made her look nearly as tall as the other women in the group. A balding young man with a pleasant face helped her into the truck—the new husband, the extension officer for one of the villages in Ocua.

Good for you, Elsa, I thought. And good for him, too.

We'd known Elsa since our first month in Chiure. We wanted to form a developmental theater group to facilitate the entry of the project into the rural villages.

We figured that the best way to explain the project to the rural folk and at the same time generate goodwill was through theater presentations. Ten young people of Chiure, Elsa, Adamo, and Mamudo among them, volunteered themselves as members.

Elsa had joined the group out of desperation, or so we assume.

Never have I known someone so temperamentally unsuited for the stage. At the first meeting of the theater group she hung in the background, unable to speak, unable to come forward to be introduced, unable, even, to take her hands away from her face and raise her eyes off the ground. She fared no better in the second meeting we had with her.

This was a training in Rural Participatory Appraisal with selected members of the theater group and several members of the

District Agriculture Department. The first item on the agenda was for everyone to introduce themselves, but it was too much for Elsa. We skipped over her and told her just to be comfortable, she was among friends, no problem. Forty-five minutes later, in the midst of a lesson, she stood up, hands clutched under her chin this time.

"My name is Elsa Mendez," she announced, and sat down like the shutting of a book.

She didn't speak again until the following day. Enough was enough.

The day after that I tossed Lunga's rubber snake into her lap, which action produced a satisfying shriek, a leap in the air, and much laughter from the rest of the group. This broke the ice, or at least cracked it. Now she talks to us, though she still grips one hand in the other and blushes like a schoolgirl.

Adamo told us Elsa's story.

She had married a boy from Palma while still in her early teens and had four children with him. They built themselves a mud hut in Chiure town and Elsa busied herself with fields and babies while her husband tried his hand in the transport business. He had no car, no bicycle, so he carried live animals on his shoulders from the rural areas into town and survived off the marginal difference in pig and goat prices that exists between town and village.

He'd had enough of this after some few years and had gone in search of work to Tanzania, leaving Elsa with four children and his little brother to care for, promising to return.

Right.

She'd managed somehow, even scraping enough money together to send her ex-husband's brother to initiation rites, without which he would have been unwelcome anywhere in Macua society.

"She a good woman," said Adamo, and meant it.

Whether she would be a good actress remained to be seen. In

the group's first play, *The Three Brothers*, Elsa had only two or three lines, and these she delivered with about the degree of woodenness one would expect from a shy, first-time thespian. We saw no clue in her as to what she would become, but she must have felt some great stirring inside herself.

She surprised us all by insisting on assuming the lead role in the group's second piece, *Two Friends and the Forest*, a play about proper forest management and control of wildfires.

"Elsa will play the wife of Nivussane? Opposite Mamudo? I don't believe it," I said.

Mamudo had made quite a name for himself in the first play with his over-the-top comic improvisations; people who don't know him assume that he is a drunkard, but he is a practicing Muslim.

"He'll blow her off the stage."

"Come and see," said Adamo, and so I did.

Elsa matched Mamudo gesture for gesture, grimace for grimace, pratfall for pratfall, punch line for punch line. All improvised. We don't give our group scripts, only general outlines and the messages to be included in the play. They take it from there.

Two Friends and the Forest went on to be presented in a hundred villages and took first place in the Provincial Theater Contest in Pemba last year. Wildfires dropped to zero in the villages in which it was presented. We decided that theater was probably the most effective public education tool we have, much better than announcements on the radio or harangues by local dignitaries. We decided we had not one but two stars on our hands.

As I drove the group to the party, the rain came down in earnest. I kept my window open in solidarity so we all got soaked. No matter.

There were beers to drink and food to eat and music to dance to when we arrived, and so we did all that, more or less simultaneously, interrupting the music only to make speeches. I spoke about how great it was to work with all of them and Ruth thanked everyone for their efforts.

Magido the veterinarian's enormous wife thanked Ruth for thanking them for their efforts and introduced herself to everyone.

Jowett thanked us for inviting him and for thanking everyone for their efforts and introduced himself to everyone as well. Elsa stood up to thank us for supporting the theater group, but we howled about the new shoes and made her promenade up and down the dance floor so we could get a good look at them, which she did with good grace.

I couldn't believe I was looking at shy Elsa Mendez with her tiny body and froggy face promenading up and down like a model, posturing and posing, the unlikeliest actress the world has ever known.

Then everyone made Ruth and me dance, like a wedding, and after that I danced with every woman present in descending order of size, beginning with Magido's wife and ending with Elsa. We did *Kwasa-kwasa* and *Marabenta* and the tango and the two-step, and a lot of un-named, un-coordinated jiggling that was nevertheless an enormous amount of fun.

Mamudo danced with everyone except his first wife. Elsa's husband didn't dance, but smiled a lot from the sidelines and did double duty on the roast goat and chicken curry. We hollered and laughed and the women looked good and felt good and smelt good, the way that African women smell when they're damp from the rain and the dancing, and I was very, very glad that I had the pick of the lot for my own.

Ruth and I danced the last dance together and then we shut down the radio and the generator and drove everyone home.

The best people on earth.

. . .

We'd given them all we had the last year and they'd more than given it back. We'd spent the year fighting against hunger and poverty and cholera and ignorance and maybe we'd even won a round or two.

So sleep well, friends, and rest tomorrow. You've earned it. Meanwhile we'll go see Michel and talk about the external project evaluation, hangovers and all.

Oog.

Addenda to Chapter 8

I AM not sure why it is so hard for me to review this chapter. It's a good chapter, a hard start but a happy ending, a tribute to colleagues and friends. It's about a Christmas party, for God's sake.

So why does reading it fill me with unease? More than unease. I can't face it, can't deal with it. I want it shredded, confetti, hung, drawn, quartered, gone. GONE. Why?

I guess there is a part of this chapter that hits buttons that I don't want hit. A part that shames me. A part that reminds me of things I wish I could erase.

The part where I mention nightclubs, girls, dancing, venereal disease. The part that talks about sex. The part that reminds me of things I did that I cannot undo.

Mind you, this party happened before all that. But some part of me knew something was wrong, even in 1999. Even earlier. Way earlier.

My first real memory of horror finds me at the top of the stairs, in Carlisle, Pennsylvania, age four or five. I guess. I am shorter than the banister, so I couldn't have been much older than that.

I am crying my eyes out. My father has just told me that every person on this earth will die someday. As will I.

I am not sure why he did that. Maybe I asked what death was, maybe someone we knew died. Who knows?

In any case my father's academic rigor demanded that his reply be nothing less than the truth. He was a professor of religious studies, born into a conservative religious family, a caring, thoughtful man who became more and more liberal the more he thought about religion, life, the universe, and everything.

I must have hit him on a bad day, a day when intellect won over compassion. Or maybe he was still in professorial mode, not parental.

Father seeks to comfort me. I remember asking what happens when you die. I have some notion that I was frightened more of the aloneness of death than anything else. No leaps, no connections, no paired electrons, nothing. I wasn't thinking of pain or guts or gore. Just being out there. Alone.

His reply doesn't help. He kneels down and gently holds me by the shoulders. Think about before you were born, he says. All those many years before we had you. That wasn't so bad, was it? All I can see in my head is life moving on without me; dinosaurs and kings, postmen and preachers, firemen and lifeguards and Sunday-school teachers. I howl even louder.

Mother arrives with thunderclouds, but I sense that her fury is for father, not for me. That may be what eventually calmed me down, that and a warm blanket, a maternal backrub, and a pillow to hug far into the night.

. . .

Fast forward ten or twelve years.

I lie in bed at my family's beach house in New Jersey. By this time I have a name for the horror that keeps me awake at night, shuddering under the hopelessness of time and the decay of all things. I am hearing too much about religion from my father. I am reading too much about science.

Back then we had the Big Bang Theory, the idea that the universe started with a bang and will end with a whimper, iron atoms vibrating helplessly in a featureless void for an unimaginably long period of time (ten to the fifty-second power years is what stays in my memory) before they too decay into their component parts and became disconnected bits of subatomic matter scattered across an infinite space.

No Heisenberg leaps, no nuclei to leap around. All the fire and fury of the newly-created universe spread so thin that it effectively becomes inexistent. Frozen there. Science and linguistics tell us that cold and darkness are constructs, that they are words invested by humans to describe the absence of temperature and light.

Father tells me that Hell is the absence of God. I ask myself where in the Hell is God in that infinite cold and darkness, that I am destined to be either present for or absent from. Somehow I miss the redemptive messages of Christianity and only hear how unworthy we are. I am.

The name I call my horror? I am a teenager, so of course it's trite. I call it the Black Beast on my Back.

I haven't yet learned that it's not a thing, but a void. An absence of light, heat, connection, touch, movement. It's what you feel in the straitjacket, in the silence and darkness of the padded room.[14] *It's the opposite of the fire and fury and excitement and infinite possibility of the Big Bang.*

It's just absence. It is only years later, after I allow myself to really look at the Beast, that I realize that it will always be there, that only death will release me from its clutches. Ok, not really release. The void will still be there. What will change is my knowledge of it.

Either life after death or blessed oblivion. On my bad days, which come more and more frequently with age,[15] blessed oblivion sounds better and better.

Years later, after I come apart, after fighting with every fiber of my being against the Beast, and against the admission that in so doing I have indeed sinned against my wife, my marriage, and myself, and that I need redemption, I go to see a shrink for the first time.

Not Lidia. Her predecessor.

She asks me why I am here and I say religion, without really thinking about it. I might as well have said science, or existence.

Welcome, reader, to bipolar depression.

So why am I telling you all this?

Half of my life has been spent running from the Beast. The other half, the part I could write about in 1999, was spent in mania, the opposite of the Beast, where the fire and fury and possibility of the newly created universe were mine to wield, where I drove myself, by any means at my disposal, to stay.

I worked hard. Obsessively. I helped people. I raised kids. I worked out. I built a farm. Hell, I even made three national parks, in places even my overlords in the WWF thought might be impossible to protect. The Quirimbas Islands and adjacent mainland in Cabo Delgado, 700 meters above sea level to 700 meters deep in the abyss. Sharks and lions, elephants and whales. The Mozambican coast of Lake Malawi, the most biodiverse lake in the world. Eight hundred or more species of fish, about a third of which had already gone extinct elsewhere in the lake due to pollution and overfishing. The offshore Primeiras and Segundas

Archipelago, the world's best shrimp fishery, home to thousands of breeding sea turtles. We used to count them from light aircraft. I had superpowers.

But the Beast was still there, unacknowledged, driving me. Driving the things I did. The brighter things I wrote about in the chapters. The darker, now, in the addenda.

I suppose that is why fire attracts me so. It may be my best tool to fight the Beast, to bring me back from absence. To bring me back to me. Red hot steel, sparks and electrons leaping madly, skin bubbling and blistering and sizzling and cracking. The smell of burnt flesh. The world in flames.

The Big Bang applied to my hand, to my forearm, to my shoulder. Sensation. Emotion. Anything better than nothingness. An imperfect cure for the void. Can you understand that?

Lidia did.

Still, it took her many years and healthy doses of modern pharmaceuticals to convince me that fire is a blessing I have to refuse. Some things we just can't do, she said. And I haven't for four years. But I think about it every day.

Less pyrotechnic was the womanizing.

An awful term that dehumanizes real live people, makes them nothing more than a foil for my own struggles. I'm not proud of it, but that's what I did. Not sleeping around, not having sex, not fucking.

Womanizing.

I used people.

It doesn't seem to lessen my guilt very much that they used me, too. Mostly for money. One or two for something more.

What did I get out of it, when it was so wrong, so squarely against everything I believed, everything I stood for, everything I taught my kids? Two things.

The first thing was that I got through the night.

Many nights. Eventually my time alone with the Beast became a thing I just couldn't do, and with me travelling constantly for the WWF, and Ruth for Oxfam, we were spending more nights apart than together. A warm body in the bed, any body, almost made the nights bearable.

The second thing I got was mania. The opposite of depression. Much better that alcohol and drugs are the body's own chemicals, the ones that you get from the thrill of the chase, the hunt, the capture. The consummation.

My friend Mike told me once that his daughter was addicted to drugs in much the same way I became addicted to womanizing. He couldn't believe an upper middle-class girl with a good education from a good suburb of a prominent mid-western city could get mixed up in that life. How do you even find people to sell to you? he asked, through the glass interview window of the rehab house that finally brought her back to him.

Dad, she said, Dad. They glow.

I know exactly what she means. Women glowed for me, too. Eventually it wasn't even difficult enough to get the hormones going, the adrenaline, the testosterone. Add other levels of risk. Fetishes. I've tried most of them. Piercings in unusual places.

I was up to fourteen at one time. I did all my own piercing, with leatherwork awls or nails that I sharpened on a grinder. It's funny, but the pain and blood were not much of an attraction for me. Mechanical injury isn't fire, though it felt like it sometimes.

I do not miss the process, but I do miss wearing the piercings. Lidia and I are still working out why,[16] though she says an unusual piercing or two does not really qualify as a mental health issue that needs to be addressed. If only I didn't long for fourteen.[17]

·　·　·

And lastly, the final step before collapse, chuck the condoms out the window.

This, mind you, when parts of Mozambique were rated as having the highest AIDS rates in the world. But that just made the thrill all the sweeter, the emotions hotter, more real, more present. I rolled these particular dice perhaps hundreds of times.

It was a Big Bang level of intensity, the hunt and hormones and adrenaline and sex and death all mixed together in one act, one act drawn out with exquisite anguish over the months until the next furtive HIV/AIDS test. No room for emptiness when the soul is full of this cocktail. And the thrill all the greater when the tests came back negative, as they always did.

What more evidence did I need that I was superhuman? Beyond mere mortals?

A God?

My mother tells me that at some point I told her I was a genius. Ruth remembers a great many similar incidents. I remember walking down the street, back ramrod straight, chest out, looking at women passing and knowing, just knowing, that I could have any one I wanted. I became invincible at work, too.

And intolerable.

Hours on and under the sea, diving and exploring under all conditions, until my pilot and boatmen complained to my supervisor. I didn't care about rest or sleep or food. When night and rain found us far offshore it only made it better.

The best was when the engine died and I stripped it at sea, at night, my success only serving to feed the legend inside my head.

My WWF colleagues who regularly came to visit from USA started telling each other to carry their own rations, because Peter won't feed you.

.   .   .

I pushed my rangers hard. Way too hard. I broke three of Abdulrahamane's ribs while demonstrating disarming techniques; blackened and closed Momade Juma's eye while teaching him to counterpunch.

When Alfredo Gonsalves finished a long foot patrol ahead of me, I brooded for three months and taught myself to do without water, just so I could leave him behind next time. Of course I made sure that we "forgot" the canteens.

When I caught another ranger accepting bribes from timber poachers, I beat him so badly that he was bedridden for three months. I can't even remember his name now. The investigation went all the way up to Ministerial level. A friend in the Ministry got the other rangers present to cover for me, saying that we were practicing martial arts and it was a "training accident."

Facing down poachers, armed only with my bare hands. And elephants, and wildfires, and crooked cops, and politicians.

It had to end. Eight years ago, on the night of 28th December, at our beautiful farm in the hills, Ruth performed perhaps the most difficult and loving act of her life and confronted me with her suspicions.

I sat in silence for perhaps fifteen minutes. She said Peter, you talk, or I am going to divorce you. And so I talked, and broke her heart.

So why don't I like this chapter? Because it reminds me of a time before, when I wasn't quite so crazy, when I could still trust myself at parties, and discos, and dancing with other women.

Lidia says that I have to avoid what she calls toxic places and toxic people. Places which will hit the old buttons, people who will trigger the old behaviors.

So this chapter marks the end of an era. The end of innocence.

The end of trust. The end of a time when a happy dance with Elsa Mendez was nothing more than a happy dance with Elsa Mendez. Even in my head.

I live more carefully now.

Swimming towards a dropoff in the Quirimbas National Park. I had the great privilege of being the first person to dive many of the sites in the Quirimbas Archipelago. Nothing beats the feeling of dropping down into the depths, one hand on the depth gauge and the other on the buoyancy regulator, knowing that you are going to be the first person ever to see whatever is coming up at you from below. (This photo was taken by a dive partner, sadly I do not remember who.)

CHAPTER 9

The Edge of the Abyss

December, 1999. In which we dive in a variety of places and discover the drop-offs and dangers of the (future) Quirimbas National Park.

L AST WEEKEND Stuart and I sailed north to explore the drop-off at the Rio Tari mouth, one last adventure before the Christmas holidays. Or rather, we went to explore the Rio Tari mouth, hoping to find a drop-off there.

I had made a point of studying the navigational maps of the Quirimbas Archipelago and systematically exploring anything that looked even vaguely interesting. Most attractive were places where the depth contours bunched together, indicating rapid changes in depth. Walls. Like climbers, divers love walls.

Pieter Jacobs, the local dive instructor and I had discovered the first of these walls near Pemba in 1997.

We had been exploring the fringing reef at the edge of the tidal flats, which at that time, 1997, was still in beautiful condition. Unfortunately a cyclone in February 1998, the El Nino Southern Oscillation of that same year, and the predations of local net fishermen would turn this reef into the underwater equivalent of the Sahel a few months later.

At the end of the reef, white sand extended seawards, feature-less except for a rippled sand bottom. We swam outward for several hundred meters anyways, until our tanks ran out. Then we surfaced and swam back.

We met our sometime dive buddies Emilio and Gareth back in the dive shop.

"There's something there, bro. I promise you. I feel it." This was Pieter.

Emilio snorted.

"Ag, man, I'm serious. Past the fringing reef, thirteen meters deep, the sand just goes north, you think it's going nowhere but if you swim out there it just gets deeper. We went out about a half a kilometer and then we had to come up. Out of air. And I felt something. An echo, a buzz. I promise you something's out there ..."

Gareth chimed in.

"I believe you felt something. Beer. Or the bends. Yer diving way too much, mate. Slow down. Get a woman."

Pieter's wife was away in Johannesburg.

"I dive a lot because it's my job, *boet*. I have clients. They give me money, I give them pleasure."

It was my turn. "Money for pleasure's prostitution, amigo, but I guess if the shoe fits ..."

Pieter rounded on me. "What about you? These clowns aren't gonna come with me ... Let's go. Today. We can have lunch and decompress and head out in three hours. Plenty of time before dark."

I never say no to a dive, so it was lunch, rest, and boat ride back to the reef. Choppy. The wind comes up most afternoons during the dry season.

Then a banana, juice, tanks on, final check and buddy check and backwards over the gunnels to meet at the bottom. We started swimming. At thirteen meters, as before, the fringing reef ended and sand sloped forever away to the north, with only the odd sea pen and sea cucumber to alleviate the rippling whiteness.

At fifteen meters, we encountered a single, isolated coral head, a mountain coral with soft coral and coral rubble around its base. Orange and white clownfish threatened us as best they could from the safety of their sea anemone nests; since they are only a few centimeters long, the effect was something like being threatened by a collection of toy French poodles.

A brilliant blue cleaner wrasse picked parasites from the skin of a rose-colored parrotfish. Another parrotfish patiently waited his turn at the cleaning station. A blue-and-white spotted stingray monitored our movements from under a growth of fire coral, only its eyes visible above the sand. There is something about these rays, particularly the protruding eyes, that suggests a headache, a queasy stomach, sincere regret for the excesses of the night before, and a desperate desire for a cup of strong, black coffee.

I gave the ray all the respect that a group of township toughs might give a drunk in the gutter. I prodded it with the haft of my diving knife while Pieter Jacobs, in his role of dive instructor, tried to look stern and disapproving. Harassment of local fauna is strictly prohibited by all major international SCUBA regulatory bodies.

Stern and disapproving doesn't come off very well through a facemask, however, and besides, he wanted to see it fly away as much as I did. The ray obliged. It shrugged the sand off its back and hoisted itself free. A wiggle of its wingtips transformed it completely and it floated off across the sand, effortlessly, a ballerina of the blue. We followed, a bit more slowly and a great deal more awkwardly, for all our fins and wetsuits and buoyancy control devices.

We found another coral head at twenty meters. This one was smaller, more nondescript, apparently less colorful. I say "apparently" advisedly, for nearly all color is filtered out at a depth of twenty meters. Only a bit of yellow and various shades of brown remain.

Unfortunately, we hadn't brought an underwater torch. A rock lobster lurked in a deep hole in the sand below, only his long antennae visible against the sand.

At 22 meters, my lips started to tingle and a shiver ran up and down my arms. Every nerve vibrated as if my skin had been sandpapered. There was no particular reason for this.

Featureless sand stretched in every direction ... but there, in front of us, it sloped downwards into darkness, into the unknown, into a great whale's mouth from which came a great whale's song like a siren's song, a song that we could not resist, a song that raised the hackles on our necks without us knowing why, a song that drew us down into darkness without us knowing why, a song that would have killed us were it not for our training.

Divers tell tales about the lure of the deep, the desire that can carry a man down and down and down until there is no going back up again. We felt it that day, felt the lure of the abyss before we ever saw it, felt the depths in front of us call to the depths within us and felt the depths within us call back, joyously, a homecoming, a reunion of kin too long parted, too long held apart by water and air and physiology and the dull weight of evolutionary time.

Perhaps something within all of us longs to go back to the sea.

This tingling wasn't a hallucination, wasn't nitrogen narcosis, the "rapture of the deep." Both of us felt it at exactly the same time. We know because we stopped and looked at each other. I thought it might be a problem with bad air, a bit of carbon monoxide pollution in the air mix, but Pieter's breathing was normal, his lips and nail beds their usual color. Carbon monoxide poisoning turns the nail beds a bright cherry red. He looked calm and his movements were slow and sure and sinuous. I suppose mine were, too.

We flashed the OK sign at each other, paused, gathered ourselves, and continued.

. . .

Nitrogen narcosis kicked in at 25 meters.

Nitrogen narcosis is a state caused by the increased concentration of nitrogen in the bloodstream due to the breathing of pressurized air. SCUBA equipment is designed to feed the diver air at the same pressure as the water surrounding him. This keeps the diver's lungs from collapsing.

The deeper the diver goes, therefore, the higher the concentration of air in the diver's lungs and bloodstream. At approximately twenty-five meters, the elevated concentration of nitrogen in the blood begins to affect the diver's judgment in the same way that drinking three beers in rapid succession might. No one really knows why.

Nitrogen has two specific effects on me. First, I lose my concentration and my edges blur.

It becomes a little harder for me to determine where I stop and the rest of the world begins.

Tasks like checking my depth gauge and air supply may be forgotten, which is one of the reasons that we dive in pairs, so that we can check on each other. A diver's training is of great help here. Routine tasks are drilled and drilled and drilled until the diver literally performs them without thinking about them: check the air every minute; check the depth gauge; check dive time remaining; check your buddy, does he look OK?

Calm, smooth, graceful, alert?

Every diver suffers from a loss of ability to concentrate at depth. Not everyone suffers from the second effect that nitrogen has on me, which is to produce an irrational fear that my mouthpiece will fall out of my mouth.

Fortunately this effect is quite controllable. At twenty-five meters I put my hand up to my regulator and held it firmly in place for a minute or two until the fear passed. Sometimes it doesn't and

I go the whole dive like that. Other people suffer from different effects. A year later, another friend of ours (another Peter) dove in the early morning on an empty stomach.

At 30 meters he felt a wave of claustrophobia, as if silvery metal walls were surrounding him on every side. He panicked and inflated his buoyancy control device, which shot him to the surface at rocket speed. The boatman said that Peter breached like a whale, surging almost clear of the water before falling back on his side.

Training saved his life, for he kept his mouth open. If he had held his breath, the expansion of the compressed air in his lungs as he rose would have blown them up like party balloons. I had once had a similar experience of claustrophobia, but I did not surface.

I just hung onto Pieter's arm until the silver metal walls went away. I think it happened because I dove on an empty stomach. I don't do that anymore. A banana or some cashew nuts before a dive is an essential part of my dive plan.

At thirty meters the sand abruptly stopped and we were flying in space, free like stingrays. No sand beneath us, just a jagged black cliff falling away into nothingness.

We looked at each other and flashed each other the OK sign, simply because divers do not have a hand sign for "absolutely incredibly mind-blowingly bell-ringingly buffalo-bellowingly beautiful fantastic out of this world no way they're going to believe us back at the dive shop why the hell didn't we dive here a long time ago we've been wasting our time, man I can't believe it!"

Pieter gave me a thumbs-down, then rolled on his side to reduce friction and blew all the air out of his buoyancy control device. He sank like a stone down the face of the cliff. I followed, a little more slowly, down past 40 meters, down where you're not supposed to go, down into the danger zone where the nitrogen feels like nine beers, or twelve, and your air lasts for only minutes and the oxygen on which your life depends can itself poison you and throw you into convulsions and paralysis and death on the seafloor, wherever the sea floor may be in the shapeless dark depths below you.

We fell past fifty meters. A stone pillar stood free of the rock wall and we swam into the cleft between pillar and cliff. Four square meters of pinkish-white sea fan hung suspended above our heads. I hung back as Pieter swam below it, then rose in the water until I could see him on the far side, as if through a lace window curtain. Two medium-sized groupers poked their heads out from under the eaves to see what all the fuss was about. They showed no fear at our presence, just tight-lipped disapproval. Most groupers are in fact friendly and inquisitive; it is not uncommon for a grouper or two to swim along with us on our dives. Not these. I suppose it takes all kinds.

Moments later our time was up. Any longer and we would not be able to surface without incurring the bends. We allowed ourselves to drift upwards, marveling at the caves and the sponges and the giant French angelfish and the myriad, tiny reef fishes. We left the cliff behind at 30 meters and rose through the open water. The current had carried us westward, and off through the blue we made out a coral tower rising through the water past the 20-meter mark. Then we were swept away.

Five meters beneath the water's surface we stopped for three minutes to decompress. Human bodies were not designed to handle changes in blood nitrogen concentration. The bloody stuff gets you drunk when it's in you and forms bubbles in your blood on its way out if you decompress too rapidly. These bubbles lodge in the joints if you're lucky, causing cramps and agonizing pain.

If you're not lucky they lodge in your brain, causing more or less the same sort of damage that strokes do. We regulate our dive time according to international standards and stop for three minutes at five meters after every dive to avoid all this. Dive time is regulated by small dive computers that we wear on our left wrists.

Five-meter stops are generally delightful. We play games with our buoyancy, breathing more deeply or more shallowly as needed, trying to float in the water as barracuda do, without moving. Waves on the water's surface cause shafts of light to dance around us like small, mythological creatures, like water sprites. Occasionally a big king mackerel will swim by, looking at us without interest or curiosity. King mackerel are not as intelligent as groupers, or maybe they're simply more task-oriented. They only really react to the presence of prey.

When our three minutes are up, we inhale deeply and rise to the surface as if ascending to heaven. Golden light shines down around us. I like to stop centimeters below the pearly gates and reach up, laying my palm flat against the undersurface of heaven, except that by the dive's end it feels like heaven is where we're coming from, not where we're going to.

That day the 5-meter stop was not delightful. We were too full of adrenaline to hang motionless. When the three minutes were up we shot to the surface, tore off our masks, and howled like dogs. It turned out to be a good thing that we were full of adrenaline. We'd drifted far out to sea and needed every bit of energy we had to swim back to the boat. Pieter's boatman had fallen asleep and lost track of us. A practice looked down upon by all major international SCUBA regulatory bodies.

I ran into Emilio on the beach the next day.

"Well?" he said. "What's there?"

I remembered the endless emptiness and felt again the pull of the great blue abyss below me. I looked north, then back at him.

"A whole lotta nothing," I said. "A whole lotta nothing at all."

All that was in 1997.

Now, in 1999, we were exploring ever northward, up into the

area that would become the future Quirimbas National Park. Local fishermen told us that the fishing at the mouth of the Rio Tari was always good, but that it had to be line fishing. "No one can pull a net there, Sr. Peter," said Abudjate. "Too many rocks in the water."

That sounded like just the place for us.

Ruth and Connie and the kids came along with Stuart and me, as it would be an all-day outing. The sail north was delightful, wind just enough for a light chop on the water, a happy gurgle along the sides of the hull. Abudjate manned the tiller while the rest of us drank coffee and had breakfast.

We had a little trouble at the Tari mouth, trouble of the good kind. We dropped anchor 100 meters off shore and found no bottom. I looked at Stuart.

"Bingo," he said.

It was a little tricky getting us into the water. We needed to be close inshore to find the drop-off, but the wind blowing from the south put the boat too close for comfort to the cliffs and the surf.

We compromised. Stuart and I suited up as we stood offshore. When we were ready, Adubjate swung us back inshore, lifting the motor from the water for a moment or two while we flipped backwards over the gunnels.

We floated for a moment to make sure Abudjate pulled clear of the coast, then swam shoreward until we saw bottom at about 15 meters. Down we went, and there was the drop-off.

The reefs were in perfect condition: what with the cliffs, the current, and the near-constant rough water, local fishermen do not come close inshore here. We drifted along for several minutes at the 15-meter mark, enjoying being pushed and pulled by the swell that reached all the way down to the bottom.

Then the edge, and the drop.

We descend along a vertical wall, down to twenty-nine meters. Deep, but a depth we were comfortable with. No need to swim as there was a long-shore current, so we fold our arms and hang there, enjoying the passing show.

A huge moray eel glares at us from the security of his cave. A little further along, two huge Napoleon wrasses, fifty kilos each, loom up from below. Instead of hanging vertically in the water, they swim with their ventral surface oriented to the cliff face, which means that they appear to be swimming along on their sides in the water. It doesn't bother them in the least and affords us quite a nice view.

They follow us for the entire dive, darting away (if such a big fish can be said to dart, that is) when we approach too closely, sneaking in close when they think we aren't looking. A school of dusky rubberlips hangs above an outcrop. These are members of the sea bass family and look exactly as their name suggests, like big dusky sea bass with even bigger vulcanized lips, brilliant yellow in color. The general effect is one of stupidity, which effect is magnified by their habit of finning in close and gaping at divers, like delegates at a village idiots' convention. When they flare their gills, we can see right through their mouths and out through their gill openings to the rock wall behind.

Pillars rise around us, eventually more than we could count. Sea fans hang from vertical surfaces. Where things are not so vertical, wire coral proliferates like coils of barbed wire. A dark shape, and then another. Finally a clear view of a blacktip reef shark. A blacksaddle grouper longer than my leg. A potato bass, longer than me. The scale of everything is off. We feel small. We feel Lilliputian.

I check my watch and find we have overstayed at depth. No matter, the sea floor is rising now as we get closer to the river mouth.

We follow it up slowly, careful of the nitrogen in our blood. At almost exactly five meters we come to a clearing of sorts with a white sand bottom. Surgeonfish and angelfish and juvenile jacks and a carousel of brilliant colors swirl around us. We sink down to the sand to sit out our decompression stop while the piscine universe spins above our heads. I am dizzy and not at all sure that it is the nitrogen.

Stu flashes the diver hand signs for a double length stop because we were down so long. I am glad that he at least has enough control to maintain dive discipline.

We swim into the river mouth itself at a depth of 2 meters, seagrass beds and pipefish and nudibranchs of every color, and surface by the boat.

Lunch and wives and kids and backflipping off the bowsprit. In the bay no one notices how much the wind is rising outside.

No one except Abudjate, that is. He makes the kids put on life jackets and insists that they sit below. Ruth and Connie join them.

We come out of the estuary to find a howling headwind and swells that take us to the limit of our sailing abilities. Stu and Abudjate are drenched and exhausted by the time we find shelter at Wimbi Beach. I am bleeding from a rope burn. Connie has vomited in a bucket.

The kids slept the whole way home.

Addenda to Chapter 9

SEAFARING FOLK underestimate the Indian Ocean at their own peril. It's not all palms and blue sky and azure waters and seashells in the sand.

Stu and I learned that on our first New Year's Day in Cabo Delgado. January 1st, 1997. We decided to picnic south of Pemba, on Chuiba Beach, for New Year's Day. A beautiful day, roast chicken and several beers were feeling just right.

We wrestled with the kids in the water and explored the tide pools. In late afternoon we were packing to leave. The tide and the wind had both risen, and there was precious little beach left to picnic on.

Two village kids ran up to us.

"Women are dying in the water."

I wasn't sure I heard right.

"Yes, women are dying in the water. One is dead already."

They pointed north along the beach. We ran that way, around a point. Far offshore, a number of heads bobbed in the waves. They saw us and waved their arms. Maybe they screamed but all we heard was the surf and the wind.

The boys pointed.

"There. They were collecting clams and oysters when the tide came in. They're stuck. It is deep between the bar and the shore."

A man came up to us.

"It's too windy to take a canoe out to them. We tried."

He pointed. A dugout canoe was stalled about 100 meters offshore. Two men paddled frantically, but the canoe would not stay nose on into the wind. As we watched it turned sideways and shipped water.

I looked at Stu.

"It's swimming then. No heroics. If we pull the canoe by the nose it will stay pointed into the wind."

"We'll need two," he said. "And some rope would be nice."

I asked for some rope but got a blank look.

"*Corda*," I said. "*Corda*."

More blank looks.

I grabbed a canoe and pulled it down the beach.

Stu swam to the one already in the water and we started the long swim out, against tide and wind and waves. Google Earth tells me the offshore bar is 2.5 kilometers from the beach at Chuiba. We felt every meter.

Another woman washed off the bar as we approached. Vanished. Nothing we could do for her. If we let go of the canoes even for a second they raced for the shore. I found seagrass underfoot a second before Stuart did. It took quite a bit of persuasion to keep the women from scrambling into the canoes. With ten women and only two canoes, we wanted them to stay in the water and hang on the sides.

In the end we had to let two women climb in. They had swallowed so much seawater they couldn't hold on.

Going back was easier. The tide had changed and was against us, but the wind and waves helped. What did not help were the panicked women. They hung vertically in the water, legs down, increasing the drag from the current. Any attempt to get them to lift their legs parallel to the water's surface led to more desperate scrambling to get into the canoe. After a while we resigned ourselves to the knowledge that sometimes brute force is the only solution.

Darkness fell as we swam back. A crowd gathered on the beach. The surf captured us and pushed us awkwardly onto the sand. Villagers swarmed around the canoes, tending their own, welcoming them back to life, to land, to warmth and hearth and home.

Stu and I stood in the shallows, hands on our knees, hearts pounding, shivering, cold, forgotten. Then one old man came up and shook my hand. Connie and Ruth found us and brought towels and shirts and hugs.

We felt a little better and walked to the pickup. It was full of people. Apparently, the two women who were in the worst shape needed to be taken to hospital, and it was assumed that we would provide this service as well.

I asked everyone to get out of the car except for the two victims and two family members, and they all did. I started the car and tried to drive away, but immediately a number of young men launched themselves into the back of the pickup. We bogged down to the axles. It was a Land Cruiser, but even a Land Cruiser can only take so much. I was genuinely furious.

I grabbed legs and jackets and pulled people indiscriminately out of the truck, tossing them onto the sand. I screamed at the by-standers to get the victims out, too, there was no way I was going to help a bunch of yellow mangy ingrate scumbags who hadn't the decency say thank you, who had the goddamn gall to jump into my truck and bog it down when I was taking their own people to the hospital.

The old man intervened.

He asked me for a shovel and I said no way was I going to give him a shovel. If they wanted their people to go to the hospital in my truck then they could pick it up themselves. So they did, about forty men together. I drove away again. This time only two boys dove into the back and I was tired of stopping, so I drove to the hospital.

We checked the women in, made them comfortable, gave their relatives some money for food and basic necessities. The police came and we made a statement.

When we went back to the car there were the two boys again, asking for a lift back to Chuiba. We said no.

Ruth was solicitous on the way home.

"I was scared," she said. "It was far, and you were very tiny out there in the ocean. Did anyone say thank you?"

"One old man shook my hand," I said.

She was quiet a while. The kids were asleep in back.

"I don't understand this place," she said. "If this had happened in Swaziland, people would thank you. People would bring you things. You wouldn't have to cook for a month."

Word did get around, though. We met the Governor some

months later at a social occasion and he asked me what it felt like to save a person's life. I had no real answer for that. It was just something that needed doing.

Several months later we went back to Chuiba to swim. A young man walked up and asked us if we were the people who had saved the women on New Year's Day.

"I recognized the car," he said. "Don't worry, now that we know it's yours, we won't break into it."

And they never did.

One final note.

My dive buddy Gareth's real name is Peter. Since there are already too many "Peters" in the story, and since he is a South African (contracted by the Ministry of Public works to rebuild roads after the war) I changed his name to Gareth in this chapter to try and reduce at least some of the confusion. It is one of those curious coincidences that happen from time to time that there were four expatriate Peters all living in Cabo Delgado Province and SCUBA diving together on a regular basis. We never mixed each other up, but nearly everyone else did (except, thanks God, Ruth and the kids).

Perhaps the most perplexed was a young man who sold fish on the beach who was convinced my name was "Hitler." I guess it does sound similar, and unusual names are not uncommon in Southern Africa. One of my fellow teachers way back in my Peace Corps days was a lovely young woman named "Deodorant Zwane." I also had a student named "Dogmeat Dlamini." When Ruth worked for Oxfam she had one colleague named "Lettuce" (*Alface* in Portuguese) and another named "Onion" (*Cebola*). I guess it's no worse than what the American musician Frank Zappa did with his children, naming them Moon Unit, Dweezil, Ahmed Emuuka Rodan, and Diva Muffin. This, of course, was in addition to passing on to them the surname "Zappa."

Aida Safire, dressed in traditional Muani attire, with gold nose piercing, hand-made by the silversmiths of Ibo Island. Aida was one of two local leaders who were instrumental in founding the Quirimbas National Park, the other being Ibo religious leader Augusto Assane Omar (pictured elsewhere). While Omar often tried to convert me to Islam, Aida maintained that I didn't have to because I already was a Muslim in my heart. She would chide Omar, saying, "God is one, brother, it is we who are divided."

CHAPTER 10

Saving the Quirimbas

December 1999. In which I organize a group of like-minded institutions and people to try to create a National Park in the Quirimbas Islands and surrounding areas. An introduction to the people and the evolution of the Park concept. A flash forward to my conviction for theft of a poacher's rifle and trophies. A flash forward to my fortieth birthday.

A CONVICTION WAS GROWING in me that something had to be done to save the wonder that was the Quirimbas Archipelago.

I wasn't sure what to do, nor how to do it. In 1997, the World Bank had initiated a $50 million Conservation Project for the Quirimbas, but as it was spread across four ministries, the combined weight of bureaucracy, both Bank and Government, doomed it from the start.

I was nominated to be on the Project Steering Committee by my provincial colleagues and we met once in mid-1997. The meeting lasted two days and was full of pie charts, statistics, roadmaps, goals, objectives, results, PowerPoint presentations, and earnest statements of intent from consultants in white shirts with button-down collars. A few wore ties. National representatives from all four involved Ministries were there, not saying very much, but nodding, and, when prompted by the consultants, strongly affirming that 80 per cent of the allocated budget would be spent in the province. Since the World Bank was involved, there of course was a substantial budget for studies on both marine and terrestrial species and habitats. Studies, in fact, would consume most of the first two years of the project. I had to say something.

I stood up.

"Look, I do appreciate the importance of these studies so that we can design the protected area properly. But we already have an emergency situation with respect to illegal resource extraction. Boats come down from Tanzania to collect live sea turtles and sell them in Mtwara or Dar-es-Salaam. Imagine a graduate student from Lisbon or Stockholm trying to tag turtles, and most of his tags end up in the rubbish bin behind the fish market in Bagamoyo. Can we not have at least a small budget for emergency patrolling and protection?"

This caused substantial muttering and whispering behind hands. It turned out that the governing legislation for protecting sea turtles dated from the colonial period, and no single institution and no clear mechanisms had been identified to govern their protection. No fines nor penalties had been defined either. The general consensus that emerged from the muttering was that it would be impossible to protect sea turtles until a formally protected area—park or reserve—had been declared. And of course the studies had to happen before that.

During the interval, the expatriate consultant moderating the meeting called me aside and told me that I was talking too much.

In retrospect, I am glad I got my two cents in because we never had another meeting. I seem to recall that half a million dollars was spent on consultancies (including a payment to John, the guy who told me to shut up) but the rest of the money went back to the Bank. Bureaucratic gridlock was so bad that no one even managed to divert any portion of the funds for individual use.

I organized a group of local leaders and provincial government officials, all interested in conservation: Nicolãu, José Dias, Cesar, Paulo, Celestino, Simba, Adriano, Aida, Omar. We called ourselves the "Working Group for Community Resource Management in Cabo Delgado" (mercifully shortened in Portuguese to *GECORENA*). We were an eclectic group.

Aida Safire and Augusto Assane Omar are local community leaders of Ibo Island, the historical town in the center of the Quirimbas National Park and the spiritual home of the Muani people.

The Muani are descended from the Swahili and were ruled by the Sultanate of Zanzibar for centuries; the tomb of an Omani princess lies on a prominent cape in the north Quirimbas. When the power of the Zanzibar sultans waned, the Muani forged for themselves an independent identity in the Quirimbas Islands, building a loose confederation of island chiefdoms and subsisting on fishing, coconuts, and trade with the interior and other islands. Most notable among the trade goods were ivory, gold, and slaves.

Slavery is an old and complex social phenomenon in East Africa, with roots in inter-tribal and inter-clan conflicts, interaction with the Arab world, with Madagascar, and later with the European powers. Poverty and famine also played its part in slavery, as they both did in cannibalism.

Only hints remain of what intertribal and inter-clan slavery looked like in the distant past. Malyn Newett, in his definitive work, *A History of Mozambique*,[18] cites a written record by an early Portuguese colonist who saw a man leading another man to town to sell as a slave.

Upon arrival at the market, a fierce argument ensured about whether the first man had the right to sell the second. Bystanders became involved. The colonist did not report the details of the debate, but he did report the final result; the prospective seller was sold into slavery himself, and the prospective slave returned home, presumably with heavier pockets and a lighter heart than when he came.

Export of slaves was already well established, though on a comparatively small scale (estimates are as high as 4000 persons/year), when the Portuguese arrived in Mozambique in 1499.

This trade was oriented to the Arab world, which had qualitatively different attitudes towards slavery than the transatlantic slave trade that followed it.

Manumission of slaves was seen as a way to garner the blessings of Allah and so slavery was not always a life sentence. There are numerous cases of slaves becoming wives and even royalty in the Arab world. And male slaves becoming stewards and viziers.

Slavery was also seen as a way out of starvation, as the social contract, as it were, of the earliest Swahili slavery implied that a slave must be cared for adequately by his/her owners. Even the use of the word "slave" is debatable in the context of the early Swahili nations; a consensus is growing that the difference between slaves and "personal clients" (dependent vassals) was minimal or nonexistent in Swahili society until the arrival of European influence.[19]

However, by 1895, a British investigator, Donald Mackenzie, wrote: [20]

European travelling into the interior of Africa has undergone a complete change since the days of Dr. Livingstone, whose expeditions were peaceful ones, and left behind them pleasant recollections. Now, armed expeditions are pouring into the interior, under the command of Europeans, who, in many cases, kill, plunder and burn the villages of the natives, almost rivalling in horror and destruction the Arab raids in quest of Slaves. One well-known German traveller [sic] is said to have burnt and plundered a village because the chief refused to send his daughter to his tent.

He also reported that porters to the interior had a death rate of 30 per cent, and that young boys were routinely mutilated and sent to "the harems in Arabia." Mackenzie also notes that:

It is a curious fact that Slaves have but very few children, owing, it is said, to the manner in which very young girls are treated by the Arabs and others; hence the necessity for the continued importation of raw Slaves to supply the demand. I was much struck with the evidence of non-increase amongst the Slaves as regards children.

I asked Aida about slavery on Ibo once, and she said, "It's over, Peter. Outlawed at Independence. But there are still some families who cannot sit with others to eat."

Slavery intensified as the Atlantic slave trade came into being following the arrival of the Portuguese, though most slaves taken from East Africa went to Brazil, not North America (Madagascar was also an important destination).

Much of the interior of northern Mozambique was depopulated; perhaps 90 per cent of the population was lost during the Atlantic slave trade, a million people "exported" and many millions more killed by conflict and drought. In 1866, David Livingstone, travelling down the Lugenda River towards the center of the Yao Kingdom at Mataka, in present day Niassa Province, passed through 50 miles of depopulated country which he described as "...still bearing all the marks of having once supported a prodigious iron-smelting and grain-growing population." He further remarked that abandoned fields abounded and that remains of forges were found "almost everywhere."[21]

•   •   •

The population of Niassa Province fell to less than 300,000. It still has not recovered, not even halfway.

Transatlantic slavery arose to serve plantation agriculture, and it was a life sentence, and generational, and intimately connected with race. No royalty here, and very few manumissions. Even Thomas Jefferson, the third president of the USA and author of the Declaration of Independence, failed to manumit the mother of his children.

The intensification of slavery went hand in hand with the ivory trade. Arab and Muani raiders from the coast ventured inland, returning with caravans of porters carrying ivory; how convenient for the raiders that the porters could now be sold into the growing Brazilian market as well.

A delegation of Americans came to Maputo one year, I think 2011 or 2012, looking into the development of a tourism route for Mozambique, similar to the one established for the Ghanaian slave forts.

I say "tourism," but that is not the right word. Pilgrimage, perhaps, for the descendants of slaves to visit the places that were significant in their history. Like a Christian going to Golgotha.

Aida was invited to attend a seminar with me, to represent the population of the Quirimbas. Someone asked her about the slave trade in the islands, and she said that yes, the slave trade was significant, and that her ancestors were very much affected.

One of the Americans asked her if her ancestors were slaves, and Aida looked away.

"No," she said. "My ancestors were the ones who sold yours into slavery."

Everyone was quiet, then the American woman came and took her hand. Somehow we all ended up standing in a circle, holding hands, silently. For quite some time.

. . .

Aida was born on Ibo Island, but ran away to Nampula to go the school, escaping a forced marriage to a much older man. She came back to Ibo as a single mother and quickly became the sort of person that a community turns to in times of trouble. She is a devout Muslim who fasts not only during Ramadan, but also every Tuesday and Friday, for reasons she explained to me several times but I have forgotten. She has made the *Hajj*, the pilgrimage to Mecca, twice, once for herself and once in the name of her mother.

She joined our group, GECORENA, for religious reasons, and to improve the lot of her people.

Augusto Assane Omar is a former military man and drunkard, who at the age of thirty-five left the military, abandoned drink, and through conscientious prayer, study, and effort earned the respect of his peers, who then elected him the president of the Cabo Delgado Islamic Alliance.

He, like Aida, joined GECORENA for religious reasons, but also took the time to study the Islamic religious texts to find a secure religious basis for the conservation of nature and wildlife.

"The Hadith are clear, Peter," Omar said. "A good deed done to an animal is like a good deed done to a human being, while an act of cruelty to an animal is as bad as cruelty to a human being."[22]

Omar was the one who introduced me to the silversmiths of Ibo Island. Gold and silver have been mined in small quantities in northern Mozambique since time immemorial, and these also found their way into the slave caravans.

Both metals were worked in the islands, and to this day a thriving community of silversmiths survives on Ibo specializing in intricate silver filigree, all made by hand using twelfth-century techniques: a rock forge with goatskin bellows; a paraffin blowpipe for welding; and lemon juice for cleansing flux.

I got to know the silversmiths well and bought entirely too many silver necklaces for Ruth. You should bring us some gold, Peter, they said. We would use gold if we had any, but no one has gold anymore.

A young relative of the Aga Khan visited Ibo shortly after the declaration of the Quirimbas National Park; I have forgotten her name. I was on hand for the visit, which provoked much speculation among the silversmiths.

As Muslims, they all knew of the Aga Khan, though they were not Ismailis themselves. At last a real payday, they told me. The daughter of a holy man, a rich holy man, is coming to see us. Surely we shall sell much. Maybe even enough to buy some gold to make a proper necklace for your wife.

Alas, it was not to be. The private jet had flown straight from Eastern Europe to Pemba, with only a brief stopover to clear customs.

No time to change money. Omar came up to me after the visit to tell me that the delegation members had convinced the silversmiths to accept Polish zloty in return for their goods; the silversmiths took it on good faith that they were not being cheated. As I was a foreigner, the only one the silversmiths knew well, I of course became responsible for exchanging the zloty for US dollars or Mozambican meticais. I failed miserably; I found no place in Mozambique nor even in South Africa that would exchange zloty for me, though there must be one, somewhere. Omar and I and a few others ended up paying the silversmiths out of our own pockets for the items bought by the delegation.

This was not our only interaction with the Aga Khan's royal family. In 2002 or 2003, Omar and I were among a delegation who received the Aga Khan's brother, Prince Amin, in Pemba. His

Highness the Prince was on a mission to establish the Aga Khan Foundation in Cabo Delgado and choose a site for a new Serena Hotel (Serena being the name of the family's hotel group).

We met him on Wimbi Beach in Pemba at sunset, when the heat had eased enough to make being on the beach an enjoyable experience.

The first words His Highness said to us were, "I say, does anyone know who won the downhill at Innsbruck?"

I may have been the only one on the beach who had a clue as to what he was talking about.

He startled me further over the next few days by demonstrating a keen interest in botany, identifying two rare herbaceous species on the dunes south of Pemba. He was perhaps the opposite of everything I expected a prince to be: gentle, intellectual, soft-spoken. Unfortunately, he decided that the sand in the Quirimbas was "not white enough" to support a Serena hotel.

He did however, deliver on the promise of support to the poor communities on the coast. The Aga Khan Foundation works there to this day, running an agricultural school and several other respected developmental projects.

Aida and Omar were instrumental in building the community consensus for the declaration of the Park. So much so, that I nominated them for the National Geographic Buffet Award for Leadership in Conservation in 2003. And they won.[23]

The Prize at that time was $25,000, and this tidy sum was duly transferred to Omar and Aida's bank accounts, $12,500 each. Both immediately used the money to repair their houses and go on the *Hajj*.

Still, something didn't sit right, with any of us. I sent a message to the Buffet Award Committee, via the WWF hierarchy, asking if there was no certificate or something like that which Aida and Omar could hang on the wall and show their grandchildren.

"We were never asked that before," came the reply, "But we can do that."

Suitably impressive certificates arrived several months later, which Omar and Aida treasure to this day. I do not know if more recent winners have received certificates.

Xavier Bacar Simba was another member of our group. Unlike Aida and Omar, he was a professional conservationist, having studied Wildlife Management in Tanzania.

Unfortunately he could find no work in conservation in northern Mozambique and was working as an agricultural extension officer at the time he joined GECORENA. He is also of coastal stock, a member of the Makwe ethnic group, another Swahili derivative. The Makwe however do not live on the islands, but rather on the mainland, along the Rovuma River. Their livelihoods include more agriculture and hunting than their Muani relatives, though the languages are mutually intelligible.

Simba brought bush skills to the group that no one else had. He grew up poor, hunting, trapping, farming, and fishing to stay alive. He was my go-to man for track, scat, and bird identification.

"Leopard," he would say to me, "Looks like dry dog feces, but it smells like a cat, and there is hair mixed in. The leopard can't digest hair."

The next time he told me, "No, Peter, not leopard this time. This one is civet. It smells a little like a cat, and there is hair, but there are also berry seeds. Civets are omnivores. Leopards don't eat berries."

And the next one, this time near the river.

"No. Not civet. Too small. And those rounded chips are crab shell fragments. Not berry seeds. This one is clawless otter."

And then, "That's not even feces Peter, and those are fish bones, not crab shells. It's a fishing owl pellet."

I both love Simba and want to strangle him. Perhaps the reason I don't is that he has an endearing weakness, and that is the tracks of the smaller members of the cat family, the genets, servals, caracals, etc.

"Ah, it's just one of the *pequenos felinos*," he would say, and refuse to examine the tracks any further.

Aida and Omar couldn't help me either as they were almost useless with tracks, scat, and birds. Although the Muani have a name for each of the 350 or so species of fish found in the islands, they really only had three names for the birds found there. *Kilongo* are the big ones, storks and the like. *Kipira* are medium-sized ones; terns, gulls, and avocets. *Kituti-kituti* are the small ones, pipers and their ilk, that race up and down the shoreline with the waves. Aida told me that these latter were named for the piping sounds they made, and that only the *kipira* were any use at all.

"They fly over the schools of tuna, and dorado," she told me. "They show us where the fish are."

I use gull and tern behavior myself to find fish, so I knew what she was talking about. She went on.

"*Kituti-kituti* are too hard to catch, and the *kilongo* are greasy and taste like rotten fish," she said.

Adriano was the Director of a local developmental NGO at the time, which we shall call OLOKALE. A charismatic leader and an extremely hard worker, he brought an intimate understanding of the development needs of the very rural people found in the remote wildlife areas.

OLOKALE had been involved in the pre-1997 fight for land rights for local people and had a strong constituent base. The institution was, however, what professional development workers refer to as a DINGO, or "Donor Induced NGO."

This made it the direct opposite of NGOs like the Environmental Association, who were simply a group of young people who cared deeply about the environment. DINGOs have their advantages and disadvantages; one advantage is that they usually start off well-funded and so can build a name for themselves and professionalize themselves relatively rapidly.

The disadvantage is exactly the same, as they tend to attract staff who are committed to a career, not necessarily the goals of the institution. When the initial donor funding is reduced or terminated, DINGOs can have trouble making it on their own. Staff drift away, assets are sold to cover operating expenses, rental offices are closed, and donor-picked boards end up presiding over exactly nothing.

Which is why OLOKALE no longer exists, yet the all-volunteer Environmental Association still does. It didn't help that Adriano got himself involved in a scandal involving a digital camera, the internet, an indiscreet friend, a young woman of barely legal age, and images of three people enjoying themselves and each other in ways that are more commonly enjoyed by only two.

He had to leave the province and so we lost him.

Cesar Augusto dos Santos was a good friend, a kind and caring man. The Provincial Director of Environmental Affairs, he was temperamentally unsuited for the rough and tumble world of post-Socialist Frelimo politics.

He was however close to the Governor, who respected his technical abilities, and thus we would eventually garner all the political support we would need. After the Quirimbas National Park declaration in 2002, he was appointed the first Park Administrator, but he was too gentle for the Wild West environment we worked in at the time. The roles of both cowboy and cavalry fell to me during his tenure, much to the dismay of the WWF institutional hierarchy (by 2002 I was working for the WWF).

I was supposed to be an "advisor," but I was temperamentally unsuited for my role as well.

"Cesar," my WWF boss said, "Cesar, please. You have to defend him. By law he is not even allowed to be on patrol with the rangers. Peter is a foreigner. He has no right to stop or search or arrest. If you don't do these things then he will. And he will get into trouble which we won't be able to get him out of."

In all fairness, I must confess that my boss was right.

I did get in trouble (in 2004 or 2005) and was saved not by my colleagues but by a clerical error.

While leading a patrol of rangers on a training mission, I arrested a group of poachers with a hunting rifle and seven gazelle carcasses, as well as other poaching equipment. The rangers and I confiscated the equipment and reported the matter to Cesar and José Dias. Then I went on a fund-raising mission to WWF in the USA for four weeks.

Upon my return I found out that the poachers had not been arrested or even charged, because they had political coverage from a highly-placed individual. Instead, I found that I had been charged and convicted in absentia of the theft of a rifle and the carcasses of seven gazelles.

I had been sentenced to six months in jail and was to be arrested on sight. Friends on the police force helped me sneak onto an airplane, thereby avoiding travel by car and the inevitable roadblocks. I made it out of the province and went into hiding for six weeks until things settled down.

It eventually turned out that the charge sheet and all the associated court documents had registered my nationality incorrectly as South African and so I was able to claim that I was not the Peter therein described; as I said in an earlier chapter, there were several Peters in Cabo Delgado at the time.

Not being a lawyer myself, I can only assume this is one of the risks of rushing cases to trial while the putative defendant is out of the country. If you don't get the details right then you have to start all over again. The poachers and their overlord were (apparently) not ready to go through all the effort and expense to have me processed a second time. I never went to jail. They got off scot-free.

Back to Cesar.

Kind as he was, he inspired loyalty and even love. This may have been inevitable given that his name means, loosely translated, *"Caesar Augustus, Beloved of the Saints."* We lost him, too, in a double tragedy.

His wife, Lia, a mestizo woman he married while studying in Brazil, died in a car accident shortly after the Park was declared. She and the Governor's wife had started a charity for children and were on the way to the official opening in Montepuez town, 100 kilometers west of Pemba. A front tire blew out and the car rolled. Lia died on the spot; no one else was hurt. Three hundred cars joined the procession for her funeral, perhaps more cars than were registered in Cabo Delgado Province at the time.

Cesar never recovered. He died two years later of a stroke, said the doctors, but those who knew him knew it was a broken heart.

GECORENA was an eclectic group. A flawed group. But we were only group we had.

Nicolau and I drafted a proposal for a "National Reserve," thinking that it might be easier to get governmental approval for a National Reserve than a National Park. It included only about a fifth of the area eventually included in the Quirimbas National Park; we hadn't yet learned that ideas need to be big enough to capture the imagination. This initial concept went through several iterations: a "National Reserve" in the islands, with another inland for wildlife; then the "Ibo National Park," a mostly-marine reserve with a little bit of the adjacent mainland, with very little area for wildlife; and finally, the Quirimbas National Park in all its glory, from the mountains of Meluco down the Montepuez river catchment to the sea, and then across the bay to include Ibo Island and ten others as well.

We sent the early "National Reserve" draft to the National Directorate of Forests and Wildlife and never heard anything back from them.

We later learned that a mid-level apparatchik had placed it in his drawer to read later and forgotten all about it.

We wrote to WWF, USAID, the European Union, various embassies, anybody we could think of. Big silence in return. The World Bank project would not engage with us as they were committed to working within government structures. For the moment, we were stymied.

Stuart and Abudjate and I sailed north again in February 2000, for my fortieth birthday. We left on Saturday the 26th, passing the Tari mouth and Ponto Diablo. Ponto Diablo treated us kindly: in English its name means Devil's Point, and most days it deserves such a name. A southerly current flows over and around a long rocky bar that extends for kilometers eastward into the ocean. This would be enough cause for turbulence, but when the wind blows hard, as it does nearly every afternoon, waves stack up here and can threaten all but the largest ships.

The traditional offering to the water gods is a slave, who is tied to a rock and thrown overboard just before crossing the bar.

We felt this to be a bit much. We offered a kilo of sorghum flour and that seemed to work just fine. We also left early in the morning and were around the point before the afternoon wind got up, which also worked just fine.

By afternoon we were in Quipaco Bay. We snorkeled over the seagrass beds and caught a *xereu* (jack) for supper, which we grilled on a charcoal grill hanging off the stern.

We slept early, lulled by the waves and a clear night sky. Squid and barracuda hunted around the boat, provoking the occasional frantic splash as smaller fry tried desperately to stay alive. Two flying fish came aboard during the night.

I woke at four, with the sunrise, to find a fish eagle perched in the rigging.

After coffee, we filled the cooler with a few more *xereu* to take home. The last one was large enough to snap my fiberglass fishing pole in two. I pulled it in hand over hand as the locals do.

As we headed out of the bay, a pod of dolphins joined us. I asked Stu to take the tiller and crawled out underneath the bowsprit, trailing one hand in the water. A dolphin rose to my hand, then another and another. Warm and rubbery.

Six hours later we arrived back at Wimbi beach, to find Ruth and Connie and the kids all there, waiting for us with a birthday picnic basket.

An overwhelming abundance of blessings. My fortieth birthday.

And the birthday of the frenzy that would consume me. I knew I was going to do whatever it took to keep the Quirimbas alive.

Addenda to Chapter 10

MOZAMBICAN LEGISLATION has changed for the better in the intervening years. New conservation legislation, some of which I am very proud to have worked on, has established clear penalties and mechanisms for the protection of sea turtles. Only one gap remains, though it is a doozy. Large-meshed gill nets, used for shark fishing, are still legal in Mozambican waters. I say shark fishing, but the real target for many of these nets is sea turtles. In any case, most sharks are endangered so there is no real justification for allowing anyone to use these nets.

How large is a large mesh? Usually just big enough to stick your head through. Should you try this at home, and I suggest that you don't, you will find that your head enters more easily than it exits, your jaw and nose being significant obstacles on the way out, though not the way in.

So it is with sea turtles and sharks, though with the (somewhat lumpy) head and flippers substituting for jaw and nose in the case of sea turtles, and the gills and the peduncles of the pectoral fins doing the same in the case of sharks. And that is how these nets work; the unwary animal blunders into them and gets stuck. Subsequent thrashing merely entangles the poor beast further.

Nets are not governed by conservation legislation, but rather by fisheries law, so there is little the Mozambican conservation community can do except lobby the Ministry of Fisheries and hope they will soon review their regulations. And write marine park management plans so these hellish devices are illegal within marine conservation areas.

Which I did with the Qurimbas.

We were on an afternoon's patrol north of Ibo in 2005. I spotted an unusual swirl in the current in the deep channel between Matemo Island and the mainland. I should note that I can give my rangers a run for their money at sea, having spent much time in boats in my youth. My skills on land however cannot be compared with theirs, as many of them are former poachers.

We headed on over and found a buoy suspended a meter or so below the water's surface. Suspicious.

Momade Anli snagged it with a boathook and we drew it onboard to find a line attached to an anchor that was attached to a large-meshed gill net that stretched away into the depths. The net had been suspended just off the bottom in deep water.

We were all furious at this; fortunately we had the authority to impound the net. It proved to be a long one. We had about 150 meters of net onboard when up came a green sea turtle, 40 or 50 kilos. When its head broke the surface it gave a great foghorn gasp. We looked at each other. Sea turtles breathe air, though greens can stay underwater for up to five hours. This one must have been trapped underwater all day, nearly drowning. It took several minutes and some tricky knife work to free it.

The great shame of it all is that a turtle of this size will yield only 5 or 6 kilos of meat. The vast bulk of the body is composed of internal organs with little muscle. And sea turtles may live for 150 years.

Some kinds of fishing are allowed in the Quirimbas, even though it is a National Park. The GECORENA team designed it that way, so that the very poor residents would feel the benefits of our collective conservation efforts.

Residents are allowed to fish with traditional, non-destructive fishing arts in most of the Park; the most common fishing art in the Quirimbas is the fish trap, which is made by weaving bamboo splits into an octagonal lattice, leaving a tapered entrance that is easy to enter but difficult to leave (somewhat like a lobster pot). This art targets herbivorous fish, which enter it in search of shelter. The trap also lets juveniles leave, as the lattice has holes large enough to insert two or three fingers into. Lastly, fish traps do not damage the substrate in the way that seining or trawling would.

The most precious marine habitats in the Park are declared as No-Fishing Zones, where adult fish can live out their lives without fear of capture and thus grow to very large size. These habitats include coral reefs, seagrass beds and areas where fish aggregate for spawning.

The relationship between fish size and egg production is geometric, not linear, and varies from species to species. Thus a 40-centimeter reef fish does not produce twice the number of eggs as a twenty-centimeter one. Rather, it produces 100 to 1000 times as many eggs. This means fish populations explode in the No-Fishing Zones.

When population pressure rises high enough, fish leave the zone and move into the surrounding waters where local fishermen may catch them. This is called the spillover effect. No-Fishing Zones are popular now in the Quirimbas as they have significantly increased overall fish catch.

"The octopi are climbing the trees now," one old man told me; octopi are one of the first species to show population increases due to their relatively short life cycles.

We still have not figured out where the Quirimbas groupers aggregate to spawn. Groupers can travel 600 kilometers, using the same underwater "trails" each year, to reach their designated spawning areas. We have had some tantalizing hints. One year an Ibo fisherman landed a 100-kilo grouper but steadfastly refused to say where he caught it. He landed another of similar size the following year.

This second year our ranger network was able to discover the general area where he was fishing, which was the seaward side of Ibo Island. Omar and the Quirimbas team convinced the population of Ibo to create a no-fishing zone of 528 hectares there in 2016, ostensibly for the protection of dolphins, but which protects all species.[24]

It is a sad reality that conservation can create a great deal of controversy. Two South African ecologists from the University of Cape Town visited the mountainous areas of the Quirimbas National Park in search of undiscovered species shortly after its declaration. After their fieldwork they visited me in the Park office to register their distress about the fact that local people were still living in the Park and making their livings off the natural resource base. They questioned this, and my credentials as a conservationist, in no uncertain terms.

Shortly thereafter a consultant from the Aga Khan Foundation criticized me strongly because a child was killed by an elephant in the Park. I tried to explain that in fact 70 per cent of our budget and ranger time was being used to reduce human/wildlife conflict, that this was one of the main objectives of the Park, and that in fact this conflict had been reduced by 95 per cent from the pre-Park days, that deaths and crop damage from wildlife had gone way down.

I tried to say that we were doing this because no one else was doing it. He was having none of that. Several days later, and by pure chance, he and Ruth were seated together on a flight from Pemba to Maputo. The consultant filled her ears with outrage that a park was declared so that elephants could kill local children.

A local parliamentarian stood up in a public meeting and said that when he was a boy, if an animal was a problem, "we just killed it ... so why don't we kill the animals in the Park?"

"*Mata*," he said, "*Mata os bichos.*"

The Ministry of Fisheries opposed the Park on the grounds that it was elitist and that we were preventing people from fishing so that tourists could benefit. Then when the fish catch in the Park started to rise due to our management efforts, senior officials (with presumably individual interests) sent a commercial factory ship into the Park to collect and package fish and crabs for the eastern market. The ship was named *Kinsho Maru* and was and is on multiple blacklists of pirate fishing vessels.[25]

We fought for two years to get the *Kinsho Maru* out of the Park, as industrial fishing is incompatible with marine conservation. During this time we forged close links with the Mozambican Navy, who also had issues with allowing an infamous, blacklisted ship into Mozambican waters. Let alone a National Park. Five times the *Kinsho Maru* was ordered out, and five times it came back in, each time with a license signed by a higher-level official.

The *Kinsho Maru* was only expelled after the Governor visited

Ibo and found thousands of dead mangrove crabs on the beach. He asked the locals what was going on and they reported that the *Kinsho Maru* was harvesting mudcrabs, packing and freezing the claws, and throwing the carcasses back into the sea. The Governor was furious over this waste of food in a province that was so poor and so hungry.

The provincial government had a plenary meeting the following Tuesday. The Governor opened the meeting by upending a sack of rotting crab carcasses onto the conference table and demanding an explanation from the Provincial Fisheries Director.

Poor Mario (Mario the ecologist who went with me to the Lurio Estuary in an earlier chapter) had no answer; he was also opposed to the presence of the *Kinsho Maru.*

At times our only friends seemed to be in the Ministry of Defense The then-Minister General Tobias Dai, a literal-minded man, read in the Mozambican constitution that the purpose of the Ministry of Defense was to defend "the people, territory, and natural resources of Mozambique."

No need for lobbying or negotiations after that. Since the constitution was clear, so was he. He would defend all of the above.

His Excellency delegated the Navy to help the Park and they became very much involved not only in fisheries enforcement, but also ranger training and even elephant/human conflict mitigation.

For many years, the Quirimbas area may have been the only place in the world where, if you had problems with elephants, you called the Navy.

Behind all the conflict, though, my friends at GECORENA and I sought and found a deeper, unifying truth, one that serves us well even today. Our approach to conservation was and is fundamentally concerned with maintaining ecosystems at the highest level of productivity possible. Forget the arguments about tourists versus fisherman, local people versus "pure conservationists."

What all humanity needs are maximally productive ecosystems. What you do with them, whether fish them or invite tourists or both, or whatever, is the second step. The first step is organizing human interaction with the natural world in such a way that ecosystem productivity (fish, crabs, crops, forests, animal biomass, ecosystem services and processes) is maximized.

We have yet to find anyone who can oppose this approach.

"Oh, your Excellency, so you are not in favor of highly productive ecosystems?"

There is no future nor political capital in that argument ...

It is relatively easy to see how "maximally productive ecosystems" is a concept that readily applies to fish and forests; a bit harder to see how it applies to large and destructive animals like elephants. Jackson et. al. addressed this issue in their seminal work, *Historical Overfishing and the Recent Collapse of Coastal Ecosystems*, an analytical review of socio- ecological studies encompassing 10,000 years of human history, from Stone Age shell middens to the collapse of the Grand Banks cod fishery in the 1990s.[26] They found that as one removes species from an ecosystem, productivity of said ecosystem invariably goes down.

They note that, to a certain extent, some species can replace others (specifically those at the same trophic level), yet these replacements always involve loss of productivity.

Elephants in Mozambique (and indeed across Africa) have filled the ecological niche of consumers of coarse grasses and herbaceous foliage, especially of trees that are out of reach of other herbivores. Their activities (including knocking over of trees and digging up roots to eat) play a key role in opening up the forest, allowing grasses to grow, reducing the dominance of tall, coarse grasses, and thus opening the way for smaller antelopes, gazelles, and other animals that require less coarse grazing to thrive. One elephant is a significant influence; a full-grown adult consumes 200–300 kilos a day of biomass and must spend twelve to eighteen hours a day eating to achieve this.

Because of this level of consumption, elephants produce impressively copious quantities of dung, which improves the soil as well as feeding a large variety of insects and beetles, including the scarab, a symbol of renewal in Egyptian mythology.

In Mozambique, humans to a large extent have replaced elephants as the dominant mammalian coarse biomass consumers (the overall champion biomass consumers in Africa are termites, by a factor of seven, but their lifecycle and role is another story, one that is less impacted by human activity, though not completely so).

Yet humans are imperfect substitutes for elephants. We do not produce nearly as much dung as elephants do (politicians excepted) as we "consume" trees and coarse grasses by burning. Much of the nutrient value of the biomass "consumed" is lost to the atmosphere as smoke and contributes to global warming. Furthermore, fires can actually burn organic material out of the soil, further impoverishing the ecosystem.

Without elephants, the *miombo* forests of Mozambique carry 3000 kilos per hectare of dry grass biomass during the dry season, practically guaranteeing destructive wildfires and loss of homes, fruit trees, crops, and human lives. A careless cigarette or cooking fire can escape and burn 100,000 hectares.

We humans do have one huge advantage over elephants, and that is that our biology does not compel us to spend twelve to eighteen hours a day eating simply to survive.

We have the freedom to alter our behavior so that we are less dependent on practices that consume our resource base and our habitats. Slash and burn agriculture can be substituted by conservation agriculture and permaculture, just as overfishing can be reversed by the establishment of no-fishing zones.

This allows humans to be less destructive, to consume less forest, to live on less land per capita, and to allow elephants the chance to roam free, to live, to inspire awe and wonder, and incidentally to cycle nutrients, open up the forest for smaller grazers, and add to overall ecosystem productivity.

Not for nothing did GECORENA call itself the "Working Group for Community Resource Management." Not "Working Group for Conservation." Not "Working Group for Wildlife Protection." Not "Working Group for the Defense of Nature." Nor any name that treated humans as anything other than an integral part of the ecosystem, as worthy of protection as all other species.

> *We wanted nothing less than to change the entire paradigm for how poor communities (and humans in general) engage with their environment. We wanted communities to reap the benefits of conservation: conservation not for the wealthy tourist, but for everyone. We wanted people to change their habits, not to make themselves poorer, but to become richer through maintenance and use of maximally productive ecosystems. And to a significant degree, we succeeded.*

Maybe I am not so bad at naming things, after all.

There is one more thing to add to the story of the World Bank Conservation Project for the Quirimbas Archipelago.

In 2004, seven years after the first and only planning seminar, I got a call from a gentleman we shall call Andrew Fletcher, the World Bank Project Manager for the Quirimbas Conservation Project. He told me that a group of project evaluators had come to Mozambique and asked if I could host them on Ibo Island for a day. I agreed, though I must confess that I was consumed with nonplussedness, if that is a word.

What the hell? The World Bank hadn't given a penny to the Quirimbas National Park.

Andrew asked me to help him convince the evaluators to extend the World Bank project for another year. A "no-cost-extension" in development lingo. A request for more time to do the work they should have been doing during these past seven years.

Hey, money for conservation is money for conservation, so of course I agreed. Still full of nonplussedness. No idea how the day would go.

I met the evaluators and Andrew on Ibo a couple of days later. I introduced them to the no-fishing zones, the nascent tourist lodges, the silversmiths, the community leaders. Andrew was quiet for most of the visit, the evaluators inquisitive and interested. I didn't ask them why they were evaluating a project they hadn't funded.

We went to lunch at Ibo Island Lodge, a new lodge in the Park run by friends of mine, Kevin and Fiona Record. The cook, Fiona's rapscallion brother James (whose life deserves a book of its own) blew our minds with fish and crabs and prawns and the indigenous coffee of Ibo Island. I figured I had done my duty to Andrew and the World Bank by that point, and besides, I had no idea what was really going on, so I sat back in my chair and closed my eyes, giving priority to digestion over social interaction and, truth be told, wakefulness.

I dozed off, yet I am sure I heard Andrew saying, "You are right, we did not invest here. I brought you here to show you what is possible, what we could do with another year's extension."

It sounded pretty pathetic, but it must have worked. The project received it's no-cost-extension. During that additional year, the Quirimbas National Park continued to receive no World Bank funding at all.

Andrew didn't call. He didn't write. And we never heard anything about the World Bank's Quirimbas Conservation Project ever again.

Ruth in full wedding regalia, dancing at our traditional wedding at the farm in Swaziland in 2012. Weddings are a process in Swaziland, with several separate steps that may be spread out over many years. This ceremony is the penultimate step, the umtsimba, during which Ruth's family officially brings her to stay at my homestead, and she formally asks my mother for permission to enter the family. My mother could not be present, so the Swazi wedding planner (yes there are such things), told us that our daughter Nelisa could fill in for her. This put Ruth in the curious position of being formally escorted to a farm that we bought together, into a house that she built and decorated, to ask her daughter if she could join the family. Of course Neli said yes. PHOTO CREDIT: *Lunga Bechtel*

CHAPTER 11

Maputo

December, 1999. In which Ruth, Lunga, Neli, and I fly down to Maputo and then head to our farm in Swaziland for the holidays.

OWN TO MAPUTO now, for the holidays.

Airplane. In-flight magazine. Cold beers and whiskey in those tiny little bottles. Plastic forks and plastic plates and plastic smiles on the stewardesses. Plastic smiles as you walk on the plane, that is, but they can't keep it up for long. This is Mozambique after all.

Pretty soon they're chatting with us and we're chatting with them and with the people next to us and those sitting two rows ahead. We know half of the people on the plane, and the half we don't know the stewardesses do. Ruth gets into an argument with the National Director of Water Affairs.

She feels that Maputo Province ought to be returned to Swaziland. Her claim is partly based on the two drinks she's had, and partly based on the fact that the Swazis occupied Maputo in 1865, throwing out the British who had thrown out the Portuguese. The Swazis stayed two years and then went home, (apparently) disgusted that the land was no good for cattle. It was good for wives, though; two of Ruth's great-grandmothers were kidnapped as children from Mozambique and married forcefully into the Swazi nation.

The Director of Water Affairs has provoked Ruth's ire by calling Swaziland the "eleventh Province." She was already feeling a bit sensitive; the plane we ride on is a Fokker 100 belonging to the Swazi National Airline. The powers that be ordered the purchase of the plane but then had no money to run it so it was leased to Mozambique. I doze off as the argument rages.

Not for nothing has the Organization of African Unity adopted the policy of not recognizing any national border adjustments on the African continent, even though current borders were defined in the colonial period with little regard for cultural or ecological or even economic reality.

Two hours later I awake in Maputo.

A fumble with the bags and a short negotiation with a taxi driver and we're on our way to the Hotel Escola Andalusia. It's night, but not too dark to see the crowds of young people cruising around, doing whatever young people do in the early evening along the *Avenido de Acordos de Lusaka* next to the airport. Whatever it is, it seems like great fun; young women in plastic heels and improbable outfits exchange flirtatious smiles with gangsta wannabees who hoot and holler and make awkward hand movements, the kind that American rap stars make, in return.

Little kids push bamboo hoops (yes, they still do this in Mozambique) or run errands for their mothers. Men gather in brightly painted shebeens, sipping beer and waiting for the roast chicken to be served. A crowd of ruffians tries to sell us stolen hubcaps as we wait for a break in traffic. We pass a brilliant yellow spaza shop called "Eco-Safari Tours, Lda." They sell tires and second-hand motor spares.

Someone has sprayed "Rod Stuard Rules," across an abandoned

warehouse wall a little further along. I look at Ruth. Her eyes are glassing over.

Clean sheets, running water, and satellite TV. I order a beer from room service and try to shift gears. Ruth takes a long, hot shower, the first she's had since August. The kids, adaptable as always, run up and down the halls and bounce on the beds and try to get me to play their favorite game, which goes by the descriptive name of "kill daddy."

There's a movie on the TV about a rich doctor and his young son and their beautiful new governess, with an actor who looks like William Hurt, but probably isn't, and an actress that probably isn't Diane Keaton.

The two manage to fall in love by the end of the movie, surviving murder attempts, the son's tantrums, and the disapproving glare of the disagreeable old housekeeper.

"Why does the old lady act like that?" asks Ruth. "Why can't she be happy that the doctor is falling in love? Why does she have to be sore about it?"

Ruth expects me to be able to interpret everything that white people do, even the things they do in movies.

I reply, "You see, Ruth, the disagreeable old housekeeper is a stock character in Hollywood. Many movies have them. It's almost expected. The old lady acts that way so that the audience can say, 'Ah, so this is the lady who plays the part of the disagreeable old housekeeper' …"

I've done my best.

I can't see why the old lady acts that way either.

"You're such a fool," she says, and I can't really disagree. Certainly I'm out of my element, but the beer helps, like grease in a gearbox, and pretty soon we feel able to go out to supper in the *Feira Popular*, down by the waterfront.

.　.　.

Culture shock continues at the *Feira*. Quite a number of the ratty old shebeens have closed. Half the *Feira* lies in darkness. The other half has gone startlingly up-market. We find a Chinese restaurant run by genuine Chinese people serving genuine *Moo Goo Gai Pan* and a French restaurant run by a genuine Frenchman serving genuine *steak au poivre* and a Bulgarian restaurant, of all things, run by a genuine Bulgarian serving genuine Bulgarian food that looks and tastes a little like Hungarian goulash.

Earnest, smart-casual international development types in 100 per cent cotton shirts crowd the tables and spill out onto the cracked cement of the sidewalk. We spy a table of tourists in shorts and sandals and floral shirts. There's not a Filipino sailor nor an overdressed young woman in sight, though sadly, still plenty of beggar boys.

We sit down anyway. The proprietor comes over with menus and beers.

"I lost all my money on bad business deals," he explains, "so my wife and I run a restaurant to make enough money to go back to Bulgaria."

Six months later, the restaurant vanishes like the shebeens did, so one hopes they made it home safely. Mozambique's loss is Bulgaria's gain, or maybe lots of people in Bulgaria cook as well as his wife does.

We order several courses and munch on bread rolls. The crowd of cotton shirts thins out. The tourists leave. Lunga and Neli cadge a few coins and run off to ride the ancient bumper cars. Ruth nudges me and points with her head.

A posse of Filipino sailors staggers in. An assortment of young women with long hair extensions and short skirts drifts out of the shadows. The food comes. Neli and Lunga come back.

We begin to feel happy. We begin to feel at home.

I'm trying, but I can't really describe Maputo, can't really capture the place on a piece of paper.

Maputo assaults the senses: the fresh salt air when the wind blows and the sticky heat when it doesn't; the look and smell of the *bairros* of the poor and the look and the smell of the indescribable women of every description who live in them and walk their streets; the way the waiter uncovers the prawns grilled in garlic and lemon while a child rummages for food in the alley across the street; the way you smell the prawns and see the ragged children and feel the guilt and know that you ought to do something about it but you don't because you've spent your entire adult life doing something about it and the ragged children are still there, and if you don't eat the prawns and drink the beer then there will be nothing of you left to do something about it tomorrow; the way you have to close your mind and close your heart close around the table, or go mad; the way the skin tingles like sandpaper as your eyes meet across the table and the way the blood races with anticipation and the way the anticipation makes the reality happen; the way that two exhausted people with grey in their hair and lines starting at the corners of their eyes make love on a hotel bed as if they haven't been married for seven years, as if they hadn't supped on cheap Laurentina beer and grilled prawns and Bulgarian meatballs in a dive down by the waterfront with bars on the windows and prostitutes clustered like parrots on the white plastic patio furniture after the tourists left, as if beggar boys in rags hadn't watched them with avaricious eyes from the shadows and stolen the scraps from the table as they walked away.

Life is cheap in Maputo, and love is cheap, and because of this both become priceless.

We shower afterwards and make love again and watch our reflections follow us in the mirror and the window glass.

Ruth falls asleep between clean white sheets, her clean brown body cleaner than it's been since August. I lean on the balcony rail, wrapped in a clean white towel, and look south across the harbor to the lights of KaTembe.

. . .

The founder of the Swazi nation, King Dlamini the First, came from there. He had gotten himself into trouble—some confusion over stolen cattle—and had had to flee across the Lubombo Mountains into what became Swaziland.

The story brings to mind the Irish sagas; there is something comforting about coming halfway around the world and discovering common values. Something comforting about coming halfway around the world and hearing the African equivalent of "The Cattle Raid of *Cu Chulainn*." Something comforting about coming halfway around the world and finding old stories alive despite all that time and invading powers have done to destroy them. Something comforting about remembering that kings after all are sometimes merely tarted-up cattle thieves.

More recently, Ruth's great-grandmothers were taken from KaTembe as prizes of war; one of them was of the *Tembe* clan, the ancestral owners of that land across the harbor.

Ruth's mother, LaNkambule, never got along with this grandmother. When Ruth's older sister Thembi (a name that means "hope") married a man of the Tembe clan several years ago LaNkambule is said to have cried out, "I thought I was rid of them when the old woman died."

No such luck, mother. At least Thembi had the luck not to become Thembi Tembe; Swazi women keep their maiden names at marriage: the prefix "La" is added as a mark of respect.

The entire family seems to have a problem with names.

I have noted earlier some of my own misadventures, though, like Thembi, I have had some lucky escapes as well. At the age of twelve my parents informed me that had I been born a girl, I would have been called "Heidi."

They told me at the same time that they had only rejected the name "Rebecca" with the greatest reluctance. Thank God for the least of favors; while Heidi Bechtel is bad, Becky Bechtel is awful, worse even than Thembi Tembe.

Ruth was not so lucky. The name Ruth is beautiful in English and fits her perfectly, evoking clear skin and intelligent eyes and the merriment of a small stream bubbling in the quiet of a green-brown hillside, a stream whose secrets must be sought for to be found.

The name Ruth, however, is unpronounceable as such for Swazis; the Swazi language lacks both the "r" and the "th" sound. "R" becomes "l" and "th" is pronounced as an emphasized, aspirated 't.' The best most Swazis can do is 'Lutsi,' for no word can end on a 't' sound (or on any other consonant, for that matter). The 'tsi' ending is therefore substituted as this sound is common in siSwati. Ruth claims her name was given to her by the famous sister Thembi when she went off to primary school.

Thembi also awarded the school names of Maureen, Portia, Felicity, and Automatic to assorted other young relatives. One wonders why the family let her get away with it for so long.

Ruth's name in siSwati is Sincinele, though no one calls her that now except her mother. The name is beautiful in siSwati, evoking clear skin and intelligent eyes, etc., etc. Sincinele, however, is unpronounceable as such for English speakers; English lacks the clicks (formed by popping the tongue of the roof of the mouth) that the Swazis inherited from the original Khoi-San inhabitants of Southern Africa.

The best that most of us can do is "Sinkinele," which sounds a bit like a name a junior advertising copywriter might come up with for a new brand of dishwashing liquid or an updated model of automatic garbage disposal.

It doesn't matter though.

Swazis thoroughly appreciate it when visitors try to speak their language. The non-Swazi who can speak some few words of siSwati, however awkwardly, will find himself treated like a member of the family wherever he goes in Swaziland. He will have easy access to government officials, paperwork will be speeded up for him, new friends will buy him drinks in bars, and the traffic police will forgive him any number of minor offences.

Ruth's mother doesn't really call her Sincinele. She shortens it (quite sensibly, in my view) to "Nele," which both saves time and avoids the troublesome click.

The problem this causes is that our daughter Nelisa is called Neli; the difference between Neli and Nele becomes indistinguishable when shouted across a maize field or even across a crowded kitchen hut. In spite of the minor confusions that result, I can truly say that naming my daughter "Nelisa" is one of the few times in my life that I have done everything exactly right.

We had nine months to argue about names. Nine months less seven days, that is, for seven days after Nelisa was conceived I put my hand on Ruth's stomach and felt a pulse that hadn't been there before, a steady throb of a pulse that whispered a wordless message of life and growth and greenness and regeneration.

"Whispered" is not really the word I want here.

I'd rather use the Portuguese *sussurrar*, as this word carries more exactly the feel of a warm pulse in the belly of an unsuspecting mother as a red sun peeps over a shoulder of mountain and dew glistens on lank Kikuyu grass.

"I'm coming," *sussurred* Nelisa, seven days old, "Ready or not, here I come."

"You're pregnant," I said to Ruth, and four weeks later the doctor said the same thing. He didn't believe our story, though (no one else does either); apparently such a thing is not medically possible. Well, maybe not, but maybe it's possible some other way.

All I know is that we had quite some time, more than most people, to select a name. We only chose one, a girl's. We didn't bother with a boy's. Don't ask me why.

It wasn't easy, though the names of our family members gave us a place to start. I have an older sister Lisa who is generally known as "Lisa." I have an adopted daughter named Licinia who was generally known as Licinia until she married; her husband now calls her "Lisa."

My brother married a woman named Felicia; her nieces and nephews call her "Fishy" until they grow out of it, but he calls her "Lisa."

My cousin Freddy was once married to a woman named Alicia, who is known as—wait for it—"Lisa."

The name Nelisa allows those who wish to, to call her "Lisa"— these might include my brother, my son-in-law, and my cousin Freddy—while Ruth's mother can call her Neli if she wants to. Furthermore, "Nelisa" is pronounceable for both English and siSwati speakers, and best of all, the name means "blessings," which in turn means that, with her birth, our cup is filled and runneth over.

And it is. I feel a stab of shame.

My exhaustion and my overwork and my stress and my burnout seem suddenly unbecoming, beneath me. Almost everyone else here—the young beggar boys, the overdressed young girls, the Filipino sailors—has a much worse time of it than I do.

Even the folks across the river in KaTembe. During the war the fighting was intense over there. Attacks were a nightly occurrence. People closed their homes and shops at dusk and boarded the ferry for Maputo, sleeping in the open on the promenade along the waterfront while rockets flashed like lightning in the sky across the harbor and shells crashed like thunder in the streets and among the palms and *Casuarinas*.

In the morning they returned, opening the shops and sweeping up the rubble and putting the coffee water on to boil and fitting the jagged edges of their fractured lives back together again for another day.

I can't stay on the balcony any longer. I go to bed and hold Ruth close. I kiss her cheeks, the faint lines at the corners of her eyes, the dark circles beneath them. She lies as if dead in my arms, only the faint *sussurra* of her breath in my ear to tell me that she still lives.

I'm not ashamed any more. She's finished, all in. So am I. Maybe we know a little bit about having to put the jagged pieces back together, too. If we don't, we'd better learn fast.

The following day we stop by the Helvetas National Coordination Office before heading home. No Christmas holiday would be complete without presents, and we find ours waiting for us in Marcus's office.

He and the boys upstairs have decided that the project must undertake a self-evaluation in early February as a prelude to the external evaluation in August.

"Here, have a look at these Terms of Reference for the Mecuburi project self-evaluation. We want you to something like this."

"But Marcus, we do something like this every year. We just did something like this in June. It's a part of our regular annual program. The Mecuburi project hasn't done any evaluation, self or external, for seven years …"

"… the Mecuburi people are going to analyze their programs using the technique of SWOT analysis. I think it's a good idea if we do, too …"

"… and the water project went seventeen years without being evaluated. We did our annual evaluation in June, then the Swiss inspector came in November, and then the country programming seminar will be held the week of February 6th, and then we evaluate again in the following week? When do we spend some time working in the rural areas? When do we spend some time working with the rural people?"

"You both have to take this evaluation process more seriously. The donors expect it. It's an essential part of any project. You know this."

"We're on holiday until the end of January. The kids go back to school then."

"You should just have enough time to prepare the evaluation when you get back ..."

"... but none to go to the villages and see how the work is going."

"So you'll have to come back a week early from holidays."

"And the kids?"

"You'll have to arrange something."

"Merry Christmas, Marcus."

"And a very Merry Christmas to both of you, too."

Francisco the Helvetas driver takes us to the border where we go through the usual struggle to get the passports stamped and the bags through customs.

We try to switch from Portuguese to siSwati. Ruth is better at these quick changes than I am. I address the Mozambican customs officials in siSwati, the Swazi ones in Portuguese. Ruth is delighted by this.

We pile back in the car, wave our passports at the guard at the gate, and suddenly we're back in Swaziland, home for Christmas.

Home for Christmas.

Mountains and cattle and men carrying war clubs and wearing animal skins because they are proud to do so. The slow formalities of the Swazi language, so different from the rough Portuguese Creole we mangle up north.

Rounder faces, heavier bones, heavier bodies, lighter skins. We meet many friends in the shopping center and even more relatives.

Ruth invites Noah to come to the farm for Christmas. He accepts, gladly. He's a bachelor cousin whose parents have passed away. He had nowhere else to go. Ruth bumps into a woman in the supermarket and says, *"Desculpa,"* which pleases me no end. I manage to find a turkey and sweetmince and brandy and Christmas pudding, which also pleases me no end. The kids find Ruth's brother Bha and the battered white four-by-four, which pleases all concerned. We pile in and head for the farm.

Addenda to Chapter 11

THIS WAS our life, when our life was good. That is to say, when I was good. Ruth was and is calm and consistent, a ready laugh and ready smile.

This life is what I lost to bipolar, and, incredibly, this is what I regained. I had help and she had strength. I found the help I needed to win back a functional approximation of sanity, and then her. She had the strength to understand and forgive. I cannot begin to explain how she did it. Maybe she will write a book some day and tell us all.

The most difficult thing for me was to understand that manic determination, the kind that forced the Quirimbas National Park onto the world, was not going to win this battle.

She had seen my mania before.

She knew what the pursuit of mania cost me, and us.

I remember a night at a lodge on Lake Niassa, midnight, holding her down, trying to force forgiveness from her as she begged me to let her go, let her leave, call the management, call a Land Rover and get me out of here. I remember the wild fear in her eyes. Like a rabbit when you catch it.

I backed off. She did not leave, I think more from exhaustion than from any real desire to stay. I woke up early the next morning, left her sleeping, and walked for hours in the hills, trying to understand what had happened, trying to understand what I needed to do.

Trying to understand what my shrink was telling me. Leaping randomly around the nucleus. Trying to connect across the space-time continuum. I cried the whole way. It didn't matter, it was raining. Some synchrony between what was happening inside me and out. And when I got back, Ruth was still there.

She had not called the management. She had not called for a Land Rover. I have never been so thankful for anything in my entire life.

Later we went snorkeling. I thought we had wonderful, healing time, appreciating together the jewel that is Lake Niassa, 700-plus species of freshwater fish, the most biodiverse lake in the entire world.[27]

When we got back, over supper that night, she told me that all she could think of the whole time was how easy it would have been for me to drown her and go live the wild life I wanted.

Courage? I am dwarfed beside her. So, I think, is everyone else I know.

In retrospect, that week may have been when the healing started. We had just spent almost three months apart. We made it through the week together. And maybe, just maybe, our electrons paired again, for a moment or two. Maybe she managed to glimpse something in me besides craziness and excess.

There was still much between us, much more I had to do to re-earn her trust. She had enormous difficulty in believing that hypersexuality was a thing. Long talks with my parents and our children may have helped her to understand that this period of my life was out of character for me.

It helped when I changed psychiatrists. She was the one who found Lidia for me, someone both of us could talk to.

I hated the pharmaceuticals. They brought me down to earth. No more flying, no more mania. I was human again. It was a terrible adjustment. At best, they made me fuzzy and stupid. Emotions all damped down, cotton wool instead of a personality. I threw them away as often as I took them.

Until one day in a hotel room in Niassa Province, bright lights started dancing on the ceiling. My ears started buzzing, which continues, to a lesser or greater degree, to this day. The world spun. I thought I was still drunk but woke up the following morning and it all started again. I had a meeting with the Governor that day about the progress on the Lake Reserve. I never made it. My colleague and good friend Papucides found me hanging onto a wall 100 meters from my hotel. I had no notion, really, of where I was, or even which way was up. Just bright lights, buzzing, and spinning.

Africa, fortunately, provides a wonderful excuse for sudden and/or prolonged incapacitation. I told Papucides that I thought I was coming down with malaria. He helped me back to my room where I dutifully took malaria medications under his watchful eye. I stayed there for three days until I felt able to face the world again. Until the floor stayed put and so did the sun, lamps, and all other nearby sources of illumination. I took my medications after that and never had such a bad bout again.

I suppose I was hallucinating, but it wasn't nearly as interesting as movies and popular fiction had lead me to believe. No voices, no phantom presences, no one telling me to kill the president (or anyone else), no discussions with absent entities.

I still get the odd hallucination, usually when I am under prolonged stress and/or extremely tired. Or whenever I take cough syrup (really, it's true).

I am vaguely resentful that my hallucinations are so dull. Bad enough to be bipolar.

Boring hallucinations only add insult to injury.

The cotton wool issue plagued me for some time. I had great difficulty concentrating at work. Medicines to control my mania drove me to depressions that I had no mental tools to handle, now that my toxic solutions were denied to me.

Getting sacked by WWF in 2012 may have been a blessing in disguise, for by then I was close to the point where I could no longer work full time, could no longer guarantee five days a week of functional presence to any actual or prospective employer.

Lidia and I adjusted my medications until we finally found a combination I could live with. Meds are really a crapshoot in bipolar. No one knows in advance what combination will work; we all are experiments of one. There is much less cotton wool now, but I still cannot manage twenty days a month. I always lose some days.

Professionally, I have taken myself to that last refuge of the scoundrel, that is, consulting.[28] I advise and do project design, management planning, and project evaluations for a wide variety of clients in the conservation field. I have been lucky enough to miss a deadline only once in five years, and that was last March, for my good friend Simon.

He knew my story and hired me anyway and was gracious enough to allow me the chance to finish the project despite my lateness.

I used the malaria excuse for years and it worked a charm. Then, on or around my fifty-fifth birthday, I decided I was tired of making excuses.

My friend and sometime colleague Dieter had offered me a long-term gig advising the IFC (the International Finance Corporation, a member institution of the World Bank Group). It was a wonderful opportunity and Dieter was and is a wonderful man, a synthetic intellect, passionate about helping the poor, able to absorb great quantities of gratuitous verbal abuse and invariably giving as good as he gets. I found that something in me would not let me take the job without informing him truthfully of my limitations.

His response was better than I ever imagined; I still advise the IFC on a part-time basis.

I decided then and there to be straight with all my clients and colleagues. I count myself doubly blessed by their invariably supportive responses. I am well aware that much of the world cannot see past the stigma of mental disease.

I understand that, even though I don't like it. Hell, even I can't see past the stigma of my own condition most days. It is only time and bitter experience that has taught me that no amount of willpower will bring me right.

I lack an essential chemical balance in my brain, the way others lack vision, or a foot. Nothing to be ashamed of, Lidia tells me, Ruth tells me, I tell myself.

I really only believe Ruth and Lidia, and then only some of the time.

I guess Ruth eventually saw the changes in my attitude towards meds and the new discipline in my life. I worked hard on establishing a routine. I traveled less and avoided going out in the evenings when I did. I tried to sleep at regular times, but too often prowled around the house at night when I couldn't. She convinced me to stay in bed and read or just rest.

I reduced my drinking, though failed to stop entirely. I tried to work during regular hours, but never really managed this. I only have two speeds, stop and go. Neither is very healthy.

One thing I never had trouble with was my exercise routine.

I had been a regular runner since age fourteen, a martial artist since my mid-twenties. Lidia encouraged me to continue this, citing multiple studies that show the value of exercise for mood stabilization.

One thing I did stop was exercising while drunk. I should say running, not exercising. Martial arts while drunk never worked out very well for me. Sprint intervals on a flat stretch of road, or the beach, now that's something else again.

It took nearly five years for Ruth to start trusting again. Five years for her to say I love you without reservation, without holding back some part of herself in self-preservation. Five years for her to feel beautiful again.

My eighteen-year-old manuscript starts to come unraveled after this chapter.

Perhaps reflecting my mental state? Only two more chapters, written over the next six months. Lots of fragmentary notes about things I wanted to remember. Nothing at all about the following twenty-some months of struggle that led to the declaration of the Quirimbas National Park, my first park, the first time I managed to bend the universe to my will on any significant scale.

A FRAGMENT FROM DECEMBER 28TH, 1999

ON SATURDAY we went to town again for the final round of shopping. The four-by-four died ten minutes after the shops closed, the Saturday before Christmas.

Boy did I freak out. I called our mechanic on the cellphone, who not only nursed my four-by-four to his garage but lent me his personal two-by-four Nissan so I could drive home with presents, food, Ruth, and our Christmas tree. If anyone asks, tell them that yes, Virginia, there is a Santa Claus. His name is José Fernandes, he's short and round with a gray mustache, and he's the general manager of Capital Motors in Mbabane, Swaziland, when he's not at the North Pole.

There had to be one more incident before Christmas, just to keep us on our toes, and there was. On the 23rd I got stuck on the road up to the farm.

The ruts had gotten so deep that José's two-by-four Nissan just bottomed out, not having the clearance of a four-by-four. I was beyond fatigue and frustration at this point. I tried reversing, going forward, rocking, swearing, calling upon the sacred name of Jesus, etc.

No dice. I jumped out and got some flattish rocks and jammed one of them under the rear tire of the truck. No dice. I jammed another. Dice. Far too many dice. The truck started to roll back down the hill.

Good, it's out, I thought. Omigod, it's falling down the mountain, I thought. I had left it in neutral, with the motor running, and had forgotten to pull the handbrake.

I tried grabbing bull bar and stopping it with my superhuman strength, but no dice. I had none. The situation called for quick thinking, but I had none of that either. I ran around the open door and tried to dive into the driver's seat. No dice.

I jumped in and bounced right out again. Onto the ground. With the door coming right at my head. I squeezed myself flat so the door could pass over me, and it did, followed by the two front wheels of the truck.

I like to think that the impact of my body on the wheels twisted them so the truck turned sideways along the hill and bumped to a stop. I was unscathed except for a gash on my leg from the under-carriage and a few tire-marks on my shirt and trousers. And a sore stomach. And boy did I feel dumb.

I drove to the farm. The wind was blowing and the stars were so low I had to duck, and a jackal barked, and instead of showering I found myself pressing my head against the window frame and feeling thankful that I had survived. Feeling thankful that we get to go to Cabo Delgado, the end of the earth, and do the things we do there and then get to come back to Swaziland, to our farm in the mountains, for Christmas and family and cool fresh water straight from the river and vegetables from the garden and milk from the cows.

Of course these sorts of incidents provoke the larger questions. Why did I live? And why do little kids in Chiure starve to death? Die of cholera? I always get stuck here.

No answer. So I threw myself into the delights of the day. Hugs. Songs. Tree with lights. Presents. Turkey. Laughter. It was great.

We had purposely not invited anyone so we could just have time together as a family. Ruth and me and the kids. The most restful Christmas we've ever had.

The last present did not come until the 26th.

Licinia, my adopted daughter, sent me an email saying that she is pregnant. I think she and her husband are both over the moon about this.

She asked me if I was ready for grandfathership. After being run over by my own truck I have to say I think I'm ready for anything. Lunga and Neli's older sisters, Tiny and Khulile, are adamant that they are not ready for auntie-ship, though.

And Ruth is much too young and beautiful to be a mother, let alone a grandmother.

A final Christmas thought. One day, when I am rich and famous, I shall open an exclusive club, the Tread Club, open only to those who have run themselves over with the car they were driving at the time. Believe it or not, I already know of one other person who qualifies.

TWO FRAGMENTS FROM FEBRUARY, 2000

I FOUND out today that our friend Charles the boatbuilder caught a boa constrictor to give to Vera for Valentine's Day. Note to self: think of some other kind of gift for Ruth.

I borrowed *Longing for Darkness: Kamante's Tales* from a friend in Nampula. I enjoyed the book as a nice counterpoint to Karen Blixen. I enjoyed it, that is, until I noticed that there was no author credit for Kamante, though the "Goodreads" website describes it thus:

> Isak Dinesen and the land and people she loved are nowhere so real and compelling as in *Longing for Darkness*, written by Dinesen's majordomo, Kamante, and now boasting a smart new cover. Readers familiar with *Out of Africa* may recognize many of the enchanting stories.

These celebrated tales and others are retold here from Kamante's perspective and are enhanced with his own drawings and letters, Dinesen's words and snapshots, and photographs by Peter Beard.

Writes Beard, "Over a period of twelve years, as if divesting himself of his possessions, Kamante put down the extra dimensions of truth which are at the heart of *Out of Africa*."[29]

Peter Beard, Karen Blixen, and (may the saints preserve us) Jacqueline Kennedy Onassis all get author credits.

Not Kamante, even though these others affirm that he "wrote" it.

Why do things like this keep happening in Africa?

From left: Abdallah the helmsman; Cesar Augusto dos Santos, first Warden of the Quirimbas National Park; Mario Carvalho, ecologist; Augusto Assane Omar, Muslim religious leader. Omar was one of two local leaders who were instrumental in founding the Quirimbas National Park.

CHAPTER 12

Darkness

Near the end of the rainy season, 2000. In which I visit the estuary again, and then go to the beach in Pemba at night and ponder.

THERE'S NEVER A break. I received word that there were problems out in the estuary, so I trundled on out there to see what was going on.

A lion had entered the village of Soma several weeks back and had consumed three of the goats of our goat-restocking project. The District Director of Agriculture had immediately authorized the killing of the lion and the local police department had issued a rifle to a local hunter, who had returned after several days with the lion's head, though not the rifle.

Now a buffalo had been seen near the village of Napulimuite, and our field officer, Amina, had encountered the same hunter with the same rifle hot on the buffalo's trail. He had been tracking for several days and had succeeded in wounding the animal.

All of this was quite illegal.

Since October, 1999, hunting *"em defesa das pessoas e bens"* can only be authorized by José Dias, the head of wildlife in the province, and animals can only be killed when they prove a danger to human life. The new law is designed to prevent the casual issue of arms which can then be retained and used for "authorized" poaching, with the choicer cuts of meat making their way as if by magic into the larders and onto the tables of district-level government officials.

The fact that a buffalo had been seen on the trail did not justify the issue of a rifle for self-protection, let alone the killing of the animal. And there is no question that the hunter's action created a danger to human life where none had existed; a wounded buffalo is perhaps the least desirable animal to have in the bush around one's village.

Fortunately, Amina knew what to do. She took the hunter's authorization and rifle numbers and reported immediately to us. She also gave the hunter an earful about careless and irresponsible hunting and sent him packing back to his village on the coast.

Amina is another of those wonderfully contradictory women one finds in Africa; elegant, slender, with bones no thicker than a bird's, she is given to wearing the *capulana* cloth and head covering of the traditional Macua woman and coloring her lips with a locally-used red dye. One cannot imagine her facing down a buffalo poacher, nor even surviving too many minutes in the hot sun, though by the time I got there with Casimiro, the poacher had gone, the buffalo had gone, and Amina, though still there, had gone on to other problems.

The first was a problem with the fisherwomen of Nimanro village. They were a group who fished for fry with mosquito nets in the shallow pools at low tide.

While they were well aware that this practice was damaging fish stocks in the entire estuary, they had refused to stop because they needed something to fill their children's bellies every day.

Adult fish were caught by the men and thus were not for family use, but for sale, and the money thereby obtained was for resolution of the man's own problems, which rarely included family food supply. After much discussion, the seven fishing villages of the estuary had agreed to ban fishing with mosquito nets.

Unfortunately, this didn't mean that the husbands were ready to contribute a few fish for the family supper. Our intervention in defense of the fishery had left the women with nothing to put on the table except maize or cassava porridge. All starch, no protein.

As so often in development, an intervention for the good of all had resulted in a worse situation for women and their children. The road to hell is paved with good intentions.

The women in the villages of the interior were having different kinds of trouble.

Rats and snails to be exact. Their crops of maize, sorghum, sunflower, and sesame had been decimated. The women had planted the crop not once but twice, but both times the young plants had been consumed. Harvests were expected to be abysmal.

We were particularly upset because we felt responsible; we had found a buyer for all the sesame and sunflower the women could produce and had lent them the seed.

The men also had a problem. We had arranged for a fish buyer to locate a one-ton icebox in the village of Sambene. Great was the joy of the fishermen, for finally they would be able to sell fresh fish, which bring three times the price of dried fish (and incidentally smell much better). Hooks were sharpened and nets repaired all up and down the coast in anticipation.

I felt pretty good, too. So much talk about making development work in the private sector and "trade, not aid," and here I was turning slogans into reality. Or so I thought. Weeks turned into months and still Sr. Ricardo and his box of ice did not appear. I went by his flat but was told that he'd gone to Beira and would be back sometime in the near future. Right.

. . .

Still another problem was brewing in Soma village itself.

The community had cut twenty tonnes of ebony on the basis of a written contract with a buyer, a timber merchant from Pemba. This was actually a very sustainable amount, representing about twenty logs. The timber had been cut in November and the buyer had sent a tractor to pull the wood out of the forest and into piles along the roadside. So far so good.

Then the timber merchant made an emergency trip to Maputo and had not returned until the rains had come. The timber could not be transported to Pemba. The merchant promised to come again at the end of May when the Megarumo River dried sufficiently to allow a lorry to splash across.

Still so far so good, except the community's patience was wearing thin. The leader of the group, who had negotiated the contract with the buyer, had been accused of treachery by his neighbors and had appealed for help in explaining the true situation to the other woodcutters.

I left the tireless Casimiro in Soma with Amina to work whatever magic he could and rushed back to town. Though I had promised Amina to sleep over a night or two in Soma, a fax had arrived from Bernard requesting a small mountain of documents for the external evaluation of the project which was to occur in July, and Ruth was starting to blow fuses.

Amina looked disappointed, but I promised her to have words with the District Director of Agriculture about the illegal hunt, and words I had.

I blew my top. It is completely un-African to shout at one's colleagues, no matter how stupidly or traitorously they behave, but I was beyond caring. We had fought so long and so hard to get poaching under control, and to get the wildfires under control, and to get funds from Helvetas to get the work done, and to get the people in Mazeze to believe in us, and here it was all coming undone because of one man's stupidity, or more probably greed, or maybe a little of both. I couldn't control myself. Paulo Mualimo, who was also on the trip, looked at me as if I was mad. Maybe I was, then, the bipolar showing.

We arrived back in Pemba well after dark. The bat hawk in Murrebue had long since retired. So had Neli and Lunga.

Ruth was lying on the bed with a cloth over her eyes and a headache. I had one, too, but the house felt too small and too confining so I drove to the beach for a jog and a swim. On the way I played a tape that my parents sent me, a tape of songs from my childhood. Two folksingers: Gordon Bok on one side, Miriam Makeba on the other. I stuck it in the car stereo without looking. A Scottish ballad. Gordon Bok. And Robert Burns.

> *Ca' the yowes to the knowes,*
> *Ca' them where the heather grows*
> *Ca' them where the burnie rows,*
> *My bonnie dearie.*

I managed the swim, but not the jog, and sat in the moonlight with too many things in my mind and too many things in my heart and not nearly enough strength in my body to see them through.

Why should I bother? Why should I care? Why give a damn about a bloody little village on a muddy great river that no one's ever heard of and no one wants to hear about, either?

The beach is white and the sand is warm and the sea is cool and the moonlight lies on the water like broken glass, and I should be here with my Ruth and some wine and nothing else in the in the whole wide world.

But instead we're falling apart, she and I, falling apart together.

> *Hark! the mavis' evening sang*
> *Sounding Cluden's woods amang ...*

But the waves murmur the things they murmured to me when I was a boy and I sat on a beach and looked over the water and yearned with every part of me to be out there in a world which maybe, just maybe, might be big enough for the things I thought and the things I dreamed and the things which lay just beyond my reach, out there in the moonlight across the water.

And I was young then, and indestructible, and there was singing and there were things to believe in and things to dream of, and all were possible.

> *... Then a-fauldin let us gang,*
> *My bonie dearie.*

And now I am forty, and not so indestructible any more, and there is too little singing and too little believing and not so much is possible, and too many things still lie out there beyond my reach, dancing in the moonlight across the water, and I think of fisherwomen and fishermen and fisher-children and dry porridge and my back hurts and my legs hurt and my head hurts and there is nothing to do but let the sand hold me and the night hide me and wait for something to happen that will let me move on, let me stop wondering what the hell I'm doing in this beautiful, godforsaken place with too much poverty and too much work to do and too little money to do it and too many requests for reports and financial statements from too many white-shirted, khaki-trousered men in too many air-conditioned offices.

If I wonder too much then I think too much and if I think too much then I might decide that I'm still here because I'm too old, too chicken-shit scared to do something else with my life, because maybe after twenty years of blood and toil and tears and sweat I don't know how to do anything else anymore, because maybe I'm too stupid to give up on dreams that I dreamed when I was a boy and many more things were possible.

I might just decide that I'm here on this beautiful, godforsaken beach because I haven't managed a white shirt and khaki trousers and an air-conditioned office. I might decide I'm here even though I don't dream any more. Then where will the strength come from to carry on? Where will the strength come from to stay?

> *We'll gae down by Cluden side,*
> *Thro' the hazels spreading wide …*

A tall figure, a low voice.

"*Boa noite, Senhor.*"

A young woman.

"*Boa noite, senhorita.*"

I'd seen her around. At the disco. At the Nautilus Hotel. She'd asked me for a lift once, then declined when she saw I wasn't alone in the car.

"*Tudo bem?*" All well?

"*Muito bem.*" All well.

She wore a long, cream-colored dress with a slit up the side, a brief halter top, platform sandals. No bra. She needed none.

"You came down for a swim?" She folded herself onto the sand beside me, like some slim, long-legged animal bedding down for the night.

"Yes, and to go for a run, but I have a headache."

I'd seen her one night on the beach with the fisherwomen, squatting on her heels, helping them sort through the minnows and the crabs, plucking them from the net and the weeds with her long, painted fingernails, depositing them gently in a basket, chatting and laughing with the ragged women while her colleagues pouted and primped and paraded for the big-bellied South Africans at the end of the bar in the Nautilus Hotel. She seemed nice.

She seemed three-dimensional.

"I decided to just sit here a while and look. I'm tired."

... O'er the waves that sweetly glide
To the moon sae clearly.

"I've seen you before. You come here at night to run and do physical training."

"Yes. I don't have time during the day."

"It's beautiful at night."

"Yes. The sea, and the stars, and the palms against the sky. I need a bit of beauty tonight."

She put her hand on my arm, but I didn't react.

"What's your name?"

"Peter. Yours?"

"Viviana."

Yonder Cluden's silent towers,
Where at moonshine midnight hours ...

"You're not from Pemba."

"How did you know?"

"You don't have a Macua accent. Yours is different, somehow."

"I'm from Lichinga, Niassa Province."

"The mountains."

"Yes."

... O'er the dewy-bending flowers,
Fairies dance sae cheery.

And so I tell her about Swaziland and she tells me about Lichinga and the mountains and her mother who left when she was young and her father who married again and stayed in Lichinga and sent her to live with her auntie in Pemba when her step-mother grew jealous.

She tells me that she has no brothers and no sisters and that she would like very much to go back to school next February, if it can be arranged, and the way she says arranged lets me know she means money. She tells me she's nineteen years old.

And I think of Viviana and what it means to be a girl from Lichinga, age nineteen, living with an auntie, and I wonder what she can possibly hope for in her life and something in me wants to be something for her but I'm already something for Ruth and she needs me and I need her and so there is nothing I can do for Viviana but talk to her under the moon as if she were my own daughter.

I ask her what she wants to study and she tells me and as we talk she pretends that she's not a prostitute, though we both know she is, and she stops rubbing my thigh and we make some kind of connection there in the moonlight with the stars dancing on the water and the phosphorescence dancing inside it, and I hurt for the things she has to live through and I wish I had another brother because she is dark and beautiful and intelligent and lonely and lost and nineteen and cruising for older men on a dark beach at the very edge of the world, so maybe she can go back to school.

Ghaist nor bogle shalt thou fear …

But thou shalt fear the dark and the men and the things they will do to your nineteen-year-old body, and you ask me how old I am and I tell you to guess and you say fifty and I laugh and you tell me you see me practicing karate on the beach at night and ask me who will get old first and I am honest and I say you and you laugh and don't believe me but I know I have spoken the truth.

Women don't last long in Cabo Delgado and prostitutes don't last long anywhere anymore.

Thou'rt to love and Heaven sae dear …

And we both know that you won't get back to school, even if you do get the money.

You will marry a slow old white man who will smell of tobacco and parade you on his arm like a trophy, or maybe a fast young one, any color, who will beat you and cheat on you, or maybe you won't marry at all and end up having kids from different men and hustling a little harder and talking a little faster in the disco at Wimbi on Saturday nights, and most probably you won't be dear to anyone at all.

> *… Nocht of ill may come thee near,*
> *My bonie dearie*

I think I would give my kingdom, if I had one, if that could only be true for you. There's something inside of you, something deep down, something that reminds me of my daughters. Something that reminds me of my wife. Something that reminds me of another slim dark woman I met in the *pantanos* of Macomia last year, a woman who made more traditional choices and ended up sleeping on a mat in the fields with no children and no husband and a body that was beautiful once but wasn't anymore.

A woman who ended up staring into the darkness with red-rimmed eyes, beating on a metal bucket and throwing stones at the elephants when they came for her rice and throwing fire at the lions when they came for her.

A woman named Fatimah Bacar who stood for all of you. You remind me of all I have and all you don't. You remind me of what is and what could be and what isn't. You remind me of hard choices and whys.

> *Fair and lovely as thou art,*
> *Thou hast stown my very heart …*

And you are dark and you are fair and you are lovely and you are completely, completely screwed up and I can't do this any more. You have taken all of ten minutes to steal my heart, and break it, or has it been twenty years?

... I can die–but canna part,
My bonie dearie.

So tell me Viviana, or anybody. Tell me this.

Where will the strength come from to carry on? Or where will the strength come from to leave?

Addenda to Chapter 12

I GUESS I did manage to write about depression after all, all those years ago. It is interesting that I did; I can see in this chapter a number of themes that haunt me to this day. Night. How overwhelming the human condition can be. Time. Space. Space-time. Prowling about. And toxic company.

I never did more than talk to Viviana during the seven or so years that I knew her. As I said, she seemed multi-dimensional, a person, not a thing to be used. I would see her now and again when I ran at night, or in a shop, or walking along the seaside in Pemba. We would wave and chat. Once I saw her parked in the dunes with a colleague. I didn't wave to her then, nor did she to me.

The last time I saw her she asked me for a lift to her new house, a mixed construction with a cement floor, cane walls, and zinc roofing. She asked me in and I said no.

It was probably innocuous. Still.

What I remember most was that she had built in a low-lying area, one that the City Council had reserved as a green zone for storm-water drainage. She was not the only one building there. I asked her about that, but she told me had a construction license from the Council itself. Some months later I was back in Pemba and drove by the spot. All the houses had been razed and there were bulldozers on the site. A small shopping mall now stands where her house once did. Green zones are apparently only for those who cannot afford to build shopping malls.

Handling depression for me turned out to be harder even than handling mania.

I had to wean myself off hormones and booze. No more prowling. No more three-day work frenzies. No more senseless risks, death-defying odds, cheap thrills, cheap companions.

Despite the drugs, despite the counseling, these were the worst of times. I remember lying on the floor in the bathroom, immobile for a day, Ruth finding me there after work and helping me to the bed.

Other days on the sofa, doing nothing, too out of it to read a book, to brush my teeth, to take a shower. I avoided people, missed meetings, didn't answer the phone, couldn't make myself leave the house.

I didn't eat. One year on our anniversary I got so nervous about going out to celebrate that Ruth said we didn't have to go.

The inertia could last for months.

I discovered fire. Specifically, fire applied to steel applied to skin.

Hand, forearm, arm, shoulder. More pressure, more coverage, more time each time. Now this brought a serious hormonal rush. Really amazing. Ruth was appalled, Lidia patient.

"Peter, there are some things we just can't do, if we're going to be healthy. They may feel good to you but they hurt those around you."

So, reluctantly, I let go of fire.

· · ·

I battled with booze. One weekend Ruth was away and I was home and I decided that I would drink all weekend. This was not the beach in Pemba. This was later. In Maputo. And it was not a roll of the dice with death. Nothing so grand. It was just whiskey and Amarula so I didn't have to be with alone by myself. With myself. Anything to take the awful knowledge of emptiness away.

I passed out on the bed on Saturday afternoon and woke at midnight with Satan's own hangover. The solution obviously was not in a bottle, but where the Hell was it?

As I grew more and more desperate I began to understand the lure of suicide.

The anguish, the futility, the emptiness of depression became unbearable. Non-existence, the Black Beast of my youth, seemed more and more a blessing to me. I came to realize that there are worse things than dying. I craved the little-death of sleep even as sleep became harder and harder for me to achieve. I woke every morning wishing that I hadn't. I started planning suicide and keeping useful items around the house, ready for the day when I couldn't go on.

Lidia made me talk about suicide, made me read about what it did to family and survivors. I couldn't do that to Ruth, nor Licinia, nor Khulile, nor Tiny, nor Lunga, nor Neli. I hung on. After years of keeping myself in mania, I had years of depression to catch up on.

So what happened? Two things.

First, we finally found a combination of drugs that keeps me largely free of deep depression. That doesn't mean I am stable: small things can send me down for a day or a week. I regularly lose two or three days when I bid on even a short contract and don't win.

The inevitable disagreements of family life, no matter how

petty, can send me to the bedroom, quiet, for three or four days. Unless of course Ruth catches me and draws me out. She's getting pretty good at it.

Second, I learned, with agonizing slowness, the meaning of moderation. Anathema to bipolars. No more stoking the hormones, for what goes up must inevitably come down.

A schedule for work, play, food, and sleep. A normal life, except I had no idea what normal felt like, and when I found out, it didn't seem right to me.

Food had no taste. Work was no fun. I had trouble motivating myself to do anything. I played video games obsessively, hoping for stimulation.

We eventually decided that I should aim for just a touch of mania during the day, leashed by anti-anxiety and sleeping pills at night so things wouldn't get out of control. This, plus heavy exercise and even heavier doses of love, has done me well the past few years. Not cured me. Bipolar is forever. We can but manage it.

Financial extravagance is an issue with bipolars and has been for me in the past. I have tried to harvest the obsessive-compulsive aspects of my personality to fight this. I have overwhelming urges to buy exercise equipment yet challenge myself not to buy unless I can achieve at least a 60 per cent discount, 70 per cent on everything that is not shoes.

This allows me to spend hours on eBay and Amazon, scratching my itch, yet actually buying relatively little. "Relatively" is a relative term however; I have at least ten pairs of athletic shoes, twenty pairs of compression tights, five swimsuits, three weightlifting belts, and I just counted nine pairs of weightlifting gloves. I gave up counting tee shirts at fifty.

The search for bargains is deliciously satisfying to my compulsive soul. Nearly as good as fire.

The only downside is that the best bargains are often on awkward colors. Who cares? I wear my fluorescent pink swim fins with pride. A $100 value, for $19.99.

It wasn't easy to get to this place, though. With my reluctant approval and Lidia's encouragement, Ruth held my credit cards for years, until I learned to be extravagant only with inexpensive things.

Of course I now love second-hand shops. I haven't bought a new dress shirt in years. There are so many good ones at Goodwill Industries.

I also go through phases where I compulsively buy ornamental plants and new varieties of fruit trees. Ruth kind of enjoys this; we have extensive gardens and experimental plots at the farm. I have a weakness for palms and succulents and cycads and other primitive plants that have withstood the rigors of evolutionary time.

Physics has also done me well. Recent work on the nature of space and time calls into question the explanations of the universe that terrified me so, for so many years. Not that there is a consensus,[30] just a growing body of evidence that time is not at all what we thought it was, nor is it what we perceive every day. Recent work by Chappell et al. (2017)[31] indicates that time may not be a free-standing fourth dimension at all but rather that...

> ...time is simply one of the properties that we abstract from the geometry of the three-dimensional space, primarily the geometrical point-like quantities as well as the areal bivector quantities.

I find everything before the comma clear enough, that time is in some way a result of the relationship of the other three dimensions. Past the comma, I am lost. Still, I think I understand enough of their paper to realize that they have managed not only a plausible explanation for why one can move freely throughout the three classical dimensions, yet only linearly through time, but also a way to unify quantum mechanics and general relativity and their respective absolute and relative views of time. All of which makes me think, for what it's worth, that they may be onto something.

I found an article from *Quanta Magazine*[32] that was a bit more digestible, though still hard going. This article suggests that space-time and the matter within it (i.e. the universe) arise from the "entanglements" (read interactions, or something close to that) of static bits of quantum information, like a complex mathematical code, that exist at the outer limits of the universe, where everything becomes so distant and disconnected from everything else that time ceases to exist. Physicists call this event "heat death."

Just as a hologram produces a three-dimensional image on a flat, two-dimensional surface, the bits of quantum information encoded on this timeless "heat death" boundary "entangle" within the bubble of our universe to produce space and time. How it does that, when everything is so disconnected, is something of a mystery. Why isn't everything inside the bubble of our universe frozen in time?

It does appear from multiple researchers that an "entangled system that is globally static [like the bubble of our universe] can contain a subsystem that appears to evolve from the point of view of an observer within it."[33]

If I get it right, we only notice time because we are inside the universe. Observers outside of the universe would not perceive time.

Just how this is supposed to work no one knows, and thinking about it for too long would likely make my head hurt. Still, for me, concerned as I am with connections and the fate of the universe, this is a wonderful improvement on the Big Bang. Entropy doesn't make everything stop, it only appears to. And in the very place where it does, the boundary where heat death overwhelms connectivity, lies not eternal darkness, but the very code that makes the universe happen. Some physicists liken it to living inside a 3D computer game.

I think the ancients, with their tales of the Phoenix, might not be so far wrong after all. And entanglement makes me think of American Indian beliefs, that emphasize the entanglement of all things in ways that the culture I grew up in does not.[34]

> The sense of the interrelationship of all of creation—of all two-legged, four-legged, wingeds, and other living, moving things (from fish and rivers to rocks, trees and mountains)— may be the most important contribution Indian peoples have made to the science and spirituality of the modern world.

Though Chief Seattle's declaration that "All things are bound together, all things connect" has been shown to be unattributable,[35] and perhaps even an invention of a movie scriptwriter in 1971,[36] there is no ambiguity nor confusion about the words of the Oglala Sioux holy man Black Elk:[37]

> The first peace, which is the most important, is that which comes within the souls of people when they realize their relationship, their oneness, with the universe and all its powers, and when they realize that at the center of the universe dwells Wakan-Tanka, and that this center is really everywhere, it is within each of us.

Of course the "universe as hologram" view is only one among several competing theories (though there is some supporting evidence in that the surface of a black hole, the event horizon, may somehow encode evidence of what lies inside).[38] It pleases me no end that other theories also have Phoenix-like properties; another personal favorite is loop quantum theory, that implies that black holes (and the Big Bang) are not singularities, but rather space-time tunnels to elsewhere, including our past and future.

Perhaps the last word on the physics of the cosmos should go to Richard Feynman.[39]

> To decide upon the answer is not scientific. In order to make progress, one must leave the door to the unknown ajar—ajar only. We are only at the beginning of the development of the human race; of the development of the human mind, of intelligent life—we have years and years in the future. It is our responsibility not to give the answer today as to what it is all about, to drive everybody down in that direction and to say: "This is a solution to it all." Because we will be chained then to the limits of our present imagination.

The last word on time, however, goes to the North Atlantic Treaty Organization. NATO.

Buccheri, Saniga, and Stuckey (2003) begin the preface to the *Proceedings of the NATO Advanced Research Workshop on the Nature of Time* with the following statement:[40]

> There are very few concepts that fascinate equally a theoretical physicist studying black holes and a patient undergoing serious mental psychosis. Time, undoubtedly, can well be ranked among them. For the measure of time inside a black hole is no less bizarre than the perception of time by a schizophrenic, who may perceive it as completely "suspended," "standing still," or even "reversing its direction."

I will remind you here that schizophrenia is closely related to bipolar disorder.[41]

A view of the Montepuez River valley and the Inselbergs of Meluco in the background. A young volunteer from the Environmental Association sits atop the rock in the foreground, braiding her hair. I was thinking of the Little Mermaid Statue in Copenhagen when I took the picture. No one else seems to see the resemblance.

CHAPTER 13

Tracks

Sometime in the dry season, 2000. In which I lead a
GECORENA team and a group of Environmental Associa-
tion volunteers on our first expedition to the mountains of
Meluco, following rumors of elephant ...

A T LONG LAST we managed to organize the large animal
count along the Rio Montepuez.
I had argued with the powers that be until they had
agreed to let me use 5000 US Dollars of Helvetas project money
to fund the study.

Ruth and I were still working for the Swiss. We had to work
hard to convince them.

> *Me to authority figure, one of many, take your pick:* "How are we
> supposed to make real improvements in the lives of these
> people when their crops are consumed by elephants ev-
> ery year? And what about human lives? There were four
> deaths from elephant attacks last month."
>
> *Authority figure to me:* "We are authorized by the donors to
> make investments in support of local initiatives, not the
> protection of wildlife."

Me: "Fine. No problem. But tell me, what investments can be made without some control of the conflicts between animals and humans? I think support of farming efforts and support to reduction in animal attacks on people is perfectly in line with donor objectives."

Authority figure: "But you and Dias and Nicolãu want to make a wildlife reserve there."

Me: "What else can you do with those mountain soils? No one lives back in there, just animals. And in summer the animals come out of the mountains and destroy the farmers' fields. Seven hundred and eighty-one fields destroyed last year. If we make a wildlife reserve, try to separate the people and the animals, we make the best use of each ecosystem. Animals in the mountains and the uninhabited forest, fields near the villages, and a buffer zone for community hunting and gathering in between. This is not rocket science. It's not even re-inventing the wheel. It's ..."

Ruth stepped in.

We didn't know at the time I was bipolar, but she did know that there were times when it was better for all of us if I would just shut up.

"It is simply resource utilization according to the theory of best practice, the UNESCO Biosphere Reserve concept as applied in Cabo Delgado. Activities such as community-based tourism along the lines of the Zimbabwean CAMPFIRE program will broaden the range of livelihoods options for the local community. Better conservation of the area will also mean more wild foods and other non-timber forest products for women and vulnerable families. The DFID livelihoods approach states clearly that dependence on a single survival strategy, like subsistence agriculture, exerts a strong negative influence on the community vulnerability context."

. . .

It was the jargon that got to them in the end. It always does with development professionals. You won't win unless you give them something to tart up their monthly progress reports.

The only condition imposed by the powers that be was that I personally had to supervise the work in the field, to "guarantee quality."

I knew they just wanted me out of their hair for a while. No matter. I wouldn't have missed it for the world.

Nicolãu called in the best of the Environmental Association field-workers to help us: Njini from Minhanha, Dio from Ngura, supervisors Paulo Mualimo and Celestino, and Amina from the Lurio Estuary in Mazeze. It was a training exercise for Amina. She was a more recent hire and had missed the course in wildlife evaluation last June. Casimiro, my right-hand man from Helvetas, also came along.

José Dias, the head of the Provincial Wildlife Department, came with his right-hand man Abdallah Mussa who came with an AK47, more for the sake of his image as a wildlife ranger than because anyone thought we needed one.

I came with a cooler box full of ice and cold drinks. Everyone thought we'd need those. Amina came with khaki bush trousers and a skin-tight pink-and-rose halter top made of some flimsy material that no one thought she really needed, but everyone was glad she'd worn. This was completely out of character for Amina. Usually she dresses in the bright *capulana* cloths, nose ring, and red lip dye of the traditional Macua woman.

She received the amount of attention that one might expect a lovely young woman in a pink-and-rose halter top to receive when she heads for the bush to count wildlife with ten red-blooded, healthy male companions.

We met at Dionisio's house in Ngura village, the jumping off point for the Montepuez River valley and the mountainous region that surrounds it. Dio had arranged for two trackers from the village to accompany us. We drove as close as we could to the grottoes along the river and set up camp. Dias had divided the area into quadrants. While the cook made supper, we set out to search the first quadrant for animal sign.

The World Wide Fund for Nature, in its useful publication *Counting Wildlife Manual*, outlines a number of simple procedures that can be used for estimating wildlife population densities.

Most of them involve walking transits, counting tracks, spoor, and sightings, and then relating them mathematically to the length of the transit walked and the size of the quadrant being sampled. We came prepared with clipboards, pens, specimen sacks, binoculars, bird books, and scientific calculators with more buttons than we knew how to use.

Dias had worked out the bearings and the transits the night before and had them marked on a topographic map. He passed out photocopies to anyone who would take one.

Dio taught us all the appropriate hand signs to use if we saw animals, poachers, or if we had to run away without making any noise. He had just completed a course on wildlife management in Gorongosa National Park and was bursting to show us what he had learned.

Abdallah slid 7.62 mm rounds into the banana clip of the AK47 with tender, loving care. We were ready for anything.

Anything, that is, except for what we found.

"*Porra!*" said Dias, who was in front.

Dio shot him a dirty look and crouched down in the best Gorongosa game guard style. He signaled all of us to crouch, too. I figured it was too late to crouch in the grass since Dias was standing up ahead there saying "*Porra!*" so I walked on up beside him.

Dio shot me a dirty look, too, much dirtier than the one he'd shot Dias.

"*Porra!*" I said, and stood transfixed.

Below us lay the Montepuez riverbed, dry as a bone in the afternoon sun.

A strip of coarse white sand snaked between ranks of blue-green sawgrass that stood defiantly at attention in the dust and the breeze. A steep red bank fell away at our feet. Bamboo and figs and fever trees fought for space on the opposite bank. A great grey granite inselberg towered over us all. A few dark shapes (lanner falcons?) whirled and twirled around its summit.

"What is it?" said Njini who, at one-point-three meters tall, could hardly see over the sawgrass.

"Down there," I said. "In the sand."

"There's nothing there," he said.

"Maybe not now," said Dias, "but there was last night."

Njini looked closer.

"*Porra!*" he said.

Elephant tracks covered every square centimeter of sand, except for those few centimeters that had monkey or suni tracks, or warthog tracks or leopard tracks or sable tracks.

Tracks on top of tracks.

A lion track partially obscured a kudu track which was itself planted squarely in the drag mark of a crocodile's tail. Clawless otter tracks led to a muddy pool and out again on the other side. Baboon feces adorned every rocky outcrop, except for those that were used by civets for the same purpose.

Dio and the village trackers argued over a smaller scat that contained bones and rodent hair. I solved the argument by smelling the freshest sample; the unmistakable pong of the genet cat solved the argument to everyone's satisfaction.

The village trackers made much of me after that, but I am an awful tracker. Genet is one of the few animals I can identify by spoor alone, and this only because genets come so often round the henhouse on the family farm back in Swaziland. I spent the rest of the trip smiling enigmatically and deferring graciously to every-one else's opinion so as not to reveal the depth of my ignorance.

We didn't want to leave the riverbank. It seemed silly to push through the bamboo and acacia thickets looking for tracks when there were so many here in the riverbed. Dias tried to argue with us about scientific methodology.

We knew he was right but were too excited to listen. Dio told us what genuine Gorongosa game guards would do in similar cir-cumstances. We all thought he was being a bit of a pain. It was Paulo, son of a Maconde hunter, who made the observation that brought us all back together.

"It's getting late," he said, "and we have no water. Let's go back and get buckets and soap. We can wash in the pools by the grotto and carry water back to camp. We walk the first transit tomorrow."

We didn't find out until the next day that Paulo is extremely uncomfortable walking in the bush without a bow and arrow in his hands. He had tried to borrow a bow in Ngura village but the owner only brought it to our camp the next morning. Apparently Paulo places no trust in Abdallah, nor in AK47s.

At the pool we men stood guard and searched for more tracks while Amina bathed. I felt that peculiar, satisfying male thrill, so rare in the modern world, that comes from the protector's role, the thrill of guarding a woman during periods of danger or vulnera-bility. Made even better by that fact that this particular period of vulnerability involved the removal of the pink-and-rose halter top, albeit just out of sight.

·   ·   ·

A pile of chalk-white droppings on a rock by the river fooled Dio, but not the local hunters.

"Crocodile?" he asked.

"No," they said. "Hyena. They come for scraps from the poachers' camp."

We walked over a rise and they showed us the remains of a meat-drying rack, slowly being devoured by termites. Dias collected and wrote down what information he could about the poachers.

We caught the same group several months later across the river in Meluco District.

It was our turn to wash when Amina finished.

"How do you count the tracks when there are so many?" I asked Dias. "It's like trying to figure out how many people were on Wimbi Beach on a Sunday afternoon by counting the number of footprints in the sand."

"I know," he said. "It's impossible. And an aerial survey won't work either. The trees are too tall and the bamboo thickets too dense. You won't see anything."

"So what do we do?"

"We walk the transits. We do the calculations. The politicians need something that looks scientific or else they won't proclaim a reserve."

"Fine. Do that. But just for my own interest. We saw tracks for how many different elephants today? Make a guess."

"Sixty. Maybe 150. Who knows? Pass the soap."

After supper we tuned in the provincial news bulletin.

We don't usually do that in the bush, but Ruth had spent the day presiding over the official opening of a school that our Helvetas project had finished building in the village of *25 de Setembro* and she was to give a live interview that night.

The trackers from the village listened intently to the entire program, then turned to me.

"*Senhor*, this Ruth on the radio, this Ruth is your wife?"

"Yes."

I couldn't keep the pride from my voice. "She works with me. She builds schools and helps people with goats and seeds and other things they need."

"This Ruth on the radio, this Ruth is black?"

They looked puzzled.

"Yes," I said, "but I married her because she is Ruth, not because she is one color or another."

A short silence. Perhaps slightly less puzzlement.

Then, "And she has built a school in this village of 25 *de Setembro*?"

"Yes."

"And will you come here to build a school in Ngura?"

"Yes, if you want us to. After the wildlife reserve has been officially declared by the government. We know that Ngura village is poor. We know there are problems. We don't expect you to worry about nature conservation when you have so many problems. For us, conservation means conservation of people, too."

I sounded a little too preachy, but only because I was speaking from the heart.

The two men sat in silence for a while. Then one pointed to where Dionisio sat by the fire, boiling water for coffee.

"He told us the same thing, that you would build a school here. We didn't believe him, but we do now. We have heard it on the radio."

The other tracker spoke up. "Tell me, *Senhor*, your wife is Mozambican?"

"No. She is a Swazi."

"She doesn't get tired of helping Mozambicans?"

I laughed.

"I don't think so. Two of her great-grandmothers were Ronga, from Maputo. And Swazis and Macondes are cousins of some kinds. Both warriors. Both live in the mountains. Both proud as leopards."

I waved to Paulo.

"Even the language is similar. Can you tell me what *ingulube* means?"

"Wild pig."

"*Imbuti?*"

"Goat."

"*Kudla?*"

"To eat."

Paulo and Njini were excited by this but the men of Ngura weren't.

The men of Ngura were Macua, the traditional enemies of the Maconde. In the old times, the Maconde raided Macua settlements for livestock and women, exactly as the Swazi had raided the Tembe and Ronga and Shangaan in the south.

Amina chose that moment to serve the coffee. She knelt where I sat and placed the tray at my feet. It was a gesture from the past, a picture out of history (except of course for the khaki trousers and the pink-and-rose halter top, still damp from the washing at the river).

Thus was Shaka Zulu served his beer. Thus were the Monomotapas served.

I thought for a moment about women and what they have meant to men over time. Sparks rose into the night sky and a lion coughed on the other side of the river.

Paulo must have read my thoughts. "Do you know the story of the Maconde nation?" he asked.

"No. Tell me."

"We come from the Great Lakes region, south of Lake Niassa. There came a time when there were too many people upon the land, a time of hunger and suffering. Two groups left, one going west, one east. The group who became the Maconde came east, through Niassa. We fought every step of the way, against the Nyanja, Massuko, Macua, everyone. It was a terrible time. We had no food. We ate what we won. If we did not win, we did not eat. Many gave their lives for a sack of *mandioca*. Many gave their lives for a handful of beans."

"When we arrived at the *Rio Rovuma*, we were less than six hundred fighting men and almost no women. Every hand was against us. Beset on every side, we sought shelter in the mountains, on the *planalto* where we live today. There we made a small space where we could rest, and eat, and sleep. But the sleep was no good, because we had no women. Our leaders called us together."

"We must know who is ours, they said, and so we tattooed our faces. We are too few to frighten our enemies, they said, and so we sharpened our teeth, so that the smile of a Maconde would give fright to our enemies. Then they pointed down the mountain. Now go, they said, and return with food. Now go, they said, and return with women. And we did."

Celestino cut in.

"You stole our women," he said.

"You stole women like me," Amina said, and everybody laughed.

Celestino and Paulo are inseparable despite tribal differences. What unites them is their dreams, I guess. Both are members of the opposition party. And founder members of the Environmental Association.

"What happened to the group who went west?" asked Dio.

"They made it to Angola," said Paulo. "Jonas Savimbi is one of ours."

Celestino and I looked at each other.

"That explains a lot," he said, and Paulo hit him with a stick. It was only partly in fun. Paulo is still too much Maconde not to take pride in a warrior's achievements. But Celestino took no offence. Paulo was a man of two worlds, a man caught between his past and his future.

Just like the rest of us.

• • •

Dawn the next day found us far up the riverbed.

Paulo walked in front. He had a curious way of walking that I had never seen before: loose-joined, hunched over, all drooping elbows and knees and short shuffling steps during which the feet never seemed to leave the ground. He moved quickly for all that, in absolute silence. The borrowed bow hung from his left hand, an arrow knocked against the bowstring.

He'd inspected the borrowed arrows carefully before we left camp, choosing the oldest and most worn.

"Ahh..." he said, "the arrow that the owner confides in," and tested the metal broadhead against his thumb.

I followed Paulo as best I could, the two village trackers on my heels.

Dias and Amina came next. Dias recorded the details of all tracks encountered in his notebook. Amina watched in silence and learned, more rapidly than anyone expected her to.

Abdallah and Njini and Dio and Casimiro were not with us. They had gone off with the rest of the group to survey another quadrant.

Paulo and the trackers missed nothing. We saw everything we'd seen the day before, plus fresh tracks of leopards and the lion we'd heard last night. A maternal herd of elephants had also passed close to the camp and we were able to make out the tracks of several young, including one track of a baby that Paulo estimated to be less than a week old, "young enough that he hasn't dropped his umbilicus" as one of the trackers said.

A little farther along, an old bull, a *kambako*, had uprooted a fever tree. His tracks were the largest we'd seen so far.

The banks on either side grew steeper and the riverbed rockier. The way narrowed and the forest crowded in around us, hemming us in, drawing us to its bosom. There was something vaguely threatening about this, an arachnid creep along the spine, the glitter of compound eyes watching from the darkness under the trees.

A hammerkop broke cover and bolted back down the riverbed towards us. It started in alarm when it saw us and dove for the shelter of a bamboo thicket.

Paulo looked at me and pointed. I knew what he wanted to say, even without the use of Gorongosa game guard hand signals. The hammerkop had been startled by some danger upriver, not by our party; it hadn't known we were there until it almost flew into us. The hammerkop had been fleeing something big enough or dangerous enough that it hadn't been aware of human intruders in its territory.

And four people had been killed by elephants last month. And we had seen the tracks of a *kambako*. And we had seen the tracks of mothers with young.

Paulo motioned with his head and we crept upstream, crouching as he did, silent as bats. Our fear sharpened our senses, made us part of the forest. Our fear made us canes of blue-green sawgrass. A crested hornbill bolted downstream as the hammerkop had, but it did not see the wild things we had become. It flapped away over our heads, croaking a protest, a complaint to the management, can't even be left alone to eat my breakfast in peace.

We rounded a bend and came out onto a rock slab. One of the trackers pointed. Urine circled slowly in a pool, a froth of bubbles still clinging to its surface.

He pointed again, but we saw nothing. He cupped his hand to his ear and we raised our heads and listened. We heard the rumble of a lorry, of a landslide, of the indigestion of God.

The stomach workings of a *kambako*, at a distance of thirty paces. We stood still and silent as the *kambako* passed away into the forest.

We arrived back in camp in mid-afternoon, footsore and weary and sorely in need of a drink and a bath, full of stories of the *kam-*

bako and the kudu family group we'd seen and the maze of potholes and waterfalls we'd discovered father on up the river. We found Abdallah and Casimiro and Celestino asleep in the shade of a *jambire*, but no Njini.

"Where is he?" I asked. Celestino managed to point straight up with his chin.

I looked. A tangle of vines formed a nest of sorts halfway between ground and treetop. An arm flopped over one side of the nest, a black-booted foot the other.

"He's sleeping up there," said Celestino. I couldn't quite believe this, so Dio pelted Njini with rocks until he hit him. This produced a satisfying thump and an even more satisfying "Uhmf," proof enough that Njini had indeed been asleep.

Dio couldn't believe it either. He tried to climb to Njini's nest and failed, so we hollered for Njini to come down and show us how he did it.

He swarmed down the vines and back up again with an ease that could only have come down to him through the corridors of evolutionary time.

Burroughs wrote Tarzan as an Englishman, but the closest thing to Tarzan I've ever seen is a short, barrel-chested Maconde who climbs trees like a full brachiator but clumps through the forest like a randy hippopotamus in heavy black boots. As a result, his group hadn't come close to any animals, though they had seen as much sign as ours did.

After lunch we challenged Paulo to prove his skill with the bow and arrow that he had carried around all day. I pegged a biscuit wrapper (Hock Guam Cream Crackers, imported from Malaysia) to a tree with thorns and paced off 30 meters. Paulo toed the mark, then dropped into his hunter's crouch, all knees and elbows and eyes sticking out in front.

Up came the short bow. He pulled and held just a moment before releasing, dropping into an even deeper crouch as he did so. The arrow buried itself in the biscuit wrapper, squarely between the "Hock" and the "Guam."

Celestino's mouth dropped open in amazement.

"Now I know why you always cut the heads off people when you take photos," he said. "A camera isn't a bow and arrows. Light doesn't jump up to a camera the way an arrow jumps off a bow. You don't have to drop at the knees when you take a picture." He added a few colorful insults in Portuguese.

I'd noticed before that Paulo has a nice collection of headless torsos and crotches in his photo album back in Pemba. After our trip to the Lurio Estuary he'd presented me with a profile of myself from the neck down, set against a lagoon and a backdrop of mangrove trees.

Celestino dug in Paulo's pack for his camera.

"Here, try to take a picture without dropping at the knees." We lined up dutifully at the base of the *jambire*. Paulo raised his camera and dropped into his hunter's crouch. We couldn't take it. We dropped too, and rolled about in the leaf mould laughing like fools until some red ants took notice and proceeded to bite us back to sanity.

We spent the evening recording and analyzing our data and preparing the maps for the next day's surveying. While we worked, Njini decided that we ought to know a little more about his love life. He'd stayed three months in Minhanha without a woman and his friends had started to worry about him.

"Come, my friend, isn't their anyone in the village that you see who could stay with you and make your bed for you in the mornings?" they would say to him.

"No, my friends, I am not interested," he would say in return.

"This is not healthy, my friend," they said. "We will bring you a girl."

And they did. One evening just after dark, Njini's friends arrived with a girl from the village.

"Here she is, my friend, for you," they said. "She will treat you well. Just make sure that she leaves before dawn."

Njini took her inside to his small, rope bed. He gazed upon her face by the candlelight and saw that she was beautiful. He touched her shoulder and found that her skin was thick and smooth and heavy, like a papaya. He touched her waist and found ... something.

"What's this?"

"What's what?"

"This, here, at your waist."

"That? Just beads."

"Beads. What for?"

Njini stripped the *capulana* from the girl's body. He bent close and counted. One, two, three, four ... eighteen strings of small, dark beads around her waist. He pulled back.

"What are these beads for?" he asked again.

"What for? I don't know what for. I just wear them. My mother told me to ..."

But Njini was having none of it.

He suspected ... well, he didn't know what he suspected, but whatever it was, it wasn't something good.

Maybe a trap. Or witchcraft. Maybe he would go mad, or fall madly in love with the girl. Or maybe parts of him would shrivel, or fall off. Or maybe ... who knows?

But not something good.

He sent the girl back to his friends who all proceeded to conclude that he was an idiot. So did we.

Amina laughed with us, but maybe not as loud as we did.

She probably knew what the beads were for. Or more likely, she was thinking of the girl. Something we should have done before we laughed so hard at the story.

It can't have been nice to be offered up like a pomegranate on a platter. Unless she wanted to be. And if that was the case then the refusal would have hurt. No way to win for her.

. . .

I awoke long before dawn.

I wanted some time alone in the forest, some time to sit on a rock and think and drink in the dew and the dawn and the pinkness of the sun reflected from high, scattered wisps of cloud, the type of cloud that tells you that rain is not far off, the type of cloud that tells you that it is time to prepare your fields and renew the thatch on your sleeping hut.

I wanted some time without authority, or Dio, or Dias, or even Amina and her pink-and-rose halter top. I wanted some time when no one wanted something from me. I crept out of my tent and started down the path.

I stopped. Paulo stood there, a dark shape in dark shadows, a sentinel. I sighed, but Paulo cocked his head at the path and shifted the bow in his hand.

It was an invitation. Somehow I knew he wanted nothing from me, knew that he was there to guard my back and nothing more, knew that his presence would take nothing away from my morning, knew that with him to guard me I could fully relax, perhaps for the first time in months.

Thank you, my friend, I thought, but I said nothing. There was no need.

I walked up the river until I found a high place, then climbed it and sat on it. The sun rose as I had expected. Doves called up and down the river. A blue-headed lizard rustled in the leaves. Crows cawed and fought over crabs in the mud. No elephants came, but I needed none.

We can do this, I thought. Me and Nicolãu and Dias and Ruth and Amina and Celestino and Dio and the people of Ngura village.

We can protect this place. We can protect these people. We can make a wildlife reserve so all can live in harmony. With the data we are collecting, the politicians will have to listen to us. With the data we are collecting, the donors will have to give us the funds.

Somehow we have become a team, even though Amina and

Dio and Celestino are Macua and Njini and Paulo are Maconde, even though some are ruling party and some are opposition, even though Ruth and I are strangers here, even though none of us has ever done anything like this before.

Something in this thing that needs to be done calls to something within each of us, and something within each of us answers. We can do it, I thought, and it needs to be done. A National Reserve to preserve this hard, harsh wonderful place forever.

I thought some more.

But why just a Reserve?

Why not a National Park? Why not the highest level of environmental protection that Mozambican law can offer?

A Reserve is only partial protection, only for some species. Why not a Park that protects them all, lizards and hornbills and lions and hippos and leopards and even the humans who live here as humans have lived here for centuries. Why not a Park, that safeguards traditional culture as well?

I sat a long time there with the sun on my face and the dew soaking through my trousers and Paulo watching from somewhere in the forest. Then a noise came from the river, away on my right. A clumping, the lumbering bumbling rumbling of a randy hippopotamus in heavy black boots.

And then a voice, shouting.

"*Ola, Paulo! Onde estão, vocês?* Where are you? Hey! Dias needs the car keys. It's time to go!"

I took a last look at the sky and the trees and the sand of the riverbed. I breathed the cool morning air, the last bit of coolness I would have until nightfall.

"We're coming!" I shouted, and started back to camp.

Addenda to Chapter 13

So NOW we arrive at the end of the book. Unbeknownst to you, my reader, we finish as we started, with a death.

My father died last month. October, 2017.

I went to the USA to visit him for two weeks. I had not spent such a long time in my parent's house since my university days, but something was whispering in the back of my consciousness that it was time to go and do this.

We had one week together for laughter, for stories, and for songs. His memory was not so good so my mother and I used old photo albums to help him make connections; to jostle him so memories of his youth fell out.

I found out that my father got his love of music from his uncle, Alpheus Umstead, who soloed on the violin with multiple church choirs.

My father couldn't remember why everyone called Alpheus "Uncle Doc," as he wasn't a doctor. I found out that my father's first instrument was, of all things, the Hawaiian guitar.

I found out that he played baseball, second base, though he said they subbed him out at every opportunity.

Sunday evening of the second week he was coughing. He did not eat that night. Apparently his Parkinson's disease had advanced enough for it to affect his throat muscles, though we only found this out later. Monday he was fading fast, losing consciousness before noon. I sang to him all afternoon, playing the guitar and singing the lining off my throat. Mother and I stayed late with him in the hospital.

He rallied on Tuesday morning, eating again, and we talked and sang, his mind clearer than it had been for many days.

By Wednesday he was worse; by Thursday he was deep in a coma, the death rattle in his throat. I sang to him again on Friday as he lay there fading on the bed.

Just like Dumi.

He died fifteen minutes after midnight. Eighteen years and one month between the death of my son and the death of my father.

What did I do with that time?

You know by now that Dias and Nicolău and I and the others birthed the Quirimbas National Park, seven-and-a-half thousand beautiful square kilometers of mountains and savannah and floodplain and islands and ocean, against all odds and for the grand sum of $60,000, perhaps the least expensive National Park ever made.

We used my boat and borrowed pickup trucks and hitchhiked. No one took a salary, just food to eat in the field. When all the fieldwork was done, the communities in agreement, the local politicians onboard, I went to the Cartography Department of the Ministry of Agriculture to collect the official maps to send to the Council of Ministers so the new National Park could be approved. It was a Friday, and I had written the Management Plan already.

All we needed were the maps, for the following Tuesday. They were not done, not even started.

I threw the base maps of the province, a drafter's table and instruments, a photocopier, and a scanner into the back of my truck. All these things belonged to the Cartography Department; I think everyone was too shocked to stop me. For the next seventy-two hours, almost without a break, I taught myself cartography.

The "official" map and coordinates of the Park went down to Maputo on the Monday night flight, in time for the Council of Ministers' meeting on Tuesday.

Today, if you look in the Government Gazette, series I, no. 22, Decree 14/2002 of June 6th, you will see the list of coordinates and one of the maps I made. In my own handwriting.[42]

You know by now that I went on to join the WWF and to work with them for ten years. I think I mentioned that I led a joint government/WWF team that created the Aquatic Reserve on Lake Niassa (Lake Malawi), starting in 2006. I led that team until the declaration of the Reserve in 2011.[43]

I am not sure whether I mentioned that I also led a government/WWF team that created a huge marine reserve in the Primeiras and Segundas Archipelago, Africa's largest marine protected area.[44] Absolutely sure I did not tell you that Ruth and I partnered with our dive buddies John Hewlett and Pedro Cruz to create the Quirimbas Archipelago's first luxury lodge, Quilalea,[45] as a way to kick-start tourism in the Quirimbas National Park. John speaks of me with great kindness in his book, *Can You Smell the Rain? (O Cheiro da Chuva)*;[46] I am sorry I have not said more about him here.

These are other stories that I may tell someday.

I am concerned now mostly with the financing of conservation, GECORENA-style conservation. I work with the World Bank Group, international donors, and various conservation organizations. I write policy and legislation for the Mozambican government. And I put my money where my mouth is. Ruth and I and several business partners own two game farms, trying to make the private sector work to maximize ecosystem productivity for the benefit of wildlife and the surrounding communities.

Though there are other areas on my "bucket list" of parks to create, the financing of existing areas seems to me more critical; conservation worldwide is woefully underfunded.

The Quirimbas National Park for example was unable to withstand the tidal wave of elephant poaching that descended from Tanzania and points north during the years 2008-15.

This wave still continues, though to a lesser extent, to this day. Most analysts attribute the recent reduction in poaching to economics. Elephants have become scarce, so the economics of poaching are no longer quite so compelling. The elephant population in the north of Mozambique during this time fell from an estimated 22,000 to just over 7000.

I still feel the guilt of my departure. By 2009 I was no longer involved in the management of the Quirimbas National Park. I had moved to Maputo to fundraise and develop new partnerships for the WWF National Office.

If I had stayed in the north would things have turned out differently? The manic in me says of course I could have made a difference; the realist says that the WWF needed money and I was the one who, willy- nilly, was out there getting it. Ridding themselves of me may have been something of a Pyrrhic victory for WWF Mozambique; funding and programs declined steeply after I left in 2012.

Sadly, WWF Mozambique remains extremely underfunded, though there is an abundance of good work for them to do if they could.

Despite humanity's collective losses, there are some wins.

The emergence of the Eastern Coyote, a hybrid coyote/wolf/dog mixture that is successfully colonizing all of the eastern USA (including urban areas) fills me with inexpressible joy.[47]

The same joy filled me when I found out that I, being of European ancestry, likely have 1.8 to 2.6 per cent Neanderthal in my genetic makeup.[48]

Adaptation rather than extinction. Nature winning a round or two. Survival over time. Connectivity along the space-time continuum.

I cannot work as I once did.

Though the passion and the fury are still there, the discipline, the moderation (that blasted word again) must also be. I understand, though still have trouble accepting, that I cannot save all the people and places and species that deserve saving.

And this brings me to the questions I did not address in the addenda to the previous chapter.

If after all, the universe is coded, an "entangled system that is globally static" then what happens to free will?

If the universe is frozen to an outside observer, then why did I fight so hard, and at such cost, to conserve some wonderful pieces of it?

It seems futile if past, present, and future are simultaneously existent. It seems futile if everything is already hardwired by the quantum data bits out there on the boundary of the universe.

And if everything is hardwired, then why was I hardwired bipolar?

These are not purely speculative nor new questions. Upon hearing of the death of a friend, Einstein wrote "People like us, who believe in physics, know that the distinction between past, present, and future is only a stubbornly persistent illusion." [49]

Richard Feynman developed the first "... timeless [time-free] description of a multitude of space-time worlds all existing simultaneously." [50] And Stephen Hawking has postulated a universe which "... would be completely self-contained and not affected by anything outside itself. It would neither be created nor destroyed. It would just BE." [51]

My friend Sam Levy, when I am down, brings me up again with an array of accumulated Jewish proverbs, prayer, and philosophy, all delivered with a hug and a smile and frequently an offer of food and/or stimulating beverages.

I don't know where he gets it all, but one must concede that the Jewish faith has had longer than most religions to amass an impressive body of wisdom. Several months ago he quoted the Lubavitcher Rebbe to me:[52]

Gifted souls enter this world and shine. All that surround them bathe in their light and their beauty. And when they are gone, their light is missed.

Challenged souls enter, stumble and fall. They pick themselves up and fall again. Eventually, they climb to a higher tier, where more stumbling blocks await them. Their accomplishments often go unnoticed—although their stumbling is obvious to all.

But by the time they leave, new paths have been forged, obstacles leveled, and life itself has gained a new clarity for all those yet to enter.

Both are pure souls, G–dly in essence. But while the gifted shine their light from Above, the challenged meet the enemy on its own ground. Any real change in this world is only on their account.

I appreciated his sentiment and it cheered me, but I am not at all sure that it is a good fit. I am certain that I am not a gifted soul (except when I am manic, when I am certain that I am). Nor am I comfortable thinking of myself as a challenged soul, when little kids die of cholera in Chiure and their parents dig roots from the forest to eat in the dry season.

But souls may have something to do with the second question.

Perhaps I was wired bipolar because God, or the quantum data at the boundary of the universe, or both (now there's an argument for you), recognized me as a particularly boneheaded soul who needed to learn the lessons on moderation and mortality that bipolar has taught me.

Or maybe the universe needed some doggone manic fool to charge headstrong into a battle that, though fundamentally important, there was little chance of winning. Or maybe all or none of the above.

Ruth and I will go and see Sam and his wife Lauren tomorrow night. We will sit on the veranda of their house overlooking the beach in Costa do Sol, a little north of Maputo, and we will talk about my father, and Sam's father, and our new grandchild, and elephant conservation, and how to help poor farmers improve their agricultural production and their lives.

The questions of free will and hardwiring will be entirely unimportant to us, enmired as we are in this universe and the (possibly merely apparent) flow of time.

What will be important, and what I will try to remember the next time I go down, is that all does not end in horror. The Beast does not exist, or at least I have vanquished him, and so I do not need fire nor adrenaline nor booze nor testosterone to keep him at bay. Neither existence nor non-existence hold any more terrors for me.

And because the Beast is vanquished, and friends surround, there is hope that God or the universe, or both, will hold my dead father and my dead son and Ruth and my children and the elephants and the Quirimbas and all living things great and small within a tightly entangled web of existence. And thus they will endure.

ABOUT THE AUTHOR

Peter Bechtel (www.peterhbechtel.com) has spent nearly his entire adult life in remote areas of Africa working to improve human lives and conserve nature. He is the founder of three major conservation areas in Mozambique: the *Quirimbas National Park*; the *Lake Niassa Reserve*; and the *Ilhas Primeiras and Segundas Marine Reserve*. He was instrumental in the establishment of the Biofund, Mozambique's only Trust Fund for the Conservation of Nature (www.biofund.org.mz). He and his wife Ruth were award-winning tourist operators with their lodge, *Quilalea Private Island*, being named "World's Number One Destination" by the BBC in 2006.

He also battles bipolar disorder and alcoholism. He makes it out of bed most days and has regained just enough control over his mania and impulses that his wife trusts him to carry a credit card. He finds sport to be a lifeline, and lifts weights regularly.

He is currently an independent consultant, providing advisory services to the World Bank Group, NGO's, and private sector clients, focussing on the rural development/nature conservation nexus. He firmly believes that ecosystem health and human livelihoods are inextricably interrelated. *Disequilibrium* is his second book, his first being an instruction manual on beekeeping, published by the Swaziland Ministry of Agriculture and Cooperatives in 1987.

Peter is devoted to his wife, children, and grandchildren, who have stuck by him through thick and thin. He is currently investigating the maritime history of the ancient Mozambican town of Angoche, in cooperation with his brother Tim and two universities in the USA and Africa. He is writing his next book about this adventure.

Peter would like to thank his wife's wonderful mother, Sellinah Nkambule, for weaving the sleeping map shown on the cover of this book.

Notes

1. Mosby's Medical Dictionary, 9th edition. © 2009, *Elsevier*. Accessed: 13/6/2016, http://medical-dictionary.thefreedictionary.com/disequilibrium.

1. Falling Apart

2. United Nations Development Programme. 1996. *Human Development Report*, 1996. New York: Oxford University Press. p. 29. Accessed: 29/5/2016, http://hdr.undp.org/sites/default/files/reports/257/hdr_1996_en_complete_nostats.pdf.
3. Ibid., p.29.
4. Gabinete do Governador da Província de Cabo Delgado. 2001. Plano estratégico do desenvolvimento 2001- 2005. Relatório apresentado ao "Segundo Conferencia de Desenvolvimento da Província de Cabo Delgado," organizado pelo Governo Provincial de Cabo Delgado, Pemba. 2001.
5. World Bank Public Data. Accessed: 29/5/2016, https://www.google.co.mz/publicdata/explore?ds=d5bncppjof8f9_&met_y=sp_dyn_le00_in-&idim=country:MOZ:AGO:ZMB&hl=en&dl=en.
6. World Bank Public Data. Accessed: 29/5/2016, https://www.google.co.mz/publicdata/explore?ds=d5bncppjof8f9_&met_y=sp_dyn_le00_in-&idim=country:MOZ:AGO:ZMB&hl=en&dl=en#!ctype=l&strail=-false&bcs=d&nselm=h&met_y=sh_dyn_mort&scale_y=lin&ind_y=-false&rdim=region&idim=country:MOZ:AGO:ZMB&ifdim=region&hl=en_US&dl=en&ind=false.

2. Not a Very Good American

7. Mashasha, F.J, *The Swazi and land partition (1902-1910)*, Collected Seminar Papers no. 17, pp. 87-107, London: Institute of Commonwealth Studies, 1974. Accessed: 31/7/2018, http://sas-space.sas.ac.uk/3669/.
8. Shillington, K. ed. *Encyclopedia of African History.* Accessed: 13/5/2016, https://books.google.co.mz/books?id=umyHqvAErOAC&pg=PA789&lpg=PA789&dq=land+buy+back+swaziland+Labotsibeni&source=bl&ots=xIlzNQexa-&sig=nJLgoE-TtAnSF4sWHn_koA-Jr-bQ&hl=en&sa=X&ved=oahUKEwiWnsOG85_NAhWrKsAKHS2x-A9wQ6AEIIDAB#v=onepage&q=land%20buy%20back%20swaziland%20Labotsibeni&f=false.
9. Mozlegal, Lda. 2004. Land law legislation. Report no. 4230/RLINLD/2004. *Maputo.* Accessed: 25/5/2-16, http://www.doingbusiness.org/~/media/FPDKM/Doing%20Business/Documents/Law-Library/Mozambique-Land-Law-Legislation.pdf.

5. Poachers

10. *Pterocarpus angolensus* (African mahogany), *Afzelia quanzensis*, and *Milletia stuhlmannii*, respectively.
11. Mackenzie, C. *Forest governance in Zambezia: Chinese takeaway! Consultancy Report for Fongza*, Oram Zambézia, and the Associação Rural de Ajuda Mutuo, Moçambique, 2004.
12. The CAMPFIRE program suffered a severe blow during Zimbabwe's political disturbances in 1999- 2000, when much land was occupied by political activists of the ruling party. Zimbabwe's tourism (and other) industries have never fully recovered.

6. Campaigns

13. Lidia tells me that suicide is common in bipolar, and studies back her up. As many as fifteen percent of people with bipolar disorder will die by their own hands, half will attempt to, and nearly eighty percent will contemplate doing so. Bloomquist, M., 2008. *Bipolar disorder and the risk of suicide.* Everyday Health., 2008.Accessed: 13/10/2017, https://www.everydayhealth.com/bipolar-disorder/bipolar-and-suicide-risk.aspx.

8. Fatigue

14. Of his five and a half years as a prisoner of war in Vietnam, John McCain wrote, "It's an awful thing, solitary. It crushes your spirit and weakens your resistance more effectively than any other form of mistreatment."

Shore, J. 2011. The absence of God: A kinder, gentler Hell? *Huffington Post* 7/1/2011. Accessed: 13/7/2017, https://www.huffingtonpost.com/john-shore/the-absence-of-god-christian-hell_b_893190.html.

15. This seems to be a typical bipolar progression. Zimney, E. 2017. The progression of bipolar disorder. *Everyday Health*. Accessed: 14/7/2017, https://www.everydayhealth.com/bipolar/webcasts/the-progression-of-bipolar-disorder.aspx.

16. Eleven to 21 per cent of persons with bipolar disorder experience co-morbid OCD [obsessive compulsive disorder] at some time during the course of their bipolar disorder. Shi, X. 2015. Obsessive compulsive symptoms in bipolar patients: a comorbid disorder or a subtype of bipolar disorder? *Shanghai Archives of Psychiatry*. Accessed: 14/7/2017, https://www.ncbi.nlm.nih.gov/pmc/articles/PMC4621291/.

17. Compared to OCD patients and bipolar disorder patients without other comorbid conditions, bipolar patients with comorbid OCD have: a) higher rates of obsessive ideas about sex and religion and lower rates of ritual checking; b) higher rates of substance abuse (including use of alcohol, sedatives, caffeine, etc.); c) more episodes of depression, higher rates of suicide, and more frequent admissions to hospitals; and d) more chronic episodes and residual symptoms. Any of this starting to sound familiar? Ibid.

10. Saving the Quirimbas

18. Newett, Malyn D., *A History of Mozambique*. Indiana University Press, 1993.

19. Thomas Vernet, Slave trade and slavery on the Swahili coast (1500-1750) in B.A. Mirzai, I.M. Montana et P. Lovejoy. *Slavery, Islam and Diaspora*, Africa World Press, pp.37-76, 2009. <halshs-00671040>.

20. Mackenzie, D., 1895. *A report on slavery and the slave trade in Zanzibar, Pemba, and the mainland of the British protectorates of East Africa: presented to the British and Foreign Anti-Slavery Society*, LSE Selected Pamphlets, 1885,LSE Library. Stable URL: http://www.jstor.org/stable/60217047 . Accessed: 24/2/2018, http://www.artsrn.ualberta.ca/amcdouga/Hist494_2014/readings/report%20slavery%20zanzibar%201895.pdf .

21. Newett, Malyn D., *A History of Mozambique*. Indiana University Press, 1993.

22. Mishkat Al-Masabih.

23. National Geographic Society, 2018. National Geographic/ Buffet awardees. Accessed: 2/3/2018, https://www.nationalgeographic.org/awards/buffett/awardees/.

24. World Wildlife Fund, WWF apoia iniciativa comunitária de criação de novo santuário marinho no Parque Nacional das Quirimbas, 27/1/2106. Accessed: 3/5/2018, https://www.wwf.org.mz/noticias/?1800/WWF-apoia-iniciativa-comunitria-de-criao-de-novo-santurio-marinho-no-Parque-Nacional-das-Quirimbas.

25. Some of the blacklists include those of Norway, New Zealand, the Northwest Atlantic Fisheries Organization, and Greenpeace. Apparently the name has been changed as it appears as the "Baroon" in the 2018 Norwegian list. It has been on the Norwegian list since 2007. The Kinsho Maru was also cited in French courts as early as 1997. Accessed: 3/5/2018, https://www.stuff.co.nz/world/south-pacific/64927953/pirate-fishing-boats-on-new-zealands-radar, and https://www.nafo.int/Fisheries/IUU, and https://www.fiskeridir.no/content/download/13193/175665/version/9/file/norwegian-black-list-260218.pdf, and http://www.fao.org/tempref/FI/DOCUMENT/cwp/cwp_23/inf4e.pdf.
26. Jackson, J.B.C., et al., Historical Overfishing and the Recent Collapse of Coastal Ecosystems. *Science*, New Series, Vol. 293, no. 5530 (July 27th, 2001), pp. 629-638. Stable URL: http://www.jstor.org/stable/3084305.

11. Maputo

27. Lake Malawi is the name the English-speaking world calls Lake Niassa. I led a five-year effort to create a Reserve and Ramsar site in the Lake and coastal mountains. The Reserve and Ramsar site were both declared in 2011, the first conservation area to be declared in this most precious of habitats. Though Lake Malawi also borders Malawi and Tanzania, a border fight means that neither country can or will declare any sort of protected area in the Lake. If the Lake's biodiversity is to be saved, it must be saved by Mozambicans. We are trying.
28. Remember the old saw about teaching? It's even more relevant for development. "Those who can't do, manage projects. Those who can't manage projects, consult ..."
29. Goodreads, *Longing for darkness: Kamante's tales from Out of Africa*. Chronicle Books, 1998, summary. Accessed: 7/16/2017, https://www.goodreads.com/book/show/74502.Longing_For_Darkness.

12. Darkness

30. For several contrasting views, see: http://theunrealuniverse.com/2-nature-of-time, accessed: 1/11/2017; https://sites.google.com/site/smithjcnparadigm/, accessed: 2/11/2017; and https://blog.frontiersin.org/2016/12/08/the-nature-of-time-an-unsolved-puzzle/, accessed: 31/10/2017.
31. Chappell, J., et.al., Time as a geometric property of space. *Frontiers in Physics*, 2016. Accessed: 31/10/2017, https://www.frontiersin.org/articles/10.3389/fphy.2016.00044/full.
32. Wolchover, W. Quantum gravity research could unearth the true nature of time. *Science, reprinted from Quanta Magazine*, 2016. Accessed: 31/10/2017, https://www.wired.com/2016/12/quantum-gravity-research-unearth-true-nature-time/.

33. Ibid.

34. *Encyclopedia of North American Indians: Religion. Accessed: 5/3/2018*, http://web.archive.org/web/20050330085408/http://college.hmco.com/history/readerscomp/naind/html/na_032600_religion.htm.

35. Clark, J.L. Thus spoke Chief Seattle: the story of an undocumented speech. *Prologue*, Vol. 18, No. 1. 1985. Accessed: 5/3/2018, https://www.archives.gov/publications/prologue/1985/spring/chief-seattle.html.

36. Mikkelson, B., Chief Seattle speech. Did Chief Seattle give the environmental speech he's become famous for? *Snopes Fact Check, 2007.*Accessed: 5/3/2018, https://www.snopes.com/fact-check/chief-seattle/.

37. Black Elk., *The Sacred Pipe: Black Elk's Account of the Seven Rites of the Oglala Sioux*, as told to J.E. Brown, 1953. Accessed: 5.3.2018, https://en.wikiquote.org/wiki/Black_Elk.

38. Merali, Z., Theoretical physics: The origins of space and time, Nature, 2013. Accessed: 2/11/2017, https://www.nature.com/news/theoretical-physics-the-origins-of-space-and-time-1.13613.

39. Popova, M., Richard Feynman on the role of scientific culture in modern society, Brainpickings, 2012. Accessed: 25/10/2017, https://www.brainpickings.org/2012/08/27/richard-feynman-on-the-role-of-scientific-culture-in-modern-society/.

40. Buccheri, R., Saniga, M., Stuckey, W.M., *The Nature of Time: Geometry, Physics and Perception.* Proceedings of the NATO Advanced Research Workshop on the Nature of Time, Springer Science and Business Media, Dordrecht, 2012.

41. A recent study concludes that "bipolar and major depressive disorder might be subtypes of schizophrenia rather than two independent disease entities." Chen X. et al., A novel relationship for schizophrenia, bipolar and major depressive disorder, Part 5: A hint from chromosome 5 high density association screen, American Journal of Translational Research, vol. 9, no. 5, 2017, pp. 2473-91. Accessed: 4/6/2017, https://www.ncbi.nlm.nih.gov/pmc/articles/PMC5446530/.

13. Tracks

42. Governo de Moçambique., Decreto no. 14/2002 de 6 de Junho. *Boletim da Republica, Serie I, no.22, 2002.pp.194-(28)*. Accessed: 8/10/2017, http://www.biofund.org.mz/wp-content/uploads/2014/12/ParqueQuirimbas-Decreto-14-2002-Criacao.pdf .

43. World Wildlife Fund. Reserva Parcial do Lago Niassa: construindo o futuro, 2017. Accessed: 1/5/2018, https://www.wwf.org.mz/?2620/Reserva-Parcial-do-Lago-Niassa-construindo-o-futuro.

44. WWF. Moçambique cria a maior Reserva Marinha de África. 2013. Accessed: 3/5/2017, https://www.wwf.org.mz/noticias/?uNewsID=1183.

45. Azura Boutique Retreats. Introduction: Azura Quilalea private island, 2018. Accessed: 1/5/2017, https://www.azura-retreats.com/quilalea-introduction.

46. Hewlett, J. *O Cheiro da Chuva*. Maputo. 2106. Accessed 28.4.2018, http://clubofmozambique.com/news/j-hewlett-can-you-smell-the-rain-2016/.
47. The Economist. Greater than the sum of its parts. *The Economist* 31/10/15. Accessed: 8/9/2016, https://www.economist.com/news/science-and-technology/21677188-it-rare-new-animal-species-emerge-front-scientists-eyes.
48. Donahue, M. New clues to how Neanderthal genes affect your health. *National Geographic*, 2017.Accessed: 31/10/2017, https://news.nationalgeographic.com/2017/10/how-neanderthal-genes-affect-human-health-dna-science/.
49. Albert Einstein Site Online. 2008. Accessed: 22/11/2017, http://www.alberteinsteinsite.com/quotes/einsteinquotes.html.
50. Actforlibraries.org. 2017. Accessed: 2/11/2017, http://www.actforlibraries.org/timelessness-time-albert-einstein-stephen-hawking-relativiy-space-time/.
51. Hawking, S. *A brief history of time*, New York: Bantam Books. 1998.
52. From the wisdom of the Lubavitcher Rebbe, of righteous memory; words and condensation by Rabbi Tzvi Freeman. Accessed 23/11/2017, https://www.chabad.org/library/article_cdo/aid/148247/jewish/Gifted--and-Challenged.htm.